GALÁPAGOS ISLANDS

LISA CHO

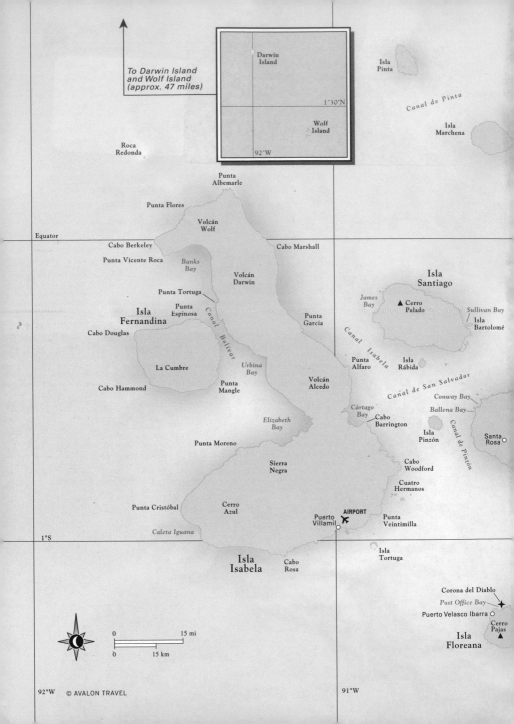

To Darwin Island
and Wolf Island
(approx. 47 miles)

Darwin
Island

1´30'N

92°W

Wolf
Island

Isla
Pinta

Canal de Pinta

Isla
Marchena

Roca
Redonda

Punta
Albemarle

Punta Flores

Volcán
Wolf

Cabo Marshall

Equator

Cabo Berkeley

Punta Vicente Roca

Banks
Bay

Volcán
Darwin

Isla
Santiago

Punta Tortuga

Punta
Espinosa

Isla
Fernandina

Cabo Douglas

La Cumbre

Cabo Hammond

Canal Bolívar

Urbina
Bay

Punta
Mangle

Punta
García

James
Bay

▲ Cerro
Pelado

Sullivan Bay

Isla
Bartolomé

Punta
Alfaro

Canal Isabela

Isla
Rábida

Volcán
Alcedo

Canal de San Salvador

Conway Bay

Ballena Bay

Elizabeth
Bay

Cártago
Bay

Cabo
Barrington

Isla
Pinzón

Canal de Pinzón

Santa
Rosa

Punta Moreno

Sierra
Negra

Cabo
Woodford

Cuatro
Hermanos

Punta Cristóbal

Cerro
Azul

AIRPORT

Puerto
Villamil

Punta
Veintimilla

Caleta Iguana

1°S

Isla
Isabela

Cabo
Rosa

Isla
Tortuga

Corona del Diablo

Post Office Bay

Puerto Velasco Ibarra

Cerro
Pajas
▲

Isla
Floreana

0   15 mi

0   15 km

92°W   © AVALON TRAVEL

91°W

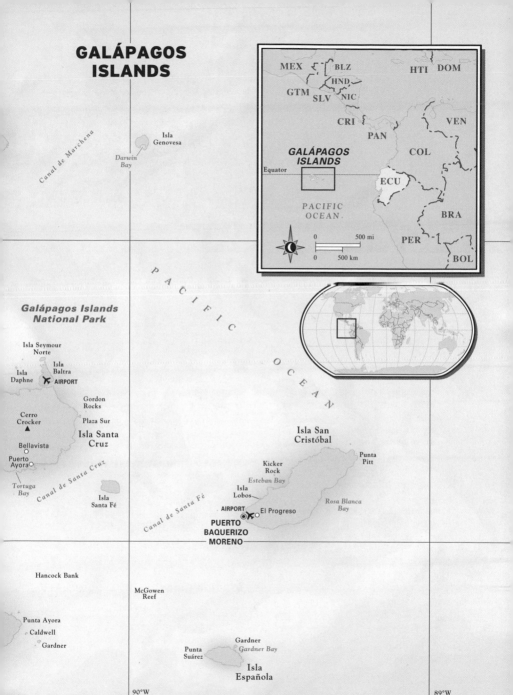

GALÁPAGOS ISLANDS

MEX
BLZ
HTI DOM
HND
GTM
SLV NIC
CRI
VEN
PAN
GALÁPAGOS
ISLANDS
COL
Equator
ECU
PACIFIC
OCEAN
BRA
0   500 mi
PER
0   500 km
BOL

Isla
Genovesa

Canal de Marchena

Darwin
Bay

PACIFIC

OCEAN

**Galápagos Islands
National Park**

Isla Seymour
Norte

Isla
Baltra
Isla
Daphne   ✈ AIRPORT

Gordon
Rocks

Cerro
Crocker   ▲
Plaza Sur

Isla Santa
Cruz

Isla San
Cristóbal

Bellavista   ○

Puerto
Ayora ○

Punta
Pitt

Tortuga
Bay

Canal de Santa Cruz

Kicker
Rock

Esteban Bay

Isla
Lobos

Isla
Santa Fé

Canal de Santa Fé

AIRPORT   El Progreso

Rosa Blanca
Bay

✈

**PUERTO
BAQUERIZO
MORENO**

Hancock Bank

McGowen
Reef

Punta Ayora

Caldwell

Gardner

Gardner

Punta
Suárez

Gardner Bay

Isla
Española

90°W

89°W

Contents

DISCOVER

DISCOVER
the Galápagos Islands

The Galápagos archipelago is one place on earth that lives up to and surpasses expectations. There are insufficient superlatives. It is unquestionably the best place on earth for wildlife-watching because the wildlife watches you as much as you watch it. The lack of natural predators has left the animals fearless. The only timid species are the fish, the food supply for so many. Every other creature on the islands is either unconcerned by the presence of visitors or is intent on communicating.

The Galápagos are also heaven for bird-watchers. Here you don't need to get up at dawn and wait with binoculars for a glimpse of birdlife in the trees. Instead, the birds proudly display themselves—the male frigates inflate their red chests to the size of a basketball, the albatross entertain with their circular clacking dance, and pelicans dive-bomb the ocean in search of lunch.

A visit to these islands changes you, as it changed Charles Darwin, who was inspired to form his monumental theory of evolution after visiting in 1835. The Galápagos region is a glimpse of what life was like before humans threw their weight around, and a reminder that when we seek out perfection, we throw a wrench in nature's works. Evidence of human activity on the Galápagos

Clockwise from top left: A helpful lava lizard eats the parasites off a marine iguana; Kicker Rock; giant tortoise at the Charles Darwin Research Station; sea lion on the beach on Plaza Sur; frigate bird in a mating display on Genovesa; an albatross.

is everywhere—the number of endemic species hunted or driven to near extinction by introduced species is alarming. But the effort of conservationists to restore the ecological balance is equally inspiring. You will return from these islands filled with a sense of wonder and a clearer view of nature's fragile beauty.

Clockwise from top left: Bartolomé; Nazca boobies rubbing beaks in a courtship ritual; hawkfish hiding in the rocks; red vesuvium on a Floreana trail.

5 TOP EXPERIENCES

1 **Wildlife-viewing:** Get a glimpse of the nearly 5,000 different species of wildlife, many of which can only be found on these rocky islands (pages 76 and 83).

2 **Bird-watching:**
The Galápagos
Islands are the best
place to see high-
diving **boobies**
(pages 92 and
page 139), bright-
chested **frigates** (page
76), and massive
albatrosses (page
139).

>>>

3 **Diving and
Snorkeling:**
Swim alongside whale
sharks, sea turtles,
hammerheads, sea
lion pups, rays, eels,
and more in the
unparalleled marine
marvels at **Kicker
Rock, Los Túneles,
Gordon Rocks,** and
the **Wolf and Darwin
Islands** (page 27).

>>>

4 **Evolution in Action:** Learn about the science and history of the Galápagos' unique ecosystem at the **Charles Darwin Research Station** (page 57), San Cristóbal's **Interpretation Center** (page 83), and the **Tortoise Reserves** on Santa Cruz (page 72).

>>>

5 **Wandering through Volcanic Landscapes:** Experience the awe-inspiring views of the archipelago through blackened lava trails in **Sierra Negra** (page 109), a forest of opuntia cactus in **Santa Fé** (page 75), and an unbelievable summit hike at **Bartolomé Island** (page 135).

>>>

Planning Your Trip

Where to Go

The Galápagos archipelago comprises 13 volcanic islands and 16 tiny islets. The total population of the archipelago is 30,000. Only four of the islands are populated: Santa Cruz (by far the largest, with 15,000 people), San Cristóbal, Isabela, and Floreana. These are the only islands that can be visited independently on shuttle ferry services. The populated areas account for only 3 percent of the archipelago's surface area, with the rest protected in the national park.

There are 70 land visitor sites and roughly the same number of marine sites. Sites on Seymour Norte, Plaza Sur, Bartolomé, Española, and Santa Fé can all be reached by either cruises or guided day trips from Santa Cruz. The other main islands in the archipelago—Santiago, Rábida, Genovesa, Darwin, Wolf, the northern part of Isabela, and Fernandina—can only be visited on cruises. Pinta

and Marchena in the north are both off-limits to visitors.

Santa Cruz and the surrounding islets receive the most visitors. San Cristóbal and Isabela also get busy in high season, and Floreana is the least visited of the inhabited islands. The more far-flung islands that are only accessible to cruises are much quieter.

Whichever islands you visit, you can see just a tiny portion of the archipelago: The 70 visitor sites represent only 0.01 percent of the total landmass, and the rest of the national park is strictly out-of-bounds to visitors.

Santa Cruz and Nearby Islands

The archipelago's tourism hub is centered around the busy but pleasant **Puerto Ayora.** Highlights include the **Charles Darwin Research Station**

Plaza Sur

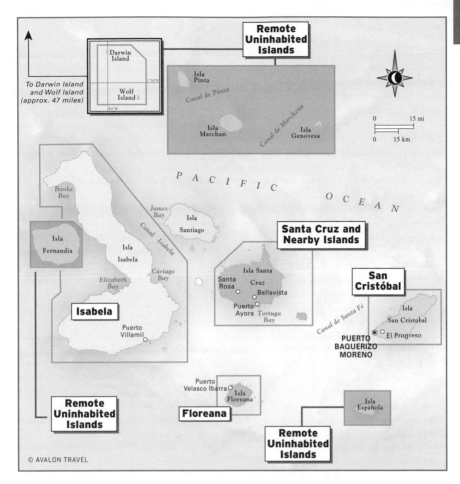

and **Tortuga Bay,** one of the islands' most beautiful beaches. Lava tunnels, craters, and giant tortoises await in the **highlands,** while surrounding islands provide excellent excursions, notably the **land iguanas** on **Plaza Sur** and **Santa Fé,** and **frigates** and **blue-footed boobies** on **Seymour Norte.**

San Cristóbal

Sea lions dominate the waterfront of **Puerto Baquerizo Moreno,** and you can walk among a large colony close to town at **La Lobería** and hike to nearby beaches and snorkeling spots. Offshore,

the trips to **Isla Lobos** and **Kicker Rock** offer unrivaled snorkeling with sea lions and sharks. At the far eastern side of the island is **Punta Pitt,** one of the few spots where all three booby species are seen together.

Isabela

Isabela is the giant of the archipelago, occupying half the total landmass. It also boasts the most dramatic landscapes, with six active volcanoes. The highlight is the **Sierra Negra** hike, which circles the second-largest crater in the world before descending to the spectacular landscape of

Volcán Chico. There are excellent boat trips to **Los Túneles** in the south and **Las Tintoreras** near town. For cruises, the western side of the island offers beautiful hiking at **Darwin Lake**, snorkeling with sea turtles and flightless cormorants at **Punta Vicente Roca**, and keeping an eye out for whales while cruising in the channel.

Floreana

Floreana's lush, peaceful ambience belies its troubled history, which has kept amateur sleuths guessing for decades. Highlights include a quirky post office and snorkeling at **Post Office Bay** and **Mirador de la Baronesa**. Offshore there is excellent snorkeling at **Devil's Crown** and **Champion Island**.

Remote Uninhabited Islands

The blackened lava trails of Santiago recall a land that time forgot. Explore this unworldly landscape in the trails around **Sullivan Bay.** The nearby islet of **Bartolomé**—a partially eroded lava formation flanked by two beaches with the black lava trails of Santiago in the distance—is the most-photographed sight in the Galápagos.

Fernandina is one of the least-visited islands, and **Punta Espinosa,** the sole visitor site, has the largest colony of marine iguanas in the archipelago and the biggest nesting site for flightless cormorants.

Española is the world's biggest breeding site for waved albatross.

Fewer boats make it to the far north, but **Genovesa** is enduringly popular for its large red-footed booby populations. **Wolf and Darwin Islands** are the preserve of experienced divers, who can enjoy the awe-inspiring sight of whale sharks from June to November.

Know Before You Go

When to Go

The Galápagos Islands are a year-round destination, and even naturalist guides differ in their opinions of the best time to visit. You can even target specific wildlife events. There are two distinct seasons in the Galápagos: rainy season and dry season, though the best time to visit largely comes down to personal preference.

Many travelers consider **wildlife** when choosing a time to visit the Galápagos. The famous waved albatross visits Española only April-November. The comical mating dance of blue-footed boobies takes place May-June. October-November is a great time to see playful sea lion pups. For divers aboard live-aboard cruises, June-November is the prime season due to the presence of enormous whale sharks.

December-April is the rainy, hot season. The weather is sunny and interspersed with periods of rain. The seas are the calmest and the water is at its warmest, and it's pleasant to swim without a wetsuit. Rain leads to an explosion of greenery on the hillsides of some islands, though the highlands and arid coastal areas don't change much. The lush green highlands of the islands stay green year-round, and the arid coastal landscapes dominated by lava rock, mangroves, and cacti don't change much either. The downside is that mosquitoes and the sun are the most intense; you may constantly feel sticky from bug repellent, sunscreen, and the humidity. This season coincides with the **busiest tourist period** around Christmas and early January.

June-October is the cool, dry season. There are fewer mosquitoes, and the temperature on land is more comfortable for most people. However, the landscapes are more barren and the sea becomes considerably rougher, so seasickness is more of a problem. You'll need to wear a wetsuit for swimming and snorkeling; the waters can be surprisingly cold. The biggest upside is that the Humboldt Current brings nutrient-rich water from the south; this means marine animals like sea lions, marine iguanas, and seabirds that feed

The waved albatross visits Española only April-November.

on fish are all more active. **June-August** is **another high season,** with many travelers coming for summer vacations.

The islands have **short low seasons** in **May** and **September.** These are the best times to secure last-minute availability, although September is often used by cruise-boat owners as an opportunity to do annual maintenance work. However, cut-price deals can be found year-round if you look hard enough and are flexible.

Passports, Tourist Cards, and Visas

Travelers to Ecuador will need a **passport** that is valid for at least six months beyond the date of entry. It is easy for most people to visit Ecuador because you don't need to apply for a visa in advance (unless you are from China or some countries in Africa). On entry to Ecuador, you will get a **tourist visa stamp** (also called a T-3) that is good for 90 days. You can apply for more time (up to 180 days) by filling out paperwork and applying for an **extended tourist visa** (12-IX). When entering Ecuador, travelers must also be able to show "proof of economic means" (a credit card is usually good enough) and a return or onward travel ticket out of Ecuador.

To enter the Galápagos, you must obtain the mandatory **$20 transit control card** from your departure airport (either Quito or Guayaquil). This helps to regulate the exact number of visitors. Upon arrival in the archipelago there is a mandatory **$100 national park entrance fee,** payable in cash. It's a hefty fee, but it helps to preserve the islands' fragile ecosystem. If you have a student or cultural visa, you pay $25, while Ecuadorians pay just $6. Note that a recent crackdown on illegal immigration means that staying beyond 90 days will result in immediate deportation.

Vaccinations

All visitors should make sure their **routine immunizations** are up to date. The U.S. Centers for Disease Control and Prevention recommend that travelers be vaccinated against **hepatitis A, typhoid fever,** and, in cases of close contact with locals, **hepatitis B. Rabies vaccinations** are also recommended for those venturing into rural areas. Proof of **yellow fever vaccination**

The *Isabela* is a mid-size cruise ship.

is necessary when entering Ecuador from Peru or Colombia, but it is a good idea no matter where you arrive from. Note that there have been some cases of dengue fever on the Galápagos recently. There is no vaccine, so wear long, light-colored clothing and use mosquito repellent.

Booking a Tour

In simple terms, the farther you are from the Galápagos, the more you pay. Cruises, land tours, and diving tours can all be arranged in your home country or through a travel agency in Ecuador. Keep in mind that when booking a tour from abroad, a **deposit** of at least $200 per person, via wire transfer or Western Union (no credit cards by Internet or phone), is usually required.

Many travel agencies in Quito and Guayaquil advertise tours, so shopping around is the way to go. Holding out for **last-minute deals** may save you anywhere from 5 to 35 percent, but be aware that it may leave you stranded as well. Some travelers with time on their hands even fly to the Galápagos, book into a cheap hotel for a few days, and take their chances on finding a last-minute cruise, saving 50 percent in some cases; but there are no guarantees.

Transportation

Transportation to the islands is generally not included in the price of a tour. Flights to the Galápagos depart from Quito and Guayaquil daily. There are two entrance **airports** in the Galápagos: one on **Baltra,** just north of the central island of Santa Cruz, and one on **San Cristóbal.** The airport on Isabela is only used for interisland flights, and there are no airports on Floreana. Make sure you're flying to the correct island to begin your tour. Prices are about $350 round-trip from Guayaquil and $400 from Quito.

If you are traveling to the islands without being booked on a tour, **Puerto Ayora** is the best place to arrange a **budget tour.** Note that getting from Baltra to Puerto Ayora is a journey in three stages involving two bus rides and a ferry ride. There are daily ferry shuttles from $30 per person one-way to the other three other ports—Baquerizo Moreno on San Cristóbal, Puerto Velasco Ibarra on Floreana, and Puerto Villamil on Isabela.

The Galápagos Islands are an expensive destination, with some of the expensive cruises costing $6,000 for a week, and the luxury all-inclusive land-based tours are not far behind. There are, however, more budget-friendly alternatives. Planning your trip independently, you could spend as little as $2,000 per person including international airfare. If you are already backpacking through Ecuador and don't have to pay international airfare, you could spend less than $1,000.

GENERAL EXPENSES

First calculate how much just getting to the Galápagos will cost you. If you are coming from the United States or Europe, it could cost you upward of $1,500. On the other hand, if you are already backpacking through South America and passing through Quito, it will cost much less (an additional $460 or so for domestic airfare and park entrance fees).

- International airfare = $500-1,200

- Accommodations, food, and airport transfer in Quito or Guayaquil = minimum $50, more if you want to stay a couple days

- Domestic airfare to Galápagos from Quito or Guayaquil = $300

- National park entrance fee = $100 (unless you're a resident of Ecuador or here on a student visa)

- Transit control card = $20

SAMPLE 10-DAY BUDGET LAND-TOUR COST

By staying in basic *hostales*, taking buses, avoiding the expensive day tours, and taking speedboat ferries, you can see the Galápagos relatively inexpensively. The 11-day Budget Backpacker itinerary can be done for around $1,000 per person, excluding the national park entrance fee, domestic airfare, and international airfare.

- Basic accommodations: $25 per person x 10 nights = $250

- Food at casual restaurants and local joints: $25 per day x 10 nights = $250

- Interisland ferries: $30 x 5 = $150

- Activities: kayak rental ($10) + bike rental ($10) + Tintoreras tour ($40) + Sierra Negra hike ($40) + splurge on day trip to Seymour Norte ($160) = $260

- Taxis to highlands ($20 per person in a group) for Santa Cruz and San Cristóbal = $40

- Water taxis: $10

- Buses: $5

SAMPLE 9-DAY HIGH-END LAND-TOUR COST

If you want to see the highlights of the Galápagos by land (including the expensive day tours), stay in luxury waterfront hotels, and fly between the islands, it can be a costly trip. The sample budget below for the Greatest Hits itinerary adds up to approximately $2,700 per person, assuming you are sharing a room, with airfare and park fees excluded. Note that the cost is in the same ballpark as a luxury-class, weeklong "last-minute" cruise in Puerto Ayora, though still cheaper than a weeklong luxury cruise booked in advance from abroad. The tradeoff is that on the cruise you will see more and spend less time every day in transit, but the land tour will have a more comfortable hotel room—and you can dive. You can also easily turn this into a midrange budget (approximately $2,000 pp) by staying in midrange hotels (halving the accommodation cost) and taking a ferry rather than the flight in between islands.

- Luxury accommodations: $150 per person x 8 nights = $1,200

- Food at nice casual restaurants geared at tourists: $40 per day x 8 nights = $320

- Interisland flight: $150

- Tours/attractions: Seymour Norte ($160) + Gordon Rocks ($170) + Bartolomé ($180) + Santa Fé tour ($160) + Kicker Rock ($150) + Española ($200) = $1,020

- Water taxis: $5

- Taxis: ($40 for tour of highlands + $25 from Baltra airport + $3 from San Cristóbal airport) = $68

Choosing a Cruise

Cruises are the traditional way to visit the Galápagos. Tour boats are organized into **four classes**—economy/tourist, tourist superior, first, and luxury. **Economy/tourist-class** boats are very basic and appropriate for those on a very limited budget; **tourist superior-class** boats are the most common in the islands, with a bit more comfort and better guides; **first class** and **luxury tours** offer gourmet food, comfortable cabins, and service that matches those in the finest hotels on the mainland, and guides are qualified scientists. Prices vary widely, but all prices should include food, accommodations, transfers to and from your boat, trained guides, and all your shore visits.

A good guide is the most important factor in your visit. All Galápagos guides are trained and licensed by the National Park Service and qualify in one of three classes, in ascending order of quality. When booking a tour, ask about your guide's specific qualifications and what language(s) he or she speaks.

Sample Itineraries

A tour of at least five days is recommended, and seven or eight days is even better, as it takes half a day each way to get to and from the islands.

There are basically three cruise itineraries: **northern, southern,** and **western.** Five-day tours include one of these areas, and eight-day tours include two; it's only possible to experience all three areas on the more expensive and rarer two-week tours. Note that the western itinerary has fewer departures and is mainly available on eight-day tours because distances are greater. Most tours start off in **Santa Cruz,** but you can also start in **San Cristóbal.** Always check the exact itinerary and the class of boat before booking.

Avoid booking "eight-day" cruises that are actually a combination of two shorter cruises; valuable time will be spent loading and unloading passengers, and the day's visits will be close to port rather than in the more spectacular remote regions.

FIVE-DAY NORTHERN CRUISE

- **Day 1:** Baltra airport, Bachas Beach
- **Day 2:** Bartolomé, Santiago, and Rábida
- **Day 3:** Genovesa
- **Day 4:** Plaza Islands, Santa Cruz (Charles Darwin Research Station, Tortuga Bay)
- **Day 5:** Baltra

FIVE-DAY SOUTHERN CRUISE

- **Day 1:** San Cristóbal (Cerro Brujo, Kicker Rock)
- **Day 2:** Plaza Islands, Santa Fé
- **Day 3:** Española (Punta Suárez, Gardner Bay)
- **Day 4:** Floreana (Post Office Bay, Punta Cormorant, Devil's Crown)
- **Day 5:** Santa Cruz (Charles Darwin Research Station), Baltra

SIX-DAY WESTERN CRUISE

- **Day 1:** Baltra, Rábida
- **Day 2:** Isabela (Punta Vicente Roca), Fernandina (Punta Espinosa)
- **Day 3:** Isabela (Tagus Cove, Urbina Bay)
- **Day 4:** Isabela (Elizabeth Bay, Punta Moreno)
- **Day 5:** Isabela (Puerto Villamil)
- **Day 6:** Seymour Norte, Baltra

EIGHT-DAY SOUTHERN AND NORTHERN CRUISE

- **Day 1:** San Cristóbal (Isla Lobos, Kicker Rock)
- **Day 2:** San Cristóbal (highlands, Punta Pitt)
- **Day 3:** Floreana (Post Office Bay, Punta Cormorant, Devil's Crown)
- **Day 4:** Santa Cruz (Black Turtle Cove), Bartolomé
- **Day 5:** Genovesa

Galápagos Islands Cruise Tours

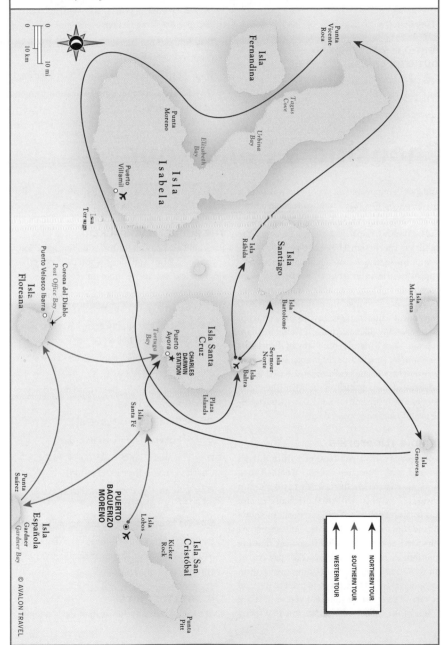

- **Day 6:** Santiago
- **Day 7:** Plaza Islands, Santa Cruz (Charles Darwin Research Station)
- **Day 8:** Baltra

EIGHT-DAY WESTERN AND SOUTHERN CRUISE

- **Day 1:** Baltra, Rábida
- **Day 2:** Isabela (Punta Vicente Roca), Fernandina (Punta Espinosa)

- **Day 3:** Isabela (Tagus Cove, Urbina Bay)
- **Day 4:** Isabela (Elizabeth Bay, Punta Moreno)
- **Day 5:** Isabela (Wetlands, Wall of Tears, Tortoise Breeding Center)
- **Day 6:** Seymour Norte, Santa Cruz (Charles Darwin Research Station)
- **Day 7:** Española (Punta Suárez, Gardner Bay)
- **Day 8:** San Cristóbal (Interpretation Center, La Galapaguera)

Choosing a Land Tour

Land tours are now the most popular way to visit the Galápagos. On a land tour, you stay in a hotel in a port town on one of the four populated islands, take day trips, and shuttle between the islands via speedboat. They are especially popular with those who are on a budget, prefer independent travel, suffer from seasickness, or want to scuba dive. There are packaged tours that include transportation, accommodation, meals, and tours, but it's increasingly easy to plan yourself and save money. There is more flexibility in planning your own itinerary, but many of the islands (for example, Fernandina, Española, Rábida, and Genovesa) are excluded from land-based visits, and many of the best sites on the other islands are also excluded. Precious time is also spent traveling to and from sites every day.

Sample Itineraries

Land tours restrict you to sites within a day's travel of four populated areas: **Puerto Ayora** on Santa Cruz, **Baquerizo Moreno** on San Cristóbal, **Puerto Villamil** on Isabela, and **Puerto Velasco Ibarra** on Floreana. The shortest land tours are five days long, but these short tours are not recommended if you are coming from abroad; in comparison to a five-day cruise, you will spend too much of your short trip in transportation. **Eight days** is preferable, and **eleven days** is the minimum if you want to see all four of the inhabited islands. Note that many

of these itineraries involve flying into one airport and flying out of another to save time.

THE BUDGET BACKPACKER

Pack light and stay on the move, exploring all four inhabited islands and focusing on the free activities and less-expensive tours on each.

- **Day 1:** San Cristóbal (fly in; Puerto Chino, La Galapaguera and El Junco by taxi)
- **Day 2:** San Cristóbal (Cerro Tijeretas, Playa Baquerizo, and La Lobería)
- **Day 3:** San Cristóbal-Santa Cruz (ferry in the morning; Las Grietas)
- **Day 4:** Santa Cruz-Isabela (Los Humedales by bike, Concha de Perla)
- **Day 5:** Isabela (Sierra Negra hike)
- **Day 6:** Isabela (Tintoreras Bay tour)
- **Day 7:** Isabela-Santa Cruz (ferry; highlands, Charles Darwin Research Station)
- **Day 8:** Santa Cruz-Floreana (ferry; highlands by *chiva*, La Lobería)
- **Day 9:** Floreana-Santa Cruz (La Botella; ferry)
- **Day 10:** Santa Cruz (splurge on a day trip to Santa Fé, Seymour Norte, or the Plazas)
- **Day 11:** Fly out of Baltra

THE GREATEST HITS

Visit the most famous sites available via land tour,

Bartolomé walkway

staying in the tourist hubs of Puerto Ayora and Baquerizo Moreno. This is also one of the most expensive itineraries.

- **Day 1:** Santa Cruz (fly in; highlands, Charles Darwin Research Station)
- **Day 2:** Santa Cruz (Santa Fé tour)
- **Day 3:** Santa Cruz (diving at Gordon Rocks, or day tour to the Plazas if you don't dive)
- **Day 4:** Santa Cruz (Bartolomé tour)
- **Day 5:** Santa Cruz (Seymour Norte)
- **Day 6:** Santa Cruz-San Cristóbal (Tortuga Bay, afternoon ferry or flight, La Lobería)
- **Day 7:** San Cristóbal (diving at Kicker Rock, or 360 tour if you don't dive)
- **Day 8:** San Cristóbal (Española tour)
- **Day 9:** Fly out of San Cristóbal

THE LANDLUBBER
People who easily get seasick can sleep in hotels and avoid long boat rides by flying between the islands and picking the tours on the inhabited islands or relatively close to port (less than 40 minutes away). The tradeoff is that interisland flights are expensive and you will miss some of the most famous sites. If your seasickness isn't that extreme, you can also consider a very large cruise ship so you can see more wildlife.

- **Day 1:** San Cristóbal (fly in; Interpretation Center and Cerro Tijeretas)
- **Day 2:** San Cristóbal (Isla Lobos tour)
- **Day 3:** Fly to Isabela (Tintoreras Bay tour, Concha de Perla)
- **Day 4:** Isabela (Sierra Negra, Playa Grande)
- **Day 5:** Isabela (bike Los Humedales and the Tortoise Breeding Center)
- **Day 6:** Fly to Santa Cruz (Tortuga Bay, highlands)
- **Day 7:** Santa Cruz (bay tour and Charles Darwin Research Station)
- **Day 8:** Santa Cruz (Santa Fé tour)
- **Day 9:** Fly out of Baltra

SURVIVAL OF THE FITTEST
Do the most challenging hikes, bikes, dives, and

kayaking trips in the Enchanted Isles; balance the calorie deficit with plenty of *pescado encocado* (seafood cooked with sweet coconut milk). To make the itinerary a little less extreme and a couple days shorter, cut out the most off-the-beaten-path activities (camping and hiking Cerro Crocker).

- **Day 1:** Santa Cruz (ferry in the morning, Tortuga Bay beach visit and kayak)
- **Day 2:** Santa Cruz (visit El Chato and Túneles de Bellavista by bike)
- **Day 3:** Santa Cruz (diving at Gordon Rocks)
- **Day 4:** Santa Cruz-Isabela (ferry in the morning; Tortoise Breeding Center and Los Humedales by bike)
- **Day 5:** Isabela (Sierra Negra or Sulfur Mines hiking tour)
- **Day 6:** Isabela (Los Túneles tour or diving at Tortuga Island)
- **Day 7:** Isabela (SUP tour to Tintoreras Bay, swimming at Concha de Perla)
- **Day 8:** Isabela-Santa Cruz (ferry to Santa Cruz; hike Cerro Crocker)
- **Day 9:** Santa Cruz (kayaking and camping at Playa Garrapatero)
- **Day 10:** Santa Cruz (return to town, swimming at Las Grietas)
- **Day 11:** Santa Cruz-Floreana (ferry in the morning; highlands, La Lobería)
- **Day 12:** Floreana (kayaking tour to Post Office Bay)
- **Day 13:** Floreana-Santa Cruz (kayaking tour to La Botella; afternoon return ferry)
- **Day 14:** Fly out of Baltra

Best Wildlife-Watching

You won't be squinting through binoculars for glimpses of wildlife in the Galápagos—the animals display themselves proudly and fearlessly, and every excursion brings unforgettable sights.

Santa Fé (page 75)

This small island midway between Santa Cruz and San Cristóbal offers trails through a forest of opuntia cacti, which grow up to 10 meters high, with **Galápagos hawks** circling overhead. Negotiate the rocky trail and cross a steep ravine to view colonies of the yellowish **Santa Fé land iguana,** endemic to the island.

Seymour Norte (page 76)

Bird-watching heaven is found on this tiny island near Santa Cruz. Decide which has the most interesting mating ritual—**boobies** marching around showing off their bright blue feet or **frigates** inflating their red chests to the size of a basketball.

Punta Espinosa, Fernandina (page 138)

Fernandina's only visitor site is home to the islands' largest **marine iguana** colony, along with a **sea lion** population and the biggest breeding site for **flightless cormorants,** birds who have swapped flying for diving to the ocean floor.

Punta Suárez, Española (page 139)

On the west side of Española is the biggest breeding site in the world for **waved albatross.** Nicknamed "albatross airport," it's the best place to see these magnificent birds take off, land, and perform their dancing mating ritual.

Darwin Bay Beach, Genovesa (page 139)

This beach is home to the largest colony of **red-footed boobies** in the Galápagos and the world.

Best Snorkeling and Diving

Punta Vicente Roca, Isabela

The Galápagos may be the best destination worldwide for watching wildlife on land, but the marine marvels underwater are beyond belief. After snorkeling with playful sea lion pups and nonchalant sea turtles or diving with hammerheads and whale sharks, the Caribbean and Red Sea simply pale in comparison.

Gordon Rocks, Santa Cruz (page 64)

One hour from Puerto Ayora, this site is for intermediate to advanced divers due to strong currents. Visibility is usually excellent, and you can watch schools of hammerheads, rays, moray eels, and sea turtles.

Kicker Rock (León Dormido), San Cristóbal (page 92)

The narrow channel between the sheer walls of this volcanic tuff cone is a prime snorkeling spot. White-tipped reef sharks, sea turtles, and rays are commonly seen in the channel, while divers go deeper to see hammerheads. A visit is combined with snorkeling among a sea lion colony at nearby Isla Lobos.

Punta Vicente Roca, Isabela (page 111)

On the western side of Isabela, this protected bay is an important resting spot for sea turtles, and you can also spot Galápagos penguins, flightless cormorants, and marine iguanas.

Devil's Crown and Champion Island, Floreana (page 128)

The jagged peaks of the submerged volcanic cone known as Devil's Crown poke out of the water—hence its ominous name. Snorkel outside the ring or in the shallow inner chamber with tropical fish and occasional sharks. A visit is usually combined with snorkeling among a sea lion colony at Champion Island.

Gardner Bay, Española (page 138)

On the northeast side of Española, this crescent beach offers snorkeling with a sea lion colony, stingrays, white-tipped sharks, and parrot fish. It's also an important nesting site for sea turtles.

Wolf and Darwin Islands (page 140)

The ultimate diving experience, open only to live-aboard dive cruises, is found around these islands in the far north. Hundreds of hammerheads can be seen off Wolf, gigantic whale sharks cruise by June-November, and bottlenose dolphins are common at Darwin's Arch.

sea lions at La Lobería, San Cristóbal

As budget tourists know, day tours can easily empty your wallet; cruises can empty your bank account. Luckily, a surprising number of sights are free to visit on your own. Check out these spots and keep an eye out for blue-footed boobies, marine iguanas, and sea lions.

Tortuga Bay, Santa Cruz (page 59)

Most travelers don't come to the Galápagos to lie on beaches but rather to watch animals lying on beaches. However, you may welcome the chance to sun yourself like a lazy iguana after a hard day of watching wildlife. The longest beach in the archipelago is a 45-minute walk from Puerto Ayora on Santa Cruz. The first beach has strong currents and is popular with surfers, but walk to the end and soak in a sheltered, shallow lagoon at Playa Mansa. In between, there is a short rocky path where you can keep your eye out for marine iguanas and blue-footed boobies.

Cerro Tijeretas, San Cristóbal (page 81)

A walking path from town winds through dry lava rock and cacti, ascending a steep hill with views of the beaches below. You can often spot frigate birds on the trees in the morning. The path then descends to a protected cove with clear water and good snorkeling.

La Lobería, San Cristóbal (page 83)

Walk an hour out of town in San Cristóbal (or take a $2 taxi) and you will find yourself walking among a huge colony of sea lions. The babies play in the sand while the moms sunbathe and the alpha males patrol the beach. The water is a bit murky and choppy, but that doesn't stop tourists and locals from wading in to snorkel.

Playa Grande and Los Humedales, Isabela (pages 99 and 107)

Puerto Villamil's town is built along a beautiful white-sand beach that just keeps getting prettier the farther west you walk, until you reach the wetlands area with lagoons, flamingos, and marine iguanas.

Concha de Perla, Isabela (page 99)

Just walk 15 minutes from town and you are ready to snorkel with sea lions, penguins, and lots of fish in this protected, mangrove-fringed cove that is free to the public.

La Lobería, Floreana (page 119)

Just a 20-minute walk from Puerto Velasco Ibarra is a rocky, lava-strewn path, fringed on either side by dramatic red vesuvium plants and cacti. At the end of the path is a protected area where snorkelers can float among sea turtles and a small sea lion colony. The west-facing point is one of the best places to watch the sunset in the Galápagos.

Visiting the Islands

There are basically two ways to see the Galápagos: on a cruise or on a land-based tour.

Cruises have historically been the most popular, and advantages include the opportunity to travel farther, cover more sites, and spend more time there without needing to get back to port at dusk. There are also many sites accessible only to cruise tours, and there is less environmental impact than staying on land, with none of the associated pollution from hotels. The drawbacks are that you are on a boat with the same group for several days with a fixed schedule, which doesn't suit everyone. Seasickness is also a factor, even on the largest cruises. With the wide choice of boat classes available, it's important to remember that, by and large, you get what you pay for. You could save a few hundred dollars by opting for the cheapest boat, but you'll end up with a guide with less knowledge, a less comfortable boat, and probably worse seasickness.

Land-based tours are becoming increasingly popular, particularly for those not suited to spending a long time on a boat. Many operators organize short tours based on one island, or you can do an island-hopping tour. However, with the wide availability of day tours in Puerto Ayora and regular ferries between the three main populated islands (San Cristóbal, Santa Cruz, and Isabela), increasing numbers of budget travelers are shunning tours and doing it themselves, saving a lot of money. Bear in mind, though, that doing it this way restricts you to day tours close to the main islands, and islands such as Genovesa, Española, Santiago, and Fernandina, as well as the better sites on Floreana and Isabela, become off-limits.

Whatever you decide to do, it's important that you don't get preoccupied with a checklist. Eight days (or even five days) in the Galápagos is an incredible experience to be savored, so don't ruin your enjoyment of it by becoming obsessed with seeing it all.

Previous: a beach yacht in front of Rábida Island; diving boat off of Kicker Rock.

Cruise Tours

Most cruises are 5-8 days. There are also four-day itineraries, but when you consider that two half days at the beginning and end are spent traveling, a minimum of five days is recommended, and eight days is preferable if you can afford it. In five days, the most common cruise itineraries start at Santa Cruz, taking in Puerto Ayora, the highlands, Seymour Norte, and Plaza Sur, then head either north or south. Northern tours usually include Bartolomé, Santiago, and Genovesa, while southern itineraries usually take in Santa Fé, San Cristóbal, Floreana, and Española. There is also a slightly less frequent and more expensive western itinerary that includes Isabela and Fernandina. Eight-day tours usually combine two of these three routes (north and west, north and south, or west and south). It's not possible to see all of the above islands in eight days, and while cruises for longer than eight days do exist, they are rare and mostly dedicated dive trips. Dive tours are the only ones that reach the most remote islands of Darwin, Wolf, and Marchena. Note that since 2012, boats have been prohibited from visiting the same site in a 14-day period (previously the limit was seven days); the goal is to protect the most popular visitor sites.

There are roughly four classes of tour boats—economy/tourist, tourist superior, first, and luxury—and trips range 4-8 days, with occasional special charters of 11 and 15 days. The rating system is far from standardized, however, and you may find tour agencies that sell cruises in different categories, such as "standard" versus "deluxe." Whatever length of tour you opt for, there's no escaping that it's not cheap. Prices range from less than $1,000 per person for a five-day tourist-class trip to $6,000 for eight days on a luxury-class vessel. Note that arrival and departure days are counted as tour days. Prices include food, accommodations, transfers to and from your boat, trained guides, and all your shore visits.

The airfare and insurance are paid separately, and you'll need to factor in tips for the crew, plus alcoholic and soft drinks on board. Note that single cabin supplements are usually very high. It doesn't hurt to ask, but you're far better off sharing a cabin.

Itineraries are strictly controlled by the National Park Service to regulate the impact of visitors on delicate sites. Every cruise has a tight schedule, and the feeling of being herded around doesn't suit everyone, but console yourself that cruises have far less impact on the environment than land-based tours; plus you get to see far more.

BOAT TYPES AND SIZES

Cruises operate on many types of boats, from small 10-passenger motor-sailboats to 100-passenger cruise ships. Each offers a very different experience, and it's important to note the differences when choosing a cruise.

Yachts

Small yachts carrying 10-20 passengers are the most intimate way to see the Galápagos Islands. Keep in mind, however, that an intimate group atmosphere you get aboard a small yacht may or may not hold true on the visitor sites. Whether there are four small yachts anchored at a site or one large cruise ship (split into several groups), you will be sharing the site with other people according to the schedules set by the national park.

Also, boats carrying 16 or fewer passengers may have only one naturalist guide. If there is only one guide and a mix of Spanish-speaking and English-speaking guests, the guide may have the irritating responsibility of repeating everything.

The smallest yachts are only 50 feet long, while the larger luxury ones are 150 feet. Out of the small yachts, some are single-hulled **motor yachts** (abbreviated M/Y), while **motor catamarans** (M/C) have two hulls for extra lateral stability, and **motor-sailors** (M/S) have both motors and sails. Note that motor-sailors are among the most photogenic boats in the Galápagos, but usually the motors do all the work. They rarely hoist their sails because of the need to get to faraway sites on schedule. There are yachts in all of the cruise boat classes, from economy class to luxury class.

Cruise Ships

While the largest cruise ships are thankfully a thing of the past in the Galápagos, there is still demand for a deluxe tour with standards comparable to good hotels on the mainland. Most of the ships are luxury class and have capacity for more than 40 passengers, and the biggest cater to 100.

The main benefit is comfort and stability: Rolling with the sea is minimized, so you're far less likely to get seasick, although it's still possible. Compared to a yacht, you will probably get a larger cabin, spacious social areas, and more amenities. Whereas shared tables are ubiquitous on yachts, it's relatively easy on a cruise ship to have a private table at meals if you're planning a romantic trip or simply don't want to socialize with strangers.

The biggest potential drawback is that you are visiting with a large number of people, so the experience feels less personal. Fortunately, cruise ships have several ways to manage groups while visiting the islands. First, they divide their passengers into smaller groups of 10-16 people, usually by language. Second, the guides manage their groups to keep a healthy distance on wildlife visits, doing the same loop trails in reverse order, for example. Third, cruise ships stagger when their groups disembark by half an hour to avoid crowding. Last, cruise ships sometimes have alternative activities, such as glass-bottom boats or kayaks; hence people may also be split among different activities. Also note that the itinerary may be less active than on small yachts. Whereas a small yacht might have both snorkeling and kayaking at a site before lunch, a

cruise ship might offer one or the other, with the additional time spent onboard.

CRUISE BOAT CLASSES

Cruises come in four basic classes: tourist/economy, tourist superior, first, and luxury. It is important to note, however, that the classification system is not regulated and there is no universal standard. You may find the same yacht advertised in two different classes by different agencies. Make sure you confirm all the important details (name of yacht, qualifications of guides, size of cabins, amenities, etc.) when booking a trip. In the past, the cheapest cruises had shared bathrooms and no air-conditioning. However, in light of the limited supply of berths aboard cruises allowed by the national park, ongoing investment has renovated or replaced many of the most basic boats. This means that cruises are becoming more expensive, but the overall quality is increasing as well.

Economy/Tourist Class

These boats are the "backpacker specials" of the Galápagos. Prices for boats in the tourist class range $1,000-2,000 per person per week, but there are frequent last-minute deals because older visitors booking from abroad tend to avoid the most basic boats. You may be lucky and have a good experience, but note that every aspect of the service on these small boats, which carry 10-16 passengers, will be basic. These boats tend to hire either Class One or Class Two guides, with less training, less knowledge, and often a poor level of English. Cabins are usually air-conditioned but tiny, with small, bunk-style beds. Some may lack hot water. The most basic had shared bathrooms in the past, though these boats have largely been upgraded and replaced. Most importantly, small boats are more prone to rocking, so seasickness is worse. Common areas are minimal, and the food will likely be uninspiring. Maintenance is also generally worse, and there is an increased risk of problems such as air-conditioning breaking down, power outages, or, more rarely, engine problems. These boats tend to be slower; most avoid the long distances to the more pristine and far-flung corners of the archipelago (Fernandina, the west side of Isabela, and Genovesa).

While these boats are popular with young backpackers, they are losing popularity to land-based tours, and there are very few of these boats around the islands now. Boats in this category include the *Darwin, Golondrina, Flamingo, King of the Seas,* and *Merak.* You should also consider that visiting the Galápagos is probably a once-in-a-lifetime experience, so paying a bit more for better service is advisable.

Tourist Superior Class

Tourist-superior-class boats are popular mid-range boats that cost $2,000-3,000 per person per week. These medium-size sailboats or motorboats hold 10-20 passengers. Everything is better quality than on the economy boats—better cabins (though still small and with bunk beds) with private bathrooms, hot showers, more varied food, and Class Two guides with a higher level of knowledge and better English. While the service is not as good as on first-class boats, overall these boats offer the best deal and attract a mixed range of clients—from backpackers to locals and older foreign travelers.

Boats in this category include *Aida Maria, Angelito, Cachalote, Daphne, Encantada Fragata, Floreana, Galaven, Nemo 1, Samba, San José,* and *Yolita.*

First Class

First-class boats cost $3,000-4,000 per person per week and are a popular and very comfortable way to see the islands while maintaining an intimate group atmosphere (mainly 16-26 passengers). They can also cover longer distances, and many include visits to the fascinating western islands of Isabela and Fernandina. Cabins are more comfortable, often with beds rather than bunks, and the decor makes the interior a pleasant place to spend time, unlike on many cheaper boats, where you want to escape the interior any chance you get. The interior is air-conditioned, and the food is excellent. These are also much sturdier yachts, so seasickness is less of a problem. Guides have to be Class Three, so they must hold a degree in natural sciences, usually biology or geology, and speak nearly fluent English.

Boats include the *Anahi, Archipell I* and *II, Beagle, Beluga, Coral I* and *II, Cormorant, Eric, Letty, Galaxy, Millennium, Mary Anne,*

Tourist-class yachts such as the 12-passenger *Encantada* are a less expensive way to see the outlying islands.

Monserrat, Odyssey, Reina Silvia, Seaman Journey, Sea Star Journey, Tip Top II, III, and IV, and *Treasure of Galapagos.*

Luxury Class

Luxury-class tours start at $4,000 per person per week and climb to over $10,000. This is the most deluxe experience possible in the Galápagos. The food is gourmet, cabins are large, and the Class Three guides are the best in the archipelago. Cabins start to resemble hotels rooms and often have an extra couch, chairs, or a desk. Some cabins have private balconies, panoramic windows, or TVs with satellite cable. Common areas include a comfortable lounge and dining area and a Jacuzzi. Food is excellent, usually buffet-style for breakfast and lunch and gourmet for dinner. Aboard the larger cruise ships you may also find Wi-Fi access, a pool, fitness center, spa, medical clinic, glass bottom boats, and professional photographer. Note, however, that you should not book these tours expecting a comparable level of luxury as found in top-class hotels on land—cabin sizes still do not compare to five-star hotels.

The large majority of luxury-class boats are cruise ships with 40-100 passengers, which have their own advantages and disadvantages.

A few exclusive yachts and catamarans carry only 20 passengers or fewer. These tours tend to attract older passengers, particularly aboard the large cruise ships.

Luxury cruise ships include the *Celebrity Flora, Endeavor II, Isabela II, Islander, La Pinta, Legend, Silversea,* and *XPerience.* Luxury yachts and catamarans include the *Camila, Celebrity XPloration, Evolution, Grace, Integrity, Ocean Spray, Origin, Passion,* and *Petrel.*

SPECIALTY CRUISES

Foreign companies sometimes charter entire cruise ships, bring their own staff, and market the tour themselves for various specialty cruises that command a premium. Cruises with the most reputable experts on Darwin, Harvard University professors, or famous birding experts are available on specific dates for a premium above the normal cost. Photography cruises typically have onboard celebrity photographers and lectures on photography techniques in the evenings. There are cruises designed for families with children, gay cruises, and singles cruises. These cruises are less common, and it is usually necessary to book well in advance for specialty tours; showing up in Puerto Ayora and

a room aboard a luxury-class cruise

looking for a last-minute deal is unlikely to be fruitful.

GUIDES

While the boat you travel on is very important, a good or bad guide can make or break your trip. There's no escaping the fact that, in most cases, you get what you pay for. The best guides usually work on the most expensive tours they can find, where they are best positioned to receive the largest tips, in addition to higher pay by the company. The good news is that all Galápagos guides are trained and licensed by the National Park Service, and they have all received further training in recent years as part of the Ecuadorian government's action to confront the islands' environmental problems. Guides are qualified in one of three classes, in ascending order of quality: Class One guides, usually on tourist-class boats and land-based tours, have the lowest level of knowledge and English; Class Two guides, on tourist- and tourist-superior-class boats, are more knowledgeable and often very good; and Class Three guides, on first-class and luxury boats, are the real experts and have all studied natural sciences at university. All guides should speak at least two languages, but Class One guides often speak little besides Spanish. Every guide has to pass rigorous examinations every three years and complete a training course on the islands every six years to keep his or her certification. When booking a tour, ask about your guide's specific qualifications and what language he or she speaks.

LIFE ON BOARD
Daily Routine

When you arrive on your boat, unless you're traveling first class or luxury, your first reaction may be: "I didn't think the cabin would be *that* small." But bear in mind that your room is really just for sleeping—you'll have far too much to look at outside on deck and at the visitor sites.

You'll meet the rest of the tour group, and your guide will introduce him- or herself and the rest of the crew before going through the

tour schedule. Guides will also explain the park rules, which you must follow, and do a safety evacuation drill.

Most days have an early start (breakfast at 7am or earlier) to give you the maximum time at the island sites (and also to get there before the day tours). Most boats tend to travel overnight to save time, and it's one of the joys of the cruise to wake up in a new place. The morning visits usually take 2-3 hours, including the *panga* (dinghy) ride to shore. Your guide will direct the group along the path or down the beach, explaining what you're seeing and filling in relevant natural-history details as you go. Be understanding if your guide seems overly concerned about keeping the group together and making everyone stick to the trail; remember that some visitors unwittingly cause damage, and the tour group is the guide's responsibility. Just because you've paid a lot of money doesn't mean you can do whatever you want. The same sentiment applies when your guides insist that you wear a lifejacket during *panga* rides; they face fines and jail time if they're caught with passengers not wearing them.

Back on board, you'll find your cabin clean and lunch ready. The midday meal is casual—a buffet on cruise ships and fixed menus on smaller vessels. You may find yourself surprisingly hungry after all that hiking and snorkeling, but don't overeat, as you may get lethargic and more prone to seasickness if the boat is traveling after lunch. Consuming lots of water and fruit is important to keep your energy and hydration levels up. Your guide will announce the departure time for the afternoon excursion; there's usually an hour's break.

Afternoon visits are similar to the morning, although it's considerably hotter, so take a hat and plenty of sunblock. Late afternoon is famously the best time for photography. Don't miss the incomparable opportunities to snorkel, for many people the highlight of their trip. Where else in the world can you swim with sea lions, turtles, stingrays, and sharks? Wetsuits are handy, especially in the cold season, but not necessary in the warm

Land Tour or Cruise...or Both?

The first decision you need to make is whether to take a cruise or a land tour. Or do you? While most travelers do either one or the other, it is also reasonably common to do both. Some travelers like a couple days to relax in the islands before flying home, and others choose to spend those days scuba diving—an activity not allowed aboard cruises with the exception of the few specialty live-aboard diving boats. If you must decide, however, the tradeoffs are below.

ADVANTAGES OF LAND-BASED TOURS

- **Avoiding seasickness** is one of the top reasons people choose land tours. However, although you do get to sleep in a comfortable hotel room on dry land, you also spend significant time in transit on small boats that are very prone to rocking. You can avoid interisland speedboat ferries by buying interisland flights instead, but some of the best day-trip sites are a 45-minute to 2-hour boat ride from port. Though you will likely be less seasick on a land tour compared to a small tourist- or tourist-superior-class yacht, you will likely be more seasick compared to being on a 50- to 100-passenger cruise ship.

- **Saving money** is another reason people choose land tours, particularly if you choose to travel independently. Your overall trip cost can be much lower, and your hotel room will likely still be nicer and more spacious than your cruise cabin.

- **You're not stuck on a boat** on a land tour. You can take a walk after dinner, grab a drink, or have extra time for souvenir shopping in the ports. You can eat at a variety of restaurants (though the gourmet food aboard first-class and luxury cruises is usually better than the restaurants in the ports).

- **You can customize your itinerary** to your interests, including hiking, wildlife visits, snorkeling, and even camping. You can travel spontaneously and independently without a fixed itinerary, booking tours just the day before as it suits your whims.

- **You can explore sights near the ports** independently; if you're lucky, you might even find yourself completely alone in nature.

- **You can scuba dive**—an activity that is not allowed on regular cruises, only on a few specialized live-aboard dive cruises.

- Land-based tours **support the local Galápagos economy** much more than cruises.

season; wearing just a swimsuit, most people can last about half an hour in the water before getting chilled.

There's usually some time before dinner to freshen up and enjoy a drink while watching the sunset (just after 6pm year-round). Dinner is the most important meal of the day, and this is your chance to fill up. Formality and the quality of the food depend on the class of cruise. After dinner, your guide will review what you saw today and preview tomorrow's schedule.

The higher-class vessels often have after-dinner entertainment; otherwise, it's a case of swapping tales with your fellow passengers. Alcohol is available, but try not to overdo it—you don't want the next morning's tour ruined by a hangover and interrupted sleep. Bear in mind that drinks are comparatively pricey and not included in the tour. You may be surprised to be nodding off by 9pm. Get plenty of rest because, after all, you didn't come to the Galápagos for the nightlife.

- **You see more of the culture** of the Galápagos when you spend time in the ports. Note, however, that the Galápagos region is not famous for its local culture, and Quito is a much better option if you really want to experience Ecuador's rich history and culture.

DISADVANTAGES OF LAND-BASED TOURS

- The Galápagos archipelago is famous for its unique wildlife and varied pristine landscapes, and **you simply don't see as much** of these on land tours. Fernandina, Española, Genovesa, Rábida, and many of the best sites on even the inhabited islands are off-limits. Some of those sites are home to animals that you won't see anywhere else in the archipelago. Visitors on a land tour don't see the waved albatross, flightless cormorant, or fur seal at all, and they also miss the largest colonies of other animals, such as the red-footed boobies on Genovesa. If you choose a shorter central-islands cruise, however, you can indeed see the large majority of the same sites on a land tour.

- **Significant daylight hours are spent in transit,** so you generally see fewer sites in the same number of days, and you may experience seasickness aboard the small boats used for day tours.

- Day tours often employ **Class One naturalist guides,** who have less knowledge and experience than the Class Two or Class Three guides found aboard the higher-end cruise ships.

- If you book day tours on your own, you will likely have a single guide with a mixed-language group, hence **all information is repeated:** once in English and again in Spanish. Note, however, that this is also true of some of the smaller cruise boats.

- Many land tours involve **island-hopping,** which requires you to pack and unpack your suitcase frequently to move to hotels on different islands. You travel between islands aboard an uncomfortable speedboat or a more pricey interisland flight.

- Though there are some eco-hotels with excellent environmental practices, **land tours usually have a larger environmental impact.** As land-based tourism grows, more workers and infrastructure on the islands are needed, and more goods are imported on cargo ships.

Land Tours and Independent Travel

Sleeping and eating on a boat is not for everybody, and if you are particularly prone to seasickness, consider a land-based itinerary. These are becoming increasingly common, both on organized tours and for independent travelers.

Note that there may be no escaping seasickness even on land-based tours because you will spend plenty of time on boats shuttling to and from the port, and they are smaller boats that roll around more. To completely avoid seasickness, you can opt for pricey interisland flights, rather than the interisland speedboat ferries, and choose the day tours that are close to port, rather than the farthest sites up to two hours away.

Most commonly you will be based in Santa Cruz, but island-hopping itineraries that take in San Cristóbal and/or Isabela are also popular. Five-day tours start at about $500 per person, and seven-day tours can cost up to $4,000 or more. You may find last-minute discounts on packages, but they are rarely as highly discounted as the cruises.

If you have decided that a land-based tour is preferable to a cruise, the next step is to decide whether or not you want to book an all-inclusive organized tour package (which includes meals, transportation, tours, and accommodations) or travel independently. While die-hard independent travelers prefer to avoid all tours whatsoever, this is often impractical in the Galápagos since many sites can only be visited by boat with a naturalist guide on a tour. For the purposes of this guide, we will refer to independent travel as when you aren't traveling with an organized multi-day tour group. You might have to buy a day tour in order to get to the uninhabited islands (since they are only accessible by boat with a licensed naturalist guide), but you buy your hotel, meals, and day tours separately, and you can also spend time walking or biking to sites near port on your own.

ORGANIZED LAND TOURS

Organized land tours are much more convenient, usually including all accommodations, tours, transportation, and meals, allowing you to focus on your vacation rather than the logistics. Some offer an excellent value due to negotiated group rates. Some organized tours have one guide for your entire trip, rather than switching every day as you book your own tours, and the guides may be more qualified depending on the tour operator who organized the trip.

Prices of Land Tours

Shopping for a land tour can be confusing because there is no classification or rating system. Land tours can range from $500 for five days to over $10,000 for a week, though most cost $2,000-4,000. Flights to and from the Galápagos, international airfare, and the Galápagos National Park entrance fee are very rarely included. Many factors make the difference between cheap and astronomically expensive land tours.

The organization of a tour determines whether you get a cohesive experience or more like a package of day tours. Nicer tours have an appointed guide or leader to accompany you throughout the trip and a defined group of guests who begin and end their trip at the same time. Other tours, particularly "customized tours," feel more like a package, where the travel agency just booked your hotel and daily activities with different providers. That would be the equivalent of independent travel, except that someone else handled the reservations.

Accommodations can be a very basic *hostal*, a luxury $400-plus hotel, or anything in between. Transportation between islands on an island-hopping tour can be aboard a public speedboat ferry ($30 each way) or more comfortable interisland flight ($130 each way). Food and the quality of naturalist guides can vary widely depending on how much the tour operator spends.

Itinerary makes a big difference in price as well because organizers of cheap and midrange land tours can't afford to buy you a spot on an expensive day yacht tour. The cheap, short five-day $500 land-based tours spend most of their time at places close to the main ports—sights that you could just as easily visit walking from town for free. Visitors on these inexpensive land tours not only miss the pristine sites accessible to cruises but also miss some of the best sights accessible by land. Moderately priced land tours usually include some of the less expensive tours that you could book yourself for $40-80: bay tours, Sierra Negra volcano, Los Túneles, or Kicker Rock. The expensive land tours include one or more day trips to neighboring islands such as Bartolomé, the Plazas, Santa Fé, or Seymour Norte; it costs independent travelers $100-180 to book these pricey excursions.

The most exclusive land tours, costing over $5,000, also have their own private day-tour yachts, which are more luxurious than the boats used by the other operators. The Finch Bay Eco Hotel's land tours include day-tour excursions aboard the 74-foot *Sea Lion* yacht, which boasts its own chef and onboard kitchen. The Pikaia Lodge's land tours have excursions aboard a 100-foot private yacht complete with a Jacuzzi and private cabins for each guest.

Types of Organized Tours

SINGLE-ISLAND HOTEL PACKAGES

Some short organized tours (five days or less) stay completely on Santa Cruz Island and take day trips into the highlands, to nearby beaches, and to some of the surrounding uninhabited islands. This is a popular approach because there are tons of sights within a day's trip of Santa Cruz, and you don't have to move hotels, but you will be missing some amazing sights on the other inhabited islands.

ISLAND-HOPPING

A very popular option is island-hopping tours that combine a stay on two, three, or even four of the inhabited islands, allowing you to see the highlights close to each port. Most island-hopping tours take speedboats between the islands, though the more expensive tours take interisland flights, sparing the discomfort and potential seasickness. A few organized tours island-hop to Floreana (which has no airport) along with Isabela or San Cristóbal. If you want to see these islands, some organized tours charter private speedboats to go directly from Floreana to Isabela or San Cristóbal, saving time and discomfort; independent travelers need to take two public ferries transferring through Santa Cruz.

DIVING TOURS

Diving tours include accommodations and daily dives; some also mix traditional snorkeling and wildlife walks with the diving. You can find diving tours that are completely based on Santa Cruz Island or island-hopping itineraries that dive off of San Cristóbal and Isabela.

MULTISPORT, CAMPING, AND SPECIALTY TOURS

Specialty land tours are increasingly organized for various groups. There are photography tours, family-friendly tours, LGBT tours, and more.

Particularly popular are **multisport adventure tours.** Multisport tours include plenty of vigorous kayaking, hiking, and biking activities along with the standard wildlife walks and snorkeling. If you prefer one particular activity, there are even specialty biking tours, kayaking tours, yoga tours, and surfing tours. These activity tours tend to attract a younger crowd and are well suited for the active adventurer.

Camping tours make it much easier to camp in the Galápagos. There are privately owned campgrounds open to the public for a fee, but they are generally far away from port and the sights. It can quickly become expensive to hire a taxi to take you from camp into town every day if you are traveling by yourself or in a pair, whereas organized tours can transport everyone by van. If you want to camp inside the national park, it becomes even better to go with an organized group; transportation is taken care of, as well as the potentially bureaucratic paperwork to get the necessary permits from the national park. Lastly, a couple of campsites on beaches are only reachable via boat; the only way to camp there is to go with an organized group that will charter a boat.

INDEPENDENT TRAVEL

Independent travel allows you to customize your trip and include just the activities that most interest you, the restaurants that you like, and the hotels or *hostales* that fit your budget. Fiercely independent travelers should be aware that independent travel in the Galápagos is not 100 percent independent; you are planning your own itinerary day-by-day, and there are several activities you can do independently, but for the most famous sights you will still be visiting in tightly controlled tour groups.

You can usually find accommodations in the ports for as little as $25 per person per night. You can obtain the deepest discounts on hotels by walking in without a reservation and negotiating. There are tour options for all budgets: Many nearby beaches and other sights are free; moderately priced boat tours and highlands trips cost $40-80; trips on day-trip yachts to the more famous sites cost up to $180. You can plan your activities as late as the day before, allowing you to spontaneously change a hiking day into a beach day if the mood strikes you. You can decide to eat wherever you like, rather than following your tour group to the designated restaurant. You can often save money compared to package tours, particularly if you travel in a small group of friends that can share taxis and negotiate hotel rates. If your timing and luck are excellent, you might even find yourself completely alone in nature in one of the beautiful places just walking distance from the port.

Keep in mind, however, that you will have to spend valuable time arranging transportation, choosing a hotel, and making reservations in tour agencies. You will have to carry around absurd amounts of cash to pay for hotels and tours. You will likely get a different naturalist guide every time you book a different day tour, making redundancy of information about animals and the islands a given. Compared to an organized land tour, you are also much more likely to end up in a mixed-language group, where your guide has to repeat everything in Spanish and English. The appealing flexibility of changing your plans quickly evaporates during high season, when the popular day tours book up a couple days ahead of time.

WHERE TO STAY

There are plenty of accommodations in the three main ports. **Puerto Ayora** on Santa Cruz has the widest range, with double rooms from just $30 per night up to $400. **Puerto Baquerizo Moreno** on San Cristóbal and **Puerto Villamil** on Isabela have a good range and are quieter. On **Floreana,** there are less than a dozen accommodations. There are only two lodges and the rest are informal family-run guesthouses. The best hotels on the islands are often booked up in high season (Christmas-Easter), but cheap accommodations are usually available in all the ports. Note that rates at the top-end hotels are very high, so you are usually better off booking an all-inclusive tour if you want to stay at this level of accommodation.

WHERE TO GO

If you've decided to island hop, there are four main ports that you can visit.

the pool at the Finch Bay Eco Hotel in Puerto Ayora on Santa Cruz

Puerto Ayora on Santa Cruz is the most touristy port and has the largest offering of day tours and activities. Tortuga Bay, Las Grietas, and Charles Darwin Research Station can easily be visited independently on foot and via inexpensive water taxi. Garrapatero beach and the highlands can be visited inexpensively by taxi. The cheapest tours are the bay tour ($35) and day tours of the other inhabited islands (Floreana, $80; San Cristóbal, $120-160; and Isabela, $80-120). More pricey trips visit nearby uninhabited small islands: A snorkeling-only trip to Santa Fé is about $100, while landing on the island costs $180. A snorkeling-only excursion to Daphne and Pinzón is $120. Trips to popular sites such as Plaza Sur, Seymour Norte, and Bartolomé cost $160-200.

Puerto Baquerizo Moreno on San Cristóbal is the second-largest town and capital of the Galápagos, though it has a smaller offering of activities compared to Puerto Ayora. You can easily walk on your own to the Interpretation Center and Cerro Tijeretas, and hike to several beaches on the edge of town. You can also visit La Lobería, which has a large sea lion colony, completely independently. There are three day tour options: Kicker Rock ($100), Isla Lobos ($80), Española ($200), or a 360 tour ($140) that visits several spots as you circumnavigate the island by boat. In the highlands, you can hire a taxi for $10 per hour and visit the freshwater lake of Laguna El Junco, the tortoise reserve La Galapaguera, and Puerto Chino beach.

Puerto Villamil on Isabela is a popular town to visit due to its relaxed vibe, beachfront location, and excellent offering of activities. You can visit a large number of attractions near town on your own; you can walk along Playa Grande, snorkel at Concha de Perla, visit the tortoise breeding center, and bike the wetlands Los Humedales. There are tours to Las Tintoreras ($40) on the edge of town and, farther out, Los Túneles ($110) and Isla Tortuga. The best hike in the islands is Sierra Negra ($35), which visits the stunning crater and moonlike landscapes.

Puerto Velasco Ibarra on Floreana is the tiniest town in the Galápagos, with only 130 residents (out of the islands' total population of 30,000). Most people visit Floreana on a day trip from Santa Cruz ($80), but visitors who stay a night or two on the island can have a unique off-the-beaten-path experience. You can visit the black-sand beach Playa Negra, La Lobería snorkeling spot, and the highlands independently by *chiva* (open-top bus). The real highlight is the excellent community-run day tours that visit La Botella ($45 pp; 2 person minimum) and Post Office Bay/Mirador de la Baronesa by kayak (cost subject to change). Bicycling tours are also in the works.

Booking and Last-Minute Deals

Booking a tour to the Galápagos can be done anywhere—from thousands of kilometers away at home in your own country to an agency in Puerto Ayora the night before the cruise leaves. Few accept credit cards, and if they do, a surcharge is usually applied. Operators in the Galápagos and Ecuador take cash, and when booking from abroad a wire transfer or PayPal is more common, so make sure to work with a reputable agency. The last two weeks in December are the busiest time of the year; be aware that many travelers book as much as a year in advance, and make your plans early for the best selection. July-August is not as crazy as winter break, but it is also a high season when there are fewer last-minute deals available.

BOOKING FROM ABROAD

Most travelers book their tours abroad before buying their international airfare to make sure they can take the cruise they want

Navigation Times on Day Tours

One of the most often cited disadvantages of taking day tours compared to a cruise is the significant amount of time spent in transit, particularly aboard the less comfortable speedboats that go to most of the destinations. The exceptions are the priciest tours leaving from Puerto Ayora to Bartolomé, the Plazas, Seymour Norte, and Santa Fé, which are aboard more comfortable day-tour yachts. Navigation times depend on the conditions at sea, but these estimates should give you some idea. Some tours are much longer when it comes to navigation time. Note that bay tours of Puerto Ayora, San Cristóbal, and Isabela are very popular, but the entire point of the tour is to coast slowly by the rocks in a small dinghy, and seasickness is rarely an issue, so navigation time is not really applicable.

DAY TOURS FROM PUERTO AYORA

- Santa Fé: 40 minutes each way

- Seymour Norte: Leaves Puerto Ayora by bus (45 minutes each way) followed by boat (30 minutes each way)

- The Plazas: 1.5 hours each way

- Pinzón and Daphne: Leaves Puerto Ayora by bus (45 minutes each way), followed by 3 hours of time on the boat in total

- Bartolomé: Leaves Puerto Ayora by bus (45 minutes each way) followed by boat (2 hours each way)

- San Cristóbal: 2 hours each way

- Floreana: 2 hours each way

- Isabela: 2-2.5 hours each way

- Bay tour and glass-bottom boat tour: none; exploring the bay by dinghy is part of the fun

DAY TOURS FROM SAN CRISTÓBAL

- Kicker Rock: 45 minutes each way

- Isla Lobos: 30 minutes each way

- Punta Pitt: 2 hours each way

- 360 tour: 4 hours round-trip; artisanal fishing tour

- Bay tour and glass-bottom boat tour: none; exploring the bay by dinghy is part of the fun

DAY TOURS FROM ISABELA

- Los Túneles: 45 minutes each way

- Las Tintoreras tour: none; coasting around the bay in a small dinghy is part of the fun within a specific vacation window. It can be impossible to book the smaller yachts directly, since they rely on travel agencies for their bookings, and you will need to go through a travel agency. It is much easier to book the large cruise ships and some of the higher-end yachts directly; most of them have their own sales team in Ecuador and the United States.

LAST-MINUTE DEALS

There are several ways to save on cruises if you have a flexible schedule and are willing to do a decent amount of legwork. You can save up to 50 percent of the total price by booking your tour last-minute in Ecuador. Even greater savings can be made booking last-minute in the Galápagos. However, bear in mind that it's very much a question of luck to get what you want. You may need to be flexible with different boats, itineraries, cruise classes, and departure dates. It might be far harder to find last-minute deals during high season (July-August) and almost impossible over Christmas (mid-December-early January). It is also harder to find last-minute deals if you are traveling with more than two people. Also note that it is impossible to book last-minute deals with some of the luxury and first-class boats; they prefer to leave cabins empty rather than discount.

In contrast, all-inclusive land tour and island-hopping operators do not generally offer last-minute discounts in the same way that cruises do. If you are traveling independently, you might find a last-minute deal on the day-tour yachts heading to Bartolomé, the Plazas, or other nearby islands, but discounts are far smaller and rarer than the last-minute cruise deals. Land-based travelers can, however, save money "last minute" by walking into hotels without reservations and negotiating.

Online and Abroad

Some travel agencies offer last-minute deals conveniently on their websites that you can book either from Ecuador or even abroad. These are usually not nearly as discounted as last-minute pricing in Quito or the Galápagos.

The larger companies that own and operate Galápagos cruises and have in-house travel agencies sometimes offer last-minute deals that you can book from abroad, even up to 30 days in advance. Discounts of up to 30 percent can be found, particularly in low season. Keep in mind, however, that if you book a last-minute cruise from abroad before you've bought your flight, you might cancel out any savings because of the higher cost of last-minute international flights.

In Quito and Guayaquil

Many travel agencies in Quito and Guayaquil advertise tours, so shopping around is a good idea. Between the two cities, Quito is much more highly recommended. There is a greater concentration of tourist agencies there, particularly in the Mariscal district, and there are tons of world-class attractions to keep you occupied while you're hunting for a deal. The more time you browse, the more likely you are to find a good deal, so it pays to be patient. The best deals come when operators are desperate to fill the last few spaces on a tour, and you can save 25-50 percent. Deposits range 10-50 percent, depending on the boat and tour operator. While booking from Quito may not be quite as cheap as booking from the Galápagos, it is more recommended because it lessens the risk of not getting the cruise that you want.

In the Galápagos

The biggest savings can be had by flying to Puerto Ayora, checking into a cheap hotel, and browsing the agencies on the waterfront for last-minute deals. Don't fly into Puerto Baquerizo Moreno if you want a last-minute cruise; although there are a few travel agencies there, they focus on day tours. Securing more than 50 percent off the original price is possible, but it's all a question of luck—and it's far less likely in high season.

Make sure to book a flight with extra days to give you more flexibility in finding a last-minute deal. Once you have your cruise booked, you can sightsee around Santa Cruz with your extra days, taking care to avoid the sights you will see on your cruise.

Ask for prices for specific boats from more than one agency; agencies receive a commission for each booking, but some may also mark the price up further. Once onboard, it is not uncommon to find differences of $200 or more in what different people have paid for the same cruise, last minute. Ensure that you get an itinerary and all the details of what you are paying for printed out. Some travelers find that they pay for what they thought was a tourist-superior boat only to get landed with a tourist-class vessel, so it's worthwhile getting the name of the boat and researching it online. Direct all complaints concerning tours, before or after, to the port captain (*capitanía del puerto*) if you booked in the islands, and to the agency directly if you booked in Quito or outside the country.

TIPPING

Don't forget to budget for the customary tips at the end of your trip. Remember that, although your tour is expensive, in a country as unequal as Ecuador, the big bucks don't filter down to the lowest level; the crew as well as the guide will very much appreciate your tip. Obviously use your own judgment on how much to give, and your tip should reflect the level of service. Between 5 and 10 percent of the price of the cruise or all-inclusive land tour is considered normal.

Tour Operators and Agencies

There are hundreds if not thousands of companies that sell cruises and land tours in the Galápagos, and deciding where to buy a tour can be daunting. Tour agencies sell a wide variety of cruises and tours and operate on commissions. In contrast, tour operators are the companies that own and operate the cruises in the Galápagos, or that organize groups for land-based tours. Specialty tour companies typically charter an entire cruise yacht for selected departures for special-interest groups.

If you want to see a wide variety of options and have someone help you choose the right one, it is best to find a reputable tour agency. If you mostly know what you want and prefer to speak with the experts on a particular boat or tour, contact the tour operator directly.

CRUISE OPERATORS

If you're interested in a particular company or specific yacht or cruise ship, many people prefer to deal directly with the owner/operating company. You can book directly with the following companies, which operate the first- and luxury-class cruises, and a small number of the cheaper boats. To book the other yachts, you need to book with an agency because they aren't set up to accept direct bookings.

Angermeyer Cruises/Andando Tours (P.O. Box 17210088, Mariana de Jesús E7-113 at Pradera, Quito, tel. 2/323-7330, www.visitgalapagos.travel) is an Ecuadorian company that builds on the experience of the Angermeyer family, one of the first families to settle the islands. They offer cruises on a wide range of vessels and are the owner/operators for the *Mary Anne*—a lovely three-masted sailing ship—and the luxury motor yacht *Passion*.

Celebrity (www.celebritycruises.com), which merged with Royal Caribbean Cruises in 1997, is a mega-cruise company best known for their experience operating very large 1,000-passenger cruises all over the world. Their Galápagos cruise ships include the *Flora, XPedition, Xperience,* and *XPloration.*

Ecoventura (www.ecoventura.com) is an Ecuador-based company with an excellent track record for running 20-person yachts (the first-class *Eric* and *Letty,* and the luxury-class *Origin*) and the live-aboard dive cruise *Galapagos Sky.* They are known for their environmental sustainability, active itineraries, and dedicated family departures. By running the yachts on identical schedules, they are able to create intimate groups of like-minded passengers.

Enchanted Expeditions (De Las Alondras N45-102 at Los Lirios, Quito, tel. 2/334-0525, www.enchantedexpeditions.com) is an Ecuadorian company founded by former naturalist guide Judy Carvhal. The company owns the first-class motor sailor *Cachalote*, the first-class motor yacht *Beluga*, and the luxury yacht *Passion*, and also books cruises on a range of other vessels.

Haugan Cruises (www.haugancruises.com) operates three intimate yet spacious catamarans: the first-class catamaran *Cormorant* and the luxury catamarans *Petrel, Camila,* and *Ocean Spray*. The catamarans have spacious cabins and Jacuzzis, but with the intimate experience of only 16 passengers each.

Klein Tours (www.kleintours.com) is a well-established company, founded in 1983. Today they are the owner/operator of the 100-passenger cruise ship *Legend* and two smaller yachts, the *Coral I* and *II,* and offer extensions in mainland Ecuador and Peru.

Lindblad Expeditions (www.expeditions.com) is best known for its partnership with *National Geographic*. Together they operate the medium-sized *Islander* and the large *Endeavor II* luxury cruise ships, which have a high standard of luxury and specialist National Geographic photographers on board.

Metropolitan Touring (www.metropolitan-touring.com) is one of the largest and most well-respected companies cruising the Galápagos. They were founded in 1953 and helped pioneer the Galápagos tourism industry. They operate high-end land tours as well as the luxury cruise ships *Isabela II, La Pinta,* and the *Santa Cruz*. They also have packages combining the Galápagos with stays at their boutique hotels in Quito (Casa Gangotena) and the jungle (Mashpi Lodge).

Silversea (www.silversea.com) is an award-winning luxury cruise company based in Italy that operates large cruises all over the world. When money is no object, travelers choose the 100-passenger *Silversea* for its European refinement, spacious suites, butler service, and included gratuities.

LAND TOUR OPERATORS

Land tours vary widely and range from just $700 at the low end up to $8,000 for the most exclusive. Note that these companies operate multi-day itineraries and are not to be confused with day-tour operators, which sell just daylong or half-day trips to independent travelers. Recommended operators for day tours can be found in the chapters for Santa Cruz, Isabela, and San Cristóbal.

Backroads (www.backroads.com) is a company well-known for adventure travel and international bicycle tours all over the world. They are headquartered in California and offer high-end multisport adventures that combine the Galápagos with the Andes in mainland Ecuador, with plenty of biking, kayaking, and hiking. There are family departures on selected dates.

GAdventures (www.gadventures) is a large international company that offers tours around the world. Their Galápagos tours are comfortably midrange and well organized. In recent years, they have become the largest supporter of Floreana's community tourism initiative; all their island-hopping triangle tours support this initiative. They are also one of the few companies to offer camping tours on private land, specifically for travelers 18-30.

Galakiwi (www.galakiwi.com) is based in the Galápagos and specializes in high-end, land-based island-hopping tours, including the complete circuit to all four inhabited islands in just ten days, with direct chartered speedboats. In addition to the multisport adventures, they offer specialized sports tours focused on biking or SUP.

Metropolitan Touring (www.metropolitan-touring.com), headquartered in Quito, offers luxury land-based tour packages. Visitors stay in their Finch Bay Eco Hotel on Santa Cruz Island and take day trips aboard their exclusive yacht *Sea Lion*. There are also island-hopping packages including a stay at the luxurious glamping Scalesia Lodge in the highlands of Isabela. They are also well-known for their cruises.

Pikaia Lodge (www.pikaialodgegalapagos.com) is a luxury eco-lodge in the highlands of Santa Cruz Island that operates the most exclusive land-based tours in the Galápagos, with seven-night tours that cost upward of $10,000 per person. These include day tours aboard their private luxury yacht, which boasts private cabins and a Jacuzzi.

ROW Adventures (www.rowadventures.com) is a worldwide adventure travel company. It is known for its unique, award-winning Galápagos Unbound island-hopping tour. This is currently the only company that organizes regular camping trips at Manglecito, a remote beach on San Cristóbal where it is impossible to camp on your own. The only access is by boat, and this tour arrives in style by ocean kayak.

SPECIALTY COMPANIES

Specialty companies charter cruise boats and operate tours on specific dates with their own sometimes famous expedition experts, or for specific interests such as families.

Cheeseman's Ecology Safaris (www.cheesemans.com) is a U.S.-based, high-end expedition travel company that has just a couple two-week-long departures per year with expert leaders. They book up far in advance.

Holbrook Travel (www.holbrooktravel.com) is a U.S.-based educational travel company that runs specialty cruises geared toward biology teachers and students.

Natural Habitat (www.nathab.com) is based in the United States and is the official partner of the World Wildlife Foundation (WWF). It offers high-end specialty cruises with expedition leaders, family cruises, photography cruises, and a two-week-long cruise covering all the major areas of the archipelago.

Nature Expeditions International (www.naturexp.com) from Florida specializes in educational adventure travel for older active travelers, including a 12-day package

that takes in Quito, the highland markets of Otavalo, and a Galápagos cruise on various first-class and luxury vessels.

Zegrahm (www.zegrahm.com) is a high-end expedition travel operator from Seattle that organizes its own chartered expeditions aboard selected yachts and cruise ships with expert expedition leaders.

TOUR AGENCIES

The advantages of booking from an agency rather than a tour operator are seeing multiple options in the same place, getting expert advice on choosing between them, and taking advantage of the customer service that many agencies are known for. The following is a list of reputable tour agencies based abroad, in Ecuador, and in the Galápagos. Though they are separated by home office location, don't think that you can't book a cruise with an Ecuador-based agency from the United States. Though most Ecuadorian tour agencies get a large part of their business from walk-in traffic for last-minute deals, they are also accustomed to handling email and phone inquiries from abroad. You can usually even call a toll-free number to speak with them. The tour agencies in Ecuador offer the widest selection of boats and land tours to choose from, and are also the best at last-minute deals. In contrast, U.S.- and U.K.-based agencies typically offer a smaller selection of cruises and land-based tours, mostly at the high end, packaged with adventures in mainland Ecuador, Machu Picchu, or elsewhere. U.S. and U.K.-based agencies often have higher prices, but they usually also include accommodations and tours in Quito or elsewhere.

United States

Adventure Associates (U.S. tel. 800/527-2500, www.adventure-associates.com) offers a curated list of luxury yachts, cruise ships, and hotel tours, along with packages that include the Amazon and the Galápagos in one trip.

GalapagosIslands.com (405 Dale Mabry Hwy. 342, Tampa, FL 33609, U.S. tel. 877/260-5552, www.galapagosislands.com) has a wide variety of cruises and land tours and an easy-to-navigate website.

In the United Kingdom

Andean Trails (tel. 131/467-7086, www.andeantrails.co.uk) is the self-proclaimed "South American travel specialist," offering tours all over South America, including a variety of cruises and land tours.

Select Latin America (tel. 20/7407-1478, www.selectlatinamerica.co.uk) has a huge range of bespoke cruise options, including sailing yachts (*Beagle, Sagitta,* and *Mary Anne*) and larger luxury cruise ships (*Eclipse, La Pinta, Isabela II*).

In Ecuador

Ecuadorian tour operators do last-minute deals. You can easily save 25 percent off the original local price at tour operators in Quito, and even greater savings compared with prices quoted in the United States.

QUITO

Quito has more tour companies than ever, and many of them are excellent. This is the best place to pick up good deals on trips to the Galápagos, and there are regular last-minute discounts. Bear in mind that not all operators in Quito have good reputations: Some overcharge and are underqualified. The following operators are recommended for their quality, professionalism, and value.

Galápagos Tours (Amazonas 2331 at Veintimilla, tel. 2/254-6028, www.galapagostours.net) offers a wide range of cruises and can also book hotels and rainforest tours.

Happy Gringo (U.S. tel. 800/269-0216, www.happygringo.com) is an Anglo-Dutch-owned company based in Quito. It has a wide selection of cruises and land tours and is known for good customer service.

Nuevo Mundo Expeditions (18 de Septiembre E4-161 at Juan León Mera, tel. 2/250-9431, www.nuevomundoexpeditions.com) was started in 1979 by a founder and former president of the Ecuadorian Ecotourism

Association. Land-based tours cost from $1,500 per person for five days.

Safari Tours (Reina Victoria N25-33 at Colón, tel. 2/255-2505, www.safari.com.ec), operating since 1993, can book last-minute spaces or make reservations online. Browse their deals of the week on the website.

GUAYAQUIL

Guayaquil has quite a few travel agencies, but not nearly as many as Quito. For Galápagos and rainforest trips, prices are similar to those in Quito, although last-minute bargains can be harder to come by.

Dreamkapture Travel (Alborada Doceava Etapa, Manzana 02, Villa 2, tel. 4/224-2909, www.galapagos-cruises.ca) is a tour agency based in a budget *hostal*, Dreamkapture Inn, in Guayaquil. They have a good selection and good prices on last-minute cruises that you can book via either cash in hand in Guayaquil or wire transfer from abroad.

Galápagos Sub-Aqua (Orellana 211 at Panamá, tel. 4/230-5514, www.galapagossub-aqua.com) is one of the best diving operators in the Galápagos and offers a range of live-aboard cruises on the *Galápagos Aggressor, Humboldt Explorer,* and *Wolf and Darwin Buddy.* Eight-day live-aboard trips run $3,500-4,500 per person. There are also five- to eight-day land-based tours, as well as day tours ($200 pp) that include two dives and the PADI training course.

Galasam (9 de Octubre 424 at Córdova, Ed. Gran Pasaje, tel. 4/230-4488, www.galasam.com.ec) offers short, cheap island-hopping land tours starting at $500 for five days, as well as a large selection of cruises.

THE GALÁPAGOS ISLANDS

Most visitors still arrive in the archipelago with their tour already arranged, but with the growing number of budget hotels and tour operators, you can find big savings by booking in Puerto Ayora. The low seasons in May-June and September-October are the best times to find cut-rate deals, but you may get lucky at any time of year. It's worth shopping around and hanging around for a few days to browse. Note that flexibility is usually essential to getting a good deal. The following operators are recommended for last-minute deals and day tours to surrounding islands such as Seymour Norte, the Plaza Islands, Bartolomé, Santa Fé, and Floreana. There are operators in Puerto Baquerizo Moreno and Puerto Villamil, but they are mainly restricted to offering day tours.

Galapagos Alternative (Darwin, Puerto Ayora, www.galapagosalternative.com) specializes in organizing custom whole-trip itineraries for different budget ranges including accommodation, tours, and transportation, depending on the interests of the group, either as a package or as a complete tour with a private guide.

Galapagos Advisor (www.galapagosadvisor) is an online agency with a well-organized list of cruise yachts and ships, including photos and itineraries that are numerically scored according to wildlife-viewing opportunities.

Galapatur (Rodríguez Lara and Genovesa, Puerto Ayora, tel. 5/252-6088, www.galapatur.

com) offers four- to eight-day tours on the *Guantanamera* and the *Yolita II,* and land-based tours from the Galápagos Islands Hotel.

Moonrise Travel (Darwin, Puerto Ayora, tel. 5/252-6348, www.galapagosmoonrise. com) is run by Steve and Jenny Divine, long-time residents of the Galápagos. They book last-minute cruises, day tours, and live-aboard diving cruises. Longtime campgrounds in the Santa Cruz highlands at Rancho Mariposa are now closed, though it's possible they may reopen in the future.

Scuba Iguana (Darwin, Puerto Ayora, tel. 5/252-6497, www.scubaiguana.com) is the most well-known and frequently recommended diving operator, run by dive master Matías Espinosa, who was featured in the *Galápagos* IMAX movie. Daily dive rates are $200 per person. They also book live-aboard cruises and diving packages.

We Are the Champions Tours (Darwin, Puerto Ayora, tel. 5/252-6951, www.wearethechampionstours.com) offers a wide range of cruises on 16 boats of all classes as well as hotel-based island-hopping tours and live-aboard dive cruises.

Recreation

DIVING

With such an astonishing array of marine life, it's no surprise that the Galápagos rank among the world's best dive destinations. The New York Zoological Society's Oceanographic Expedition sent divers to the islands for the first time in 1925, and they've been returning ever since. In 1998, protection of the land sites was extended to a marine zone 74 kilometers offshore, and there are now some 60 dive sites around the archipelago, many of them closed to nondivers.

If you're dreaming of getting your PADI certification and heading straight here, however, be advised that diving in the Galápagos is not for beginners. Local dive schools offer

PADI training, but it is overpriced and far from the best place to learn. You are better off not only learning elsewhere but also getting a few dives under your belt first. Currents are strong, and visibility is often poor, ranging 10-25 meters (half that of the Caribbean). Many dives are in unsheltered water, meaning that holding on to coral is not only permitted but is essential. It is not ideal for the health of the coral, but it is certainly important for your health. There have been diving accidents here—some people get so excited by what they are seeing that they lose track of time and distance. Luckily, there is a decompression chamber in Puerto Ayora.

For those with sufficient experience, the

diving is world-class. Schools of fish stretch out for what seems like eternity, and you're almost guaranteed close encounters with a variety of sharks—small white-tipped reef sharks, larger Galápagos sharks, the dramatically shaped hammerheads, and, off the more remote western islands, enormous whale sharks. When you add to this extended periods following manta rays, marine iguanas, and the surprisingly fast penguins, the diving in the Red Sea or the Caribbean will pale in comparison.

The law requires that every boat in the Galápagos must be either a nondiving cruise boat or a dedicated dive boat, so divers are forced to choose between live-aboard charters, which are very expensive, or a land-based tour with day trips to dive sites. The latter option is becoming more popular because it's far cheaper, but note that you will be restricted to sites within easy reach of Santa Cruz, San Cristóbal, and Isabela.

Santa Cruz has the most dive sites and the greatest number of dive agencies, with access to **Santa Fé, Gordon Rocks, Daphne Minor, Mosquera, Seymour Norte, Cousins Rock,** and excellent sites off the coast of **Floreana.** San Cristóbal has relatively fewer: **Kicker Rock,** the **Caragua wreck, Roca Este, Roca Ballena,** and **Islote 5 Fingers.** Isabela has **Isla Tortuga** and the more advanced sites **La Viuda** and **Cuatro Hermanos.**

Most of the other dive sites in the archipelago at Española, Isabela, and off Marchena can only be experienced on a live-aboard cruise. The most spectacular diving is around Darwin and Wolf, but this requires a minimum experience of 50-100 dives. These islands are a full day's sail north of the main island group. Schools of hundreds of hammerheads can be seen off Wolf, and gigantic whale sharks cruise slowly by between June and November. Bottlenose dolphins are common at Darwin's Arch.

The best diving is during the cold season (June-November). Temperatures drop to 15°C in the cold season, when a six-millimeter wetsuit with hood, booties, and gloves becomes necessary. It's best to bring all your own equipment, as renting it locally is expensive and can cause problems because many itineraries go straight to the boat. Bring a mask, dive alert whistle, and sausage or scuba tuba. Boats supply tanks, air, and weights.

Because most visitors depart by plane, you must leave a day free at the end of your dive trip to avoid possible decompression problems (most dive tours spend the last day on Santa Cruz).

Dive Operators

Choosing the right dive company is essential for your own safety. Most operators in Puerto Ayora and Puerto Baquerizo Moreno are reputable, but there are some who will take your money without asking questions. You are strongly advised to steer clear of any operator who doesn't ask you in detail about your experience. For example, any operator willing to take novices to Gordon Rocks should be avoided completely. The best operators ask you to fill out a detailed questionnaire to assess experience.

Most large Galápagos tour agencies can book dive trips aboard the small number of equipped boats. A PADI Open Water certificate is essential, and some companies ask for a minimum number of dives, although this depends on the difficulty of the site. A PADI Open Water course generally costs around $450 per person for a four-day training course.

Live-Aboard Dive Tours

Live-aboard cruise options are very limited and are usually booked months in advance. There are currently only six live-aboard cruises, and each carries only 16 passengers. At present, the two best companies are **Ecoventura** (U.S. tel. 800/633-7972, Guayaquil tel. 4/283-9390, www.ecoventura.com), operating the *Galapagos Sky,* and **Aggressor** (U.S. tel. 800/348-2628, www.aggressor.com), operating the *Galapagos*

Aggressor I and *II.* Prices per person are $5,000 for a week.

SNORKELING

If diving is not for you, don't worry: The Galápagos also rank as one of the world's best snorkeling destinations. Sea lions, marine turtles, stingrays, reef sharks, marine iguanas, flightless cormorants, and a vast array of tropical fish can all be seen at dozens of snorkeling sites throughout the archipelago. Most cruises and day tours include use of snorkels and fins, but you can also rent them from most operators in the ports or bring your own.

A couple of good sites are within easy walking distance of the ports, where you can go on your own, such as **La Lobería** on Floreana, **Concha de Perla** on Isabela, and **Cerro Tijeretas** on San Cristóbal. Travelers on cruises will have daily opportunities to snorkel at a wide variety of excellent sites inaccessible to day tours, including **Punta Vicente Roca** on Isabela, **Devil's Crown** and **Champion Island** on Floreana, and **Punta Espinosa** on Fernandina. Some of the best snorkeling sites available on day trips include **Isla Lobos** and **Kicker Rock (León Dormido)** on San Cristóbal, **Bartolomé, Pinzón,** and **Los Túneles** on Isabela. Many tour agencies in the ports can arrange these day trips.

SURFING

While it may seem a little odd to come to the world's top wildlife-watching destination and spend your time catching waves, the Galápagos Islands are a popular place for surfers—mainly locals but some international surfers, too. Restrictions have made surfing more difficult; the national park has closed some of the best spots to surfers, and others can be difficult to reach due to a lack of tours. The best time of year for surfing, as on the mainland, is December-May.

The center of surfing in the archipelago is **San Cristóbal,** which has a few good sites within easy access of Baquerizo Moreno. The island picks up north and south Pacific swells

on the northwest and southwest coasts. **Punta Carola** is the best north swell, a 10-minute boat ride from the port. **El Cañon** is also close to town. The best south swells are **La Lobería** and **Tongo.** If you get a group together to do a day tour, a more remote spot is **Manglecito** near Kicker Rock (León Dormido).

On **Santa Cruz,** there are a few beaches close to Puerto Ayora, including **La Ratonera** near Charles Darwin Research Station, along with **Tortuga Bay.** West of Puerto Ayora, there are good swells at **Cerro Gallina** and **Las Palmas,** although picking up tours to these sites can sometimes be difficult.

On **Isabela,** you can stay on the beachfront and walk right out into prime surfing territory on Playa Grande.

Surfing Rentals, Classes, and Tours

Most surfers bring their own gear, but you can rent boards from various operators. In Puerto Baquerizo Moreno, try **Dive and Surf Club** (Herman Melville, Puerto Baquerizo Moreno, tel. 8/087-7122 or 8/634-7256, www.divesurfclub.com), which offers a full day of surf classes at Puerto Chino for $70 per person. In Puerto Villamil, the best place in town is **Galapagos Bike & Surf** (Escalesias at Tero Real, tel. 99/488-5473 or 5/252-9509, galapagosbikeandsurf.com). In Puerto Ayora, board rentals are more difficult to come by, and operators frequently open and close, so ask locally. A useful website based in mainland Ecuador is www.galapagosurf.net, which has detailed surfing information and occasional tours. A Quito-based operator, **Surf Galápagos** (Amazonas and Veintimilla, Quito, tel. 2/254-6028, www.surfgalapagos.com), also offers specialist surfing tours.

HIKING

Although much of your time in the Galápagos is spent either on the water or in the water, there are plenty of good hiking trails, most of which are strictly regulated. Most visitor sites have trails ranging from a few hundred meters to a few kilometers. However, many of them

Negra, the second-largest volcanic crater in the world. There are two trails—one that takes four hours and a longer one that takes about seven hours.

CAMPING

Camping in the Galápagos can mean very different things: basic tent camping in the national park, camping on privately-owned land for a fee, or glamping at luxury tented safari camps. Camping in the national park can be spectacular, but it is quite unpopular due to the limited number of sites where it is allowed, the small number of tours available, and logistical challenges for independent travelers. Note that visitors used to camp right on the beach in town in Puerto Villamil on Isabela, but due to changing regulations this is no longer permitted.

camping at El Garrapatero Beach on Santa Cruz

can be muddy or along uneven, rocky routes, so make sure you come equipped with good walking shoes. In most cases, tennis shoes or sneakers are sufficient, but for longer hikes in the highlands, such as Sierra Negra on Isabela or Cerro Crocker on Santa Cruz, walking boots are more advisable.

All three major ports have pleasant walks nearby. From Puerto Ayora there are short hikes to **Las Grietas** and **Tortuga Bay.** From Puerto Baquerizo Moreno there are walks to **Cerro Tijeretas (Frigate Bird Hill), Playa Baquerizo** and **La Lobería** beach, and from Puerto Villamil there are hikes to the **Centro de Crianza (Tortoise Breeding Center)** and farther along to the **Muro de las Lágrimas (Wall of Tears).**

Inland on Santa Cruz, more serious hikers can tackle the five-hour climb from **Bellavista** to **Media Luna.** On San Cristóbal, there is good hiking in the highlands around **Laguna El Junco** and at **Punta Pitt.** Isabela boasts perhaps the most famous hike on the islands, along the trail to **Sierra**

Camping Tours in the National Park

Camping is allowed by the national park at **El Cura** and the hike-in site **sulfur mines** on Isabela, but there are no regular tours to El Cura or the sulfur mines; you can organize your own private tour with tour agencies on Isabela with advance notice and a large budget. The remote beaches **Puerto Grande** and **Manglecito** on San Cristóbal are only accessible by boat. **ROW Adventures** (www.row-adventures.com) is currently the only tour operator that organizes regular camping tours in the national park on Manglecito beach.

There are plans to start camping tours at **Mirador de la Baronesa** on Floreana; contact **CECFLOR** (tel. 5/253-5055, reservas.postofficetours@gmail.com) for future availability.

Independent Camping in the National Park

There are only two sites where you can camp independently in the national park: **El Garrapatero Beach** on Santa Cruz and **Puerto Chino** on San Cristóbal. To camp at these sites, you need a permit in advance from the national park. Most would-be campers are deterred by the onerous application process, hordes of mosquitoes, expensive taxi rides, and excess baggage (no travel agencies rent tents). If you're willing to brave the mosquitoes and paperwork, however, you have a decent chance of having a deserted beach all to yourself, with only the sound of crickets and waves at night.

To camp, you need to obtain prior permission from the Galápagos National Park, which is a bureaucratic process. There is no online application; you must submit the papers in person at the national park office of the island where you want to camp at least 48 hours before camping but no more than 15 days in advance. The required papers are in Spanish only and downloadable from the national park website (www.galapagos.gob.ec/acampar-en-galapagos/): an application form and a template letter requesting the permit. Print out the papers at home and bring a photocopy of your passport. The cost is $10 per person for the application, which is good for up to two nights of camping. Keep in mind that you'll spend much more on taxis to and from the campsite ($40 round-trip) compared to the camping permit. There's also a small

chance that you'll fly in with all your gear and be denied the permit due to ocean conditions during your stay; the national park does not issue camping permits during periods of dangerous surges or tides.

Private Land

The easier alternative is to stay at campsites on private property. You will still need a taxi to get to and from these campsites, but you don't need to get a permit. There are reasonably priced campgrounds with facilities in the highlands of Isabela at **Campo Duro** (road to Sierra Negra, tel. 98/545-3045, www.galapagoscampoduroecolodge.com.ec), where you can bring your own tent and sleeping bag or use theirs for an extra fee.

Glamping

At the luxury end, there are glamping-style tents at the **Galapagos Safari Camp** (Finca Palo Santo, Salasaca, tel. 2/204-0284, www.galapagossafaricamp.com) on Santa Cruz, in the highlands where giant tortoises roam. The safari-inspired glamping tents at **Scalesia Lodge** (tel. 2/256-6090, scalesialodge.com) are deep in the highland forest of Isabela.

Santa Cruz and Nearby Islands

Look for ★ to find recommended
sights, activities, dining, and lodging.

Highlights

★ **Tortuga Bay:** Quite possibly the most beautiful **beach** in the Galápagos, Tortuga Bay has a long sandy expanse and a sheltered, mangrove-lined lagoon (page 59).

★ **Gordon Rocks:** This is the most popular dive site accessible via day tour due to its schools of **hammerhead sharks.** Strong currents make it suitable only for intermediate to advanced divers (page 64).

★ **Tortoise Reserves:** No Galápagos trip would be complete without seeing **giant tortoises** in their natural habitat—this site is by far the easiest place to spot them (page 72).

★ **Santa Fé:** See the larger **Santa Fé land iguana,** endemic only to this island (page 75).

★ **Plaza Sur: Land iguanas** meander through a dry landscape of cacti and red vesuvium plants, while **sea lions** rest on the rocks (page 76).

★ **Seymour Norte:** This island is the best place to see the impressive mating display of the red-chested **frigate bird** year-round. It's also home to a large population of land iguanas and **blue-footed boobies** (page 76).

© AVALON TRAVEL

S anta Cruz is the economic, tourist, and geographic center of the Galápagos. It's the best base from which to explore surrounding islands on day tours and pick up last-minute deals.

Many of the island's attractions can be seen independently.

Puerto Ayora is the archipelago's largest port and tourism hub, with the widest selection of hotels and restaurants. Many people stay in Puerto Ayora during their entire visit to the Galápagos, using it as a base to explore the central islands.

On the edge of town is **Charles Darwin Research Station,** the most convenient place to view giant tortoises up close. A 45-minute walk west of Puerto Ayora is the sandy expanse of **Tortuga Bay,** the longest beach in the Galápagos. The brackish waters of **Las Grietas,** fissures in the lava rocks that make for a relaxing, cool dip, are another short hike from town.

In the verdant highlands, several attractions make an interesting day trip: Two 30-meter-deep craters called **Los Gemelos** (The Twins) have abundant birdlife. East of Bellavista are the **lava tunnels** formed by the solidified outer skin of a molten lava flow, as well as the beautiful beach **Playa Garrapatero.** The biggest highland attraction is the huge **tortoise reserves,** where these giants roam in their natural habitat.

Near Santa Cruz Island are several small islands that can be visited as day-trip tours. Some of the most popular day trips leave for the iconic Pinnacle Rock on **Bartolomé,** to see land iguanas on **Santa Fé** and **Plaza Sur** islands, observe nesting frigate birds on **Seymour Norte,** and take advantage of the excellent snorkeling with sharks, turtles and sea lions at **Pinzón.** In addition, day trips leave for the populated islands Isabela, San Cristóbal, and Floreana, though staying the night is often a better idea.

Santa Cruz also has the most dive agencies. Divers frequently see schooling hammerheads at **Gordon Rocks,** and there are several other excellent options for diving day trips: **Floreana, Seymour Norte,** and **Daphne** are among the most popular.

Previous: a land iguana on Plaza Sur; El Chato Tortoise Reserve. **Above:** a frigate bird on Seymour Norte.

Santa Cruz and Nearby Islands

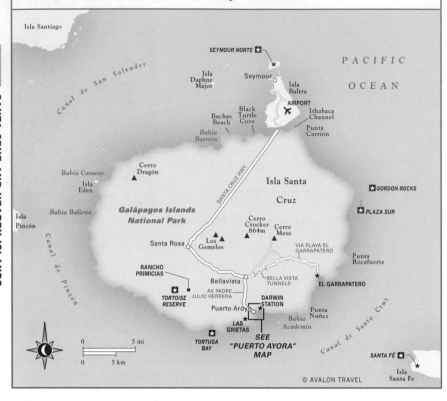

Puerto Ayora

If you're expecting to come to the Galápagos and stay in a deserted island paradise far from other humans, Puerto Ayora will come as something of a surprise. With a permanent population of about 18,000 and thousands more temporary residents and travelers, this is the bustling hub of the archipelago. The waterfront is filled with tourist eateries, travel agencies, gift shops, and hotels. While conservationists may wish the port away, blaming its expansion for the islands' environmental problems, it's hard to dislike Puerto Ayora. Set in a sheltered bay lined with cacti and filled with dozens of anchored yachts, the town is a

pleasant place to be based for a few days. The docks are particularly attractive, with a jetty that is lit up at night. To the east near Banco del Pacífico is a small fish market that attracts dozens of pelicans and a small colony of sea lions looking for scraps that fishers are happy to supply.

The facilities here are the best in the archipelago: hotels of all levels, from budget to seriously overpriced; a wide selection of good restaurants; reputable tour operators; and plenty of gift shops. If you're traveling independently, it makes a lot of sense to stay here to pick up day tours or last-minute cruises.

Puerto Ayora

To Casa Natura

LAUNDRY

To Galápagos National Park Office and Charles Darwin Research Station

ISLA FLOREANA
LAS FRAGATAS
LAS PIQUEROS
SANCHEZ

GALÁPAGOS SUITES

CAFE DEL MAR

GALERIA AYMARA

CHOCOLÁPAGOS

CEMETERY

GALÁPAGOS JEWELRY

OMG COFEE

SCUBA IGUANA

HOTEL SILBERSTEIN

AVE CHARLES DARWIN

RED MANGROVE HOTEL

MORNING GLORY

12 DE NOVIEMBRE
RABIDA

To Ingala Office, Highlands, Ferry to Baltra and Bus Terminal

AEROGAL

MUNICIPAL MARKET

GALÁPAGOS SUB-AQUA

DOCK

ANGELIQUE GALLERY

FISH MARKET

Academy

PLAZAS
LARA

CÁMARA DE TURISMO

BANCO DEL PACIFICO

Bay

IL GIARDINO

HOTEL SOLYMAR

BAMBU GALÁPAGOS INN

INDEFATIGABLE

MOONRISE TRAVEL AGENCY

EMETEBE

AV.
BALTRA

ANKER MAR

ISLA GRILL

LA GARRAPATA RESTAURANT

LA PANGA DISCOTECA & BONGO BAR

MUNICIPAL TOURISM OFFICE

12 DE FEBRERO

LOS AMIGOS

ESTRELLA DEL MAR

ITUR (TOURIST OFFICE)

PACIFICTEL

GALÁPAGOS NATIVE

TAME

HOTEL GARDNER

HOSTAL CORMORANT

POLICE STATION

MONTALVO

KIOSKOS FOOD STALLS

BINFORD

HOSTAL COSTA DEL PACIFICO

LAN

THE ROCK

CHARLES

KIOSKOS FOOD STALLS

AVE CHARLES DARWIN

To TORTUGA BAY

HOTEL SANTA FE

TOMAS DE BERLANGA

GALÁPAGOS DELI

CHARLES BINFORD

LO & LO

NAUTI DIVING

CROSSMAN HOTEL

HOSTAL VISTA AL MAR

SONDOLOS

PORT CAPTAIN

BRITO

HOSPITAL

WC

Parque San Francisco

HOTEL FIESTA

CASA DEL LAGO

CHURCH

EL DESCANSO DEL GUIA

0   500 yds

Laguna las Ninfas

SUPERMERCADO PRO-INSULAR

0   500 m

CARGO DOCKS AND WATER TAXIS

TOURIST JETTY

To Angermeyer's Waterfront Inn and Finch Bay

© AVALON TRAVEL

However, note that Puerto Ayora has its drawbacks—there's too much noise and traffic, especially the countless white-truck taxis shuttling around town. Go just a block or two inland, and you'll find unattractive piles of construction debris and half-finished building projects. Day tours by boat are increasingly very expensive. More serious are the problems with the water supply, and the construction of a decent sewage treatment facility is long overdue. The water supply here is dirtier than in mainland Ecuador (which is hardly a benchmark), so don't drink it, and use bottled water to clean your teeth.

SIGHTS

TOP EXPERIENCE

Charles Darwin Research Station

At the Charles Darwin Research Station (Av. Charles Darwin s/n, Puerto Ayora, tel. 05/252-7013 ext. 101, darwinfoundation.org, 7:30am-5pm, free admission), the primary attraction is the **Tortoise Breeding Center Fausto Llerena.** The center opened in the 1960s as a place for endangered subspecies to be hatched and cared for until they can be safely released into the wild. Adult giant tortoises of different species and land iguanas are easy to spot among the rock enclosures. Tiny giant tortoises of different subspecies are nurtured and protected in mesh-top boxes until their shells harden. One of the boxes contains baby tortoises from the island of Española. This is the station's biggest success story: After the population had fallen to only 14 individuals, conservationists have been able to breed and repopulate thousands of tortoises to the island. The biggest failure is also on display: the meticulously preserved body of **Lonesome George**, the last surviving member of the Pinta Island species, which became extinct in 2012.

In addition to the breeding center, the research station complex houses buildings dedicated to scientific research; unfortunately, these are closed to the public. However, a small visitors center has a mixed bag of exhibits about the tortoises and other Galápagos flora and fauna. There's also a small beach just outside the station, **Playa de la Estación** (7am-6pm daily), that is a good place to relax

and spot the occasional marine iguana. It's easy to visit the Charles Darwin Research Station on your own; it's just a 15-minute walk east of Puerto Ayora. If you plan to visit San Cristóbal and Isabela Islands, note that the tortoise breeding centers aren't terribly different from each other; you may want to pick just one.

MAPRAE (Museum of Pre-Columbian Art in Virtual Reality)

This museum (Darwin at Binford, tel. 5/252-5197, www.maprae.com, $8; hours vary daily) has augmented-reality virtual artifacts from the Valdivia, Chorrera, and other pre-Columbian cultures that are rendered in 3-D using an iPad with recorded audio explanations. Though the artifacts aren't physically present, the museum is a decent place to escape the afternoon heat, and the pre-Columbian information is interesting.

Laguna de las Ninfas

At dusk mysterious bubbles rise to the surface of the **Laguna de las Ninfas** (7am-6pm daily, free), named after the nymphs that just might take a dip at night. Mangroves and a raised wooden walkway surround the

Charles Darwin Research Station

turquoise lagoon. Swimming is not allowed, but you can often see fish and other critters swimming among the mangrove roots and birds flitting about the branches. It is not a must-see, but the lagoon is only a 10-minute walk west of the center of town and is a pleasant place for a relaxed afternoon stroll.

Playa de los Alemanes

Playa de los Alemanes, or German Beach, is a small beach conveniently located a short water taxi ride ($0.80 each way) from Puerto Ayora. It is not the most pristine beach, nor is there much wildlife to be seen, but it is the most easily accessible place to sunbathe and swim near Puerto Ayora, and makes a good sunbathing stop on the way to Las Grietas. The beach is right in front of the Finch Bay Eco Hotel, but it's open to the public. To get there, take a water taxi from the pier and walk past the Angermeyer Waterfront Inn for five minutes.

Academy Bay

This is the bay bordering Puerto Ayora. While it may look just like a mooring place for boats and cruise ships from town, you can explore additional areas by dinghy on the bay tour (see Tours).

Las Grietas

Las Grietas is a swimming hole nestled between red rock cliffs and easily accessible from Puerto Ayora if you're traveling independently. The calm turquoise water is surrounded on both sides by stunning 20-foot cliffs, and you can even see a few colorful fish swimming around. The swimming hole is at least twice as long as it appears; to get to the second half that far fewer tourists visit, you need to scramble over two sections of treacherous, slippery rocks. If you're feeling adventurous, there's a short underwater tunnel on the right side of the channel that goes under the second rocky scramble. To get your bearings, hike the short **bay trail** that veers left from the main path and has viewpoints over Las Grietas as well as Academy Bay.

To get to Las Grietas from Puerto Ayora,

take a water taxi across the bay ($0.80 each way) and head inland past Finch Bay Eco Hotel; it's then an easy 15-minute walk along a well-maintained trail. There is a staircase to enter the swimming hole. Bring water shoes for climbing over the rocks. Las Grietas is popular among locals and is included as part of all the bay tours. Go early in the morning or climb the rocks to the second half if you want to avoid the crowds.

★ Tortuga Bay

Galápagos tours can have hectic schedules, so you may welcome the chance to lie on a pristine beach for a few hours. Luckily, one of the most beautiful beaches in the Galápagos is only a 45-minute walk from Puerto Ayora.

Take Binford out of town to the west, up the steps, and past the national park guard post, where you need to sign in and where you can buy refreshments. Follow the paved path through cactus forest 2.5 kilometers to the beach. Finches and a variety of other birds can be seen along the path.

At the end of the path is a spectacular beach, **Playa Brava,** one of the longest in the archipelago. Note that the sea is rough here, so it's good for surfers but usually dangerous for swimmers. For a gentle soak, walk along to the right for another 15 minutes to the very end of the beach and turn inland past a group of marine iguanas to find a smaller shallow lagoon and **Playa Mansa,** where marine turtles come to lay their eggs. Don't miss the short, rocky **iguana path** to the left of the lagoon, where marine iguanas and blue-footed boobies rest. During most of the day the water can be quite cloudy, so content yourself with sunbathing and swimming in this idyllic spot. If the sun is shining and the water is calm and clear, you can see tortoises, white-tipped reef sharks, and stingrays by swimming around the bay. It's a long way around the periphery, so bring fins. You can also rent kayaks ($10 pp) and ride along the mangroves lining the bay.

Note that the beach closes at 5pm, so you should set out earlier than 3pm to have enough time to enjoy it. There are no facilities, so bring water and refreshments, and be sure to take the trash back with you. Those wishing to avoid the walk to Tortuga Bay can take a boat ($10 each way), which departs from the dock at 9am or noon and returns after a couple hours.

TOURS

Puerto Ayora's tour agencies line the blocks near the boardwalk, making it very easy to book any tour—as well as rent bikes, purchase ferry tickets, and book last-minute cruises. However, on occasion different agencies charge different prices for the same tour and yacht, so get quotes from at least two agencies before booking.

The tours on Santa Cruz island, such as the bay tour and highlands tour, only take half a day, and you can usually find both morning and afternoon departures. The other tours take a full day, leaving early in the morning and returning late in the day. Full-day tours must be booked the night before at the latest, but tours sometimes fill up, making it necessary to book a couple days in advance, especially in high season. You can also book ahead of time from abroad to ensure that you get on the tours you want, though prices tend to be higher.

Highlands Tours

The **highlands tour** ($45) goes to El Chato Tortoise Reserve, the nearby lava tunnels, and Los Gemelos collapsed craters. Alternatively, you can see many of these sights independently with a taxi driver for about $40 for a half day, divided among your group.

Bay Tours

The half-day **bay tour** ($35) takes in several highlights near Puerto Ayora. Bay tours go to the small islet **La Lobería** and observe the small colony of sea lions. Depending on conditions, the tour includes a snorkel here or in the shallower waters of **Punta Estrada** in the bay. From there the boat coasts by the cliffs to look for blue-footed boobies and other seabirds before you disembark for a short walk to **Canal del Amor,** a lookout point where you can observe white-tipped reef sharks resting in the shallows, and a rather generic beach, **Playa los Perros**. The tour concludes with a visit to **Las Grietas**, an excellent swimming hole near port; this site can also be visited easily on your own. Tours leave at 9am and 2pm every day and take about four hours. Tip:

A blue-footed booby overlooks Tortuga Bay.

Artisanal Fishing Tours

Artisanal fishing is fishing with a pole, as opposed to commercial fishing, fishing with nets, sports fishing or long-lining.

Artisanal fishing tours were created to transition residents of the islands out of fishing and into the tourism industry, where conservationists felt they would have less ecological impact. For tourists, the experience is quite similar to the day tours (and the fishing tours last all day, too). Contrary to what you might think, the primary attraction is snorkeling at a number of excellent spots. The secondary attraction is a visit to a pretty beach site, though the beaches don't have much wildlife. Fishing feels a little like an afterthought rather than the focus of the tour. Guides cast out a fishing pole and drive around for about 20 minutes. If you catch something, it means fresh ceviche for the boat, but many boats return empty-handed due to the short time fishing and the wrong time of day (not early morning or dusk, which are better for fishing).

The most notable differences between artisanal fishing tours and day tours are the sites they visit and the boats. Artisanal fishing tours depart on smaller boats that hold a maximum of 10 guests (compared to 16 on a day tour). There is considerable variety in the artisanal fishing tour boats, though they are generally smaller and less comfortable than the day tour yachts.

Artisanal fishing tours operate in all three of the main ports. Confusingly, they visit destinations that overlap with day tours (such as Santa Fé on Santa Cruz). The difference is that the day tour will disembark for a hike and wilderness viewing and then snorkeling; the artisanal fishing tour will snorkel and fish in the vicinity. In other cases, new sites such as Los Túneles and El Finado on Isabela, and Bahía Rosa Blanca on San Cristóbal, have been authorized by the national park exclusively for artisanal fishing tours. For years cruises were able to offer exclusive visits to cruise-only sites in the far reaches of the archipelago; land-based tourism finally has its own exclusive territory as well.

Request free fin rental from your tour agency when you buy the ticket. Not all agencies provide them for the half-day trips, and you will see many more fish if you're moving faster while snorkeling. The boats for the bay tour are small and generally slow because distances are short; some ($40 pp) have a glass bottom for observing marine life.

Day Tours

Full-day tours from Puerto Ayora to nearby uninhabited islands are the most desirable tours and are also the most expensive.

A day trip to **Seymour Norte** ($160-250) has a walk among colonies of nesting frigate birds and a snorkel along cliffs. A day trip to **Plaza Sur** ($140-250) includes a walk on the island to see land iguanas and sea lions. A day trip to **Bartolomé** ($160-250) features climbing the hill for the famous view of Pinnacle Rock and snorkeling in the bay. Day trips to **Santa Fé** ($160-250) land on the island to see the Santa Fé land iguana, endemic only to

that island, followed by snorkeling, though a cheaper artisanal fishing trip ($120) that only includes snorkeling is also possible. Each of these tours features a secondary, less famous beach as a spot to rest and relax after the main visit; these beaches tend to change between tour operators and days of the week. The range of prices depends primarily on whether you book a luxury or regular yacht; there is also some fluctuation depending on whether you are in high or low season.

These day tours operate aboard "day-tour yachts." These are a step up in comfort from the speedboats—typically with tables outside, booths inside, an area for sunbathing on the stern of the yacht, and a bathroom for changing out of wet clothes. A couple luxury-class yachts offer more even more amenities, such as hot food cooked onboard, the stability of a catamaran, and a couple cabins for taking a nap. Since tourism on Santa Cruz is more developed than on the other islands, these yachts are also more comfortable than you will find on day tours from the ports on Isabela and San Cristóbal. Always ask which yacht when booking a tour and try to get pictures if possible.

There's no consistent class ranking for day tour yachts, and it's worth double-checking since boats change frequently. Currently the most luxurious day tour yachts are the *Sea Lion* (Finch Bay Eco Hotel, tel. 5/252-6297, www.metropolitan-touring.com), *Adriana* (tel. 99/171-6411, www.adrianagalapagos. com), and *Promesa* (Galapagos Daily Tours, Baltra at Tomás de Berlanga, tel. 5/252-7337). Standard day tour yachts include the *Española* (www.espanolatours.com.ec), *Altamar* (tel. 5/252-6430, galapagosaltamartours.com), and *Sea Finch* (tel. 99/980-3147, www.seafinch.com).

Artisanal Fishing Tours

An artisanal fishing tour to **Pinzón** ($120-150) does not land on the island but includes excellent snorkeling. Tours to **Daphne** ($120-150) are also snorkel-only; of the two, Pinzón is considered a superior snorkeling spot, though there are a couple boats that visit both Pinzón and Daphne on the same tour.

There are also artisanal fishing tours to snorkel at **Santa Fé** ($120); unlike other day tours, they do not land on the island to see the endemic iguanas.

Inhabited Islands Tours

It's usually best to skip these day tours of the inhabited islands. Compared to day tours of the uninhabited islands and the artisanal fishing tours, the tours visit less spectacular sights for a similar cost and further navigation time. Compared to island-hopping (staying on the inhabited islands and taking local tours), these day tours have a very rushed schedule. Furthermore, they skip some of the top sights that you could visit via tours while based in the towns, notably Los Túneles and Sierra Negra on Isabela, and Post Office Bay and La Botella on Floreana. Lastly, significant time is spent in navigation (two hours each way) aboard uncomfortable speedboats (the same used for public transportation between islands).

If you're very pressed for time and are dead set on seeing the other inhabited islands, day tours leave Puerto Ayora most days to Floreana, San Cristóbal, and Isabela. Day trips to **Floreana** cost $80-100 and visit the tortoise breeding center, the highlands, La Lobería, and the beach. Day trips to **San Cristóbal** go to either Kicker Rock ($160) or Isla Lobos ($140), as well as La Lobería. Day trips to **Isabela** cost $80 and visit the *humedales* (wetlands), the tortoise center, and the beach, or for $120 also visit Tintoreras.

Tour Operators and Agencies

Most of the offices are on or near the main road, Avenida Darwin. Recommended agencies for day tours include **Galápagos Voyager** (Darwin at Colón, tel. 5/252-6833, galapagosvoyages2008@hotmail.com), **Moonrise Travel** (Darwin, tel. 5/252-6348, www.galapagosmoonrise.com), **We Are the Champions Tours** (Darwin, tel. 5/252-6951, www.wearethechampionstours.com), **Galapatur** (Rodríguez Lara and Genovesa, tel. 5/252-6088), and **Galápagos Deep** (Indefatigable and Matazarno, tel. 5/252-7045, www.galapagosdeep.com).

RECREATION
Surfing

Surfing is not quite as popular in Puerto Ayora as in San Cristóbal, but board rentals are available in town nonetheless. Popular places include **Tortuga Bay** and **La Ratonera** (past Playa de la Estación), which are accessible on foot from town. Boards are available to rent in town (approximately $20/day).

Cerro Gallina and **Las Palmas** are only accessible by boat; you book a tour with one of the specialty surfing tour companies such as **Surf Galapagos** (Amazonas N23-71 and Wilson #304A, Quito, tel. 2/254-6028, www.surfgalapagos.com).

Kayaking

Kayak rentals are available in three locations

in Santa Cruz—the dock (for exploring the bay), Tortuga Bay (where you can kayak among mangroves), and El Garrapatero Beach. Rentals cost $10 per person.

SUP

You can rent SUP boards to go around the bay for $25 for the day at **Galadventure Tours** (tel. 5/252-4119, www.galadventure.com).

Biking

Biking is a fun, off-the-beaten-path way of visiting the highlands.

The easiest ride is to take the bus or taxi to Bellavista (6 kilometers) or Santa Rosa (15 kilometers), then take a long **downhill ride to Puerto Ayora**. Buses for Santa Rosa ($1.50) and Bellavista ($1) leave Mercado Central; some have bike racks and others allow bikes on board in the back, so check with the driver. There is a protected bike lane that separates the frequent taxi and bus traffic. This lane ends shortly after Santa Rosa, so biking past there isn't recommended. You can, however, take a detour along **Guayabillos**, a paved road reminiscent of a country lane that passes numerous farms and houses before it loops back to the main highway. There's no bike lane, but practically no traffic either. It is not

marked, but it's the only paved road on the right side of the road on your way back, between Santa Rosa and Bellavista.

If you're up for a challenge, from Santa Rosa, descend five kilometers via the bumpy dirt road to **El Chato** or **Rancho Primicias**, visit the giant tortoises, ascend back to Santa Rosa, and ride mostly downhill to Puerto Ayora. This section is only possible when it hasn't been raining recently.

Another fun option is to take the bus to Bellavista, bike to **El Garrapatero** beach (14 kilometers), and catch a taxi back. From Bellavista, it's a scenic climb (seven kilometers, 100-meter climb) along verdant highland farms to the tiny town of Cascajo, where you can buy water and ice cream. From there, it's another seven kilometers of easy descent to the beach; it's interesting to watch the change of scenery from the green highlands to the low, arid coast. There are more challenging rides possible as well; the entire route is 21 kilometers each way (this is the biking portion of the Galápagos Challenge triathlon). The ascent from the beach back to Cascajo isn't recommended; it's a sweaty and unrewarding slog.

For all of the longer routes, a couple shops in town have good rental bikes, but many of

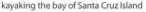
kayaking the bay of Santa Cruz Island

The Galápagos Challenge

Once a year the best athletes from the islands, Ecuador, and abroad gather on Santa Cruz Island for the archipelago's biggest athletic event—the **Galápagos Challenge**. The challenge is two days long and has two grueling events: the first day is an Olympic triathlon, and the second day is a full marathon. Both events are scored individually, and the times are added together to find the winners of the Galápagos Challenge.

The triathlon includes swimming across Academy Bay (1.5 kilometers) in Puerto Ayora, biking to El Garrapatero Beach and back (42 kilometers), and running a 10-kilometer route in town. The marathon running route crosses the island from the Ithabaca Channel dock all the way to Puerto Ayora (42 kilometers). There is also a half marathon (21 kilometers) and a 10-kilometer running route.

If you think you would like to run, bike, and swim across the enchanted islands, you can find more information at www.galapagoschallenge.com.

them are clunkers; if you're going on unpaved roads, you should try to find one with shocks. Most bike rental places open at 8am; if you want to start a long ride earlier, get the bike the day before.

Diving

Diving tours can be booked at specialist diving operators. Day tours are becoming more popular among divers because live-aboard cruises are very expensive and are no longer allowed to mix diving with land visits. Note that although you can learn to dive on the Galápagos, it's expensive. More importantly, the strong currents and predominance of drift dives mean it is better suited to more experienced divers. Academy Bay and La Lobería are popular beginner dive sites near Puerto Ayora. There are also good sites for novices and intermediate divers at Santa Fé, Seymour Norte, and Floreana, while Gordon Rocks is definitely for more experienced divers. Most diving tours meet in Puerto Ayora, then take a 45-minute bus ride north to Ithabaca Channel (provided by the diving operator), where the boat departs for the dive site. A couple of diving tours visiting dive sites south of Puerto Ayora leave directly from Puerto Ayora.

Day tours cost from $170 to $200 per person for two dives per day, although there are sometimes last-minute discounts.

There are several reputable local dive specialists. **Galápagos Sub-Aqua** (Darwin, Puerto Ayora, tel. 5/252-6350 or 5/252-6633, Guayaquil tel. 4/230-5514 or 4/230-5507, www.galapagos-sub-aqua.com) is the longest-operating dive center on the islands, with 20 years of experience and a good safety record.

Scuba Iguana (Darwin, tel. 5/252-6497, www.scubaiguana.com) is one of the most highly respected operators and is run by dive master Matías Espinosa, who was featured in the *Galápagos* IMAX movie. Daily dive prices start at $200 per person and fill up well in advance. They also book live-aboard trips.

Academy Bay Diving (Darwin, tel. 5/252-4164, https://academybaydiving.com) and **Nauti Diving** (Darwin, tel. 5/252-7004, www.nautidiving.com) are also reputable.

There is a decompression chamber in the main hospital in Puerto Ayora; your dive operator will help you in the event of an emergency.

★ GORDON ROCKS

The most famous site you can visit via day tour is **Gordon Rocks,** where schools of hammerheads are frequently seen, just 45 minutes away from Ithabaca Channel. Due to the strong currents, it is only recommended for experienced divers with 30 or more dives under their belt.

Gordon Rocks is famous for schools of hammerhead sharks.

NORTH OF SANTA CRUZ

Seymour Norte, Mosquera, and **Daphne** are other places within 30 minutes of Ithabaca Channel. Seymour Norte sometimes has strong currents, and it is home to many species of sharks. Daphne is a drift dive with moderate currents. Mosquera is in relatively calm waters above a sandy area with Galápagos eels.

Farther north, **Beagle Rocks, Bartolomé,** and **Cousins Rock** are off the coast of Santiago (90 minutes by boat from Ithabaca Channel). Divers at Beagle explore three large rocks and can often find manta rays and reef fishes. Bartolomé has moderate currents and a variety of reef fishes, sharks, and rays. Cousins normally does not have strong currents; it's home to seahorses, barracudas, sharks, and sea lions.

FLOREANA

The dive sites **Champion Island, Punta Cormorant,** and **Enderby** are right off the coast of Floreana, and are home to Galápagos sharks, white-tipped reef sharks, and sea turtles. Ironically, you can only dive there via a day trip from Puerto Ayora (two hours), because there are no local diving agencies on Floreana.

NIGHTLIFE

The downstairs disco **La Panga** (Darwin and Berlanga, no phone, 8pm-2am daily) and upstairs bar **Bongo Bar** (Darwin and Berlanga, no phone, 7pm-2am daily) are the best places to have a big night out. La Panga often has a $10 cover charge on the weekend and pumps out mainly electronic music. Otherwise most visitors simply linger in one of the many appealing waterfront restaurants for after-dinner drinks. **Santa Cruz Brewery** (Berlanga at 12 de Febrero, no phone, 4:30pm-midnight daily, beers $6) is a cozy hideaway inland, with craft brews made in Santa Cruz and tea infusions.

However, the best thing to do at night in Puerto Ayora is simply to stroll the illuminated **dock** after dark. Locals and visitors relax on the numerous benches and peer over the rails to see schools of tiny fish, sharks, and rays that are attracted by the light. You can also check the plaza by the fish market on Saturday nights; the folkloric dancers of **Centro de Danza Galápagos** sometimes put on an excellent show.

SHOPPING

Puerto Ayora has the best souvenir shopping in the archipelago. You're never more than a few meters from a souvenir store here, and most sell postcards and the obligatory Galápagos-branded T-shirts and hats. Some stores also sell collectible stamps, handicrafts, woodcarvings, ceramics, and jewelry. The biggest concentration of stores is found along Avenida Darwin toward the Charles Darwin Research Station. Prices are reasonable by U.S. standards but inflated by Ecuadorian standards. Expect to pay about $10 for a T-shirt or hat, although some negotiating is possible. Some of the smaller stores a few blocks inland tend to be a bit cheaper because they receive less business. There are also more high-end boutiques, particularly along the north end of Avenida Darwin, where you can find handmade arts and crafts and jewelry.

One fun stop is the colorful **Angelique Gallery** (Darwin and Indefatigable, tel. 5/252-6656, 9am-1pm and 3pm-9pm Mon.-Sat., 3pm-8pm Sun.), featuring the work of U.K. expat Sarah Darling. Her wild imagination captures the islands in vivid swirls of color, painted on mirrors, silk pillows, and scarves. She also makes handcrafted jewelry using silver, black lava stone, and other natural materials from mainland Ecuador.

Galápagos Jewelry (Darwin and Piqueros, Darwin and Indefatigable, tel. 5/252-6044, www.galapagosjewelry.com, 9am-12:30pm and 3pm-9pm daily) sells moderately pricey jewelry, but it's popular enough that it actually has two locations on Avenida Darwin. The designer is from the Galápagos, and the elegant creations feature iconic local animals in high-quality, shining sterling silver.

At the end of the block, **Galería Aymara** (Darwin and Piqueros, tel. 5/252-6835, www.galeria-aymara.com, 8am-noon and 3pm-7pm Mon.-Sat.) hosts a collection of high-end artwork from different Latin American artists. Expensive Peruvian tapestries, masks made by indigenous communities in Panama, and Ecuadorian jewelry are some of the highlights.

FOOD

Puerto Ayora has the best selection and variety; it has both the cheapest and the most expensive meals in the archipelago. The $5 *almuerzos* (lunches) are the cheapest meals you'll find in Galápagos. On the higher end of the spectrum, there is a wide variety of international restaurants, some even with gourmet tasting menus. The highest concentration of international restaurants is along the touristy *malecón* (promenade), where it's easy to browse the options.

Snacks and Coffee

OMG Galápagos (Darwin at Piqueros, tel.

098/916-9540, 7:30am-7:30pm Mon.-Sat., 3pm-7:30pm Sun., espresso drinks $4) single-sources coffee beans from farms in the highlands of Santa Cruz and roasts and grinds them on-site. In addition to the espresso drinks, there are snacks, coffee for sale by the pound, and pay-by-the-pound frozen yogurt. In the afternoon, it's one of the few places to enjoy the comfort of air-conditioning.

Chocolápagos (Darwin and Marchena, tel. 096/738-9575, 10am-5pm Mon.-Sat.) makes artisanal truffles on-site with chocolate from mainland Ecuador. The owner is from the Galápagos and is a certified chocolatier who studied in Buenos Aires. They also offer one-hour demonstrations of the chocolate-making process by reservation for $15.

For homemade ice cream, check out **Galápagos Deli** (see below).

Ecuadorian and Seafood

The cheapest places to eat are where the cooks prepare a two-course *almuerzo*, or a lunch where you only have one or two options. The food is usually unspectacular but can be reasonably tasty and quite filling. The first course is usually a soup, followed by fish, chicken, or beef with a mound of rice, a tiny bit of vegetables, and watery sweetened juice.

Opposite the ferry docks, **El Descanso del Guia** (Darwin, tel. 5/252-6618, 6:30am-7:30pm daily, fixed lunch $5, entrées $8-12) is the preferred choice of guides, as its name (Guides' Rest) suggests. Fill up on large plates for breakfast or lunch (chicken, fish, and meat staples), washed down by a wide range of fresh juices. The two-course set meals are great value.

For casual, inexpensive dining with fresh fish, head a couple of blocks inland to the string of small kiosks ★ **Los Kioskos** along Charles Binford east of Avenida Baltra. In the evening, the street gets very busy with locals and tourists wolfing down cheap, tasty specialties. For dinner, you can pick a whole fresh fish, particularly the bright red brujo, or lobster and langostino in season, and choose how you want it cooked. Either roasted or *encocado* (coconut sauce) is particularly good. You can also find grilled seafood skewers and decadent *cazuelas* (mixed seafood in a thick, plaintain-peanut stew). For lunch, several of the stalls serve a passable fixed-course *almuerzo* for $5. Among the kiosks, **Servisabroson** (Binford, tel. 5/252-7461, lunch and dinner daily, fixed-menu lunch $4, entrées $10-13) is one of the best for *almuerzos*.

Lo & Lo (Berlanga and Baltra, tel. 5/252-4681, breakfast, lunch, and dinner daily, breakfast $3-7, entrées $7-15) is one of the more popular casual local places. The breakfast specialty *bolon con bistec* (a fried plantain ball served with beef stew) is best if you wake up with a roaring hunger. For lunch, they have *seco de chivo* (goat stew) and *bollo de pescado* (plantain mushed with fish steamed in a banana leaf).

La Garrapata (Darwin and Tomás de Berlanga, tel. 5/252-6264, 9am-10:30pm Mon.-Sat., set lunch $4, entrées $7-15) is the town's longest-running touristy restaurant, with an attractive open-air setting and a mix of Ecuadorian meat and seafood specialties, such as fish in coconut and octopus in garlic, as well as a range of Italian pastas.

International

The **Galápagos Deli** (Berlanga and Baltra, no phone, 7am-10pm Tues.-Sun., $5-10) is a cute café and pizzeria just behind the main strip that feels more like California than Italy. The pizzas are a good value, the salads are fresh and larger than most, and the sandwiches are made with fresh ingredients on homemade bread. There are many good vegetarian options. Wash it down with an espresso and finish off with homemade *maracuya* (passion fruit) ice cream. It is also one of the few cafés with free Wi-Fi.

★ **Il Giardino** (Darwin and Binford, tel. 5/252-6627, www.ilgiardinogalapagos.com.ec, 8:30am-11:30pm Tues.-Sun., entrées $7-14) is the most popular Italian restaurant in town. The polished wood tables and lush greenery give it a relaxed garden café atmosphere. It does a wide range of Italian specialties, from homemade *panini* and crepes to spicy shrimp, seared tuna, and salmon. Afterward, don't miss the fresh ice cream sundaes and sorbet.

The Rock (Darwin and Naveda, tel. 5/252-7505, www.therockgalapagos.com, 8:30am-11pm Tues.-Sun., entrées $8-18) is a casual gastropub that has quickly become popular. Named after the first-ever Galápagos bar established on Baltra in the 1940s, it serves up a hodgepodge of international food from Mexican quesadillas to teriyaki fish fillets along with plenty of juices, shakes, and cocktails to wash it all down.

Isla Grill (tel. 98/462-7240, http://islagrill-galapagos.com, noon-10pm Tues.-Sun., entrées $13-25), located on the main strip, is the best touristy grill house in Puerto Ayora. The specialties are large cuts of grilled meat and seafood platters with heaping sides. Pizzas and large salads round out the menu. The rustic casual atmosphere and smell of barbecue contrast sharply with Almar, its upscale sister seaside restaurant.

Almar (Red Mangrove Hotel, Darwin, tel. 98/462-7240, http://almargalapagos.com, 7am-10pm daily, entrées $15-25) is most known for the fantastic views of the harbor and the resting sea lions and marine iguanas that frequent the dock connected to the restaurant. Come on a sunny day or at sunset for the best views on the elegant polished wood patio. The menu has a wide variety of international and seafood specialties with mostly local ingredients, and there's a large cocktail menu.

★ **Anker Mar** (Binford at Plazas, tel. 05/252-4994, 6pm-10pm Tues.-Sun., entrées $18-27) is run by Galápagos chefs who trained with the best in Napa Valley. They brought the region's famed farm-to-table and haute cuisine concepts back to their hometown. Though serving fish purveyed from the archipelago is hardly unique (even the humble *kioskos* serve locally caught fish), this restaurant features other ingredients, presentation, and creativity that are leaps and bounds ahead of the other restaurants in town. There is a small menu of à la carte plates. The tender brujo fish ceviche is the best in town. The roasted octopus has spirals of seafood artfully arranged on pureed yucca, with touches of herbs and sharp accents of pickled tomatoes. If you can't choose, it's easy to try everything with the chef's six-course tasting menu ($55).

Self-Service

Cooking is quite possible in Puerto Ayora. The **Supermarket Pro-Insular** (Darwin and Malecón, 8am-9pm daily) is by far the biggest supermarket in town and is conveniently located by the pier. For a more local shopping experience, head to the **Municipal Market** (Baltra and Calle No 55, 5:30am until they run out, daily); the stands sell fresh fruit, vegetables, and eggs (though most of the produce is imported from the mainland and less than fresh). Saturdays, if you can wake up and get to the market at 5am, you can find the local farms selling their produce until it runs out. To buy fresh fish, lobster, and langostino, head to the **fish market** (Darwin and Indefatigable, open morning and evening daily).

ACCOMMODATIONS

Puerto Ayora has every conceivable level of accommodations, and you can pay anything from $20 per person to more than $200 per person. Many of the cheap and midrange places charge higher rates via online platforms like Booking.com, so it's cheaper to reserve via email or phone.

Under $50

If you're not picky, you can find a decent room in Puerto Ayora in a central location for $25-30 per person without breakfast. Unless noted, rooms include Wi-Fi, private bathrooms, hot water, and air-conditioning.

If you don't need air-conditioning, **Los Amigos** (Charles Darwin, tel. 05/252-6265, $15 s, $30 d, no breakfast) has the cheapest rooms in town. Some have shared bathrooms as well, but they are popular for being clean and right on the main strip.

Hostal Morning Glory (Darwin at Floreana, tel. 099/680-5789, jmarcox@gmail.com, $20 s, $40 d, breakfast $5) is the cutest and also one of the cheapest budget options. Hand-painted panels decorate small, colorful rooms, all tucked behind a building along the main strip and centered around a small garden with recycled furniture.

Vista al Mar (Baltra at Binford, tel. 05/252-4109, $30 s, $50 d, no breakfast) has just a couple non-objectionable, centrally located rooms with lukewarm showers and a sunny patio. The real reason to stay here is that bike rental, snorkels, and fins are all included with your room. If you plan to rent those items frequently, this place quickly becomes a steal.

A good choice if you want to cook is the **Crossman Hostal** (Binford and Montalvo, tel. 5/252-6467, www.crossmanhotel.com.ec, $20 dorm, $30 s, $50 d, no breakfast), located by Laguna Las Ninfas, a 10 minute walk from town. It is one of the few places in town to offer dorms (though the price isn't that cheap) and a shared kitchen.

Estrella del Mar (12 de Febrero at Charles Darwin, tel. 5/252-6427, estrellademar@andinanet.net, $30 s, $50 d, no breakfast) is easily the cheapest hotel on the waterfront; some of the rooms even have ocean views. Guest rooms are relatively simple but have cable TV, air-conditioning, a mini-fridge, and hot water; it fills up quickly.

$50-100

Hotels in the midrange are quite comfortable and include the basic amenities of Wi-Fi, hot water, and air-conditioning. Compared to the budget options, you can get a more spacious room and nice decor, and many include breakfast.

There are passable air-conditioned rooms at **Hotel Gardner** (Tomás de Berlanga and 12 de Febrero, tel. 5/252-6108, $35 s, $60 d). The interior rooms are rather gloomy, but rooms with windows facing the exterior are adequate.

A great centrally located choice is ★ **Hostal Flightless Cormorant** (Darwin and 12 de Febrero, tel. 05/252-4343, hostalcormorant2016@outlook.com, $30 s, $60 d, breakfast $5), right on the main drag. The comfortable rooms are a fine value for the location, and a few even have large windows. The dining room and lounge are surprisingly nice, and you can relax on lounge chairs overlooking the bay. If you want to cook, it is hard to beat the well-equipped shared kitchen.

Hidden in a side street by the municipal market is the little six-room **Bambu Galápagos Inn** (Parque Alborada at Isla Duncan and Albatros, tel. 5/252-4085, elbambugalapagos@hotmail.com, $60 d, $75 t, $75 suite, no breakfast), which has the most attractive rustic-style rooms in this price range. There is no breakfast, but there is a small shared kitchenette for preparing simple meals.

Hostal Costa del Pacifico (Berlanga at Isla Plazas, tel. 05/252-6222, costadelpacificogalapagos.com, $45 s, $70-80 d, $105 t, no breakfast included) has clean, modern rooms in a central location. Though it's a little generic, the balconies and nice closet area makes it stand out in this price range.

A couple blocks inland is ★ **Galápagos Native** (Berlanga and 12 de Febrero, tel. 5/252-4730, www.galapagosnative.com.ec, $60 s, $70-90 d), with friendly service, spotless and spacious guest rooms in cheery colors, and breakfast next door at Villa Luna included. The only downside is some street noise; request a room on the second floor.

$100-200

These hotels have transparent pricing with minimal bargaining possible, so it is recommended to book in advance.

At the west end of town, inland from the docks near Laguna de las Ninfas, **Casa del Lago** (Moises Brito and Juan Montalvo, tel. 5/252-4116, $115 s, $140 d) is a cute family-run place with a bohemian vibe, with bougainvillea vines climbing up the walls. Its colorfully decorated guest rooms are rustic and equipped with built-in kitchens.

Worth the short walk north of town, ★ **Hotel Fiesta** (Moises Brito and Juan Montalvo, tel. 5/252-6440, www.galapagoshotelfiesta.com, $100 s/d, $140 t, $156 q) feels much more like a desert paradise retreat than a party as its name suggests. It has 28 elegant guest rooms, all with locally crafted furniture and mini-fridges. The regular rooms are located in the main building overlooking a pool and lounge area, while triples and quads are in quiet cabanas in the back. The hotel is in front of Laguna de las Ninfas, and guests can even walk along the mangroves on a private wooden walkway that extends partway around the lagoon. There is Wi-Fi throughout.

For a more intimate setting and personalized service, **Galápagos Suites** (Cucuve and Floreana, tel. 5/252-6209 or 9/744-8110, www.galapagossuites.com, $110 s, $138 d, $179 t) is a friendly, family-run place with just six modern guest rooms, each spacious and with a private balcony and a hammock. The hotel has a small patio and green space where you can peruse the neatly labeled endemic plants. Note that despite the name, rooms do not have kitchens or separate sitting areas.

If you are looking for suites with a kitchen, **Hotel Santa Fe** (tel. 5/252-6419, www.santafegalapagos.com.ec, $117 d, $159 suite) is an excellent choice. Rooms are large and immaculate. Suites have a small sitting area, a fully equipped kitchen, and a balcony overlooking the pool. The hotel is a short walk away from the main strip, but the local market is just a block away, making cooking very convenient. The owners also run the tour agency Galapagos a la Carte, where you can create your own custom package of accommodation in the hotel and day tours.

Over $200

The rest of the hotels in and around Puerto Ayora are mostly top-end venues popular with tour groups. You are better off booking these as part of a tour rather than independently, because the daily rates are higher.

On the main strip, German-owned **Hotel Silberstein** (Darwin and Los Piqueros, tel./fax 5/252-6277, www.hotelsilberstein.com,

$240 d) is an elegantly designed Mexican-style villa with charming arches, a tropical courtyard, a swimming pool terrace, and spacious guest rooms with solar-heated water. The hotel is part of a larger tour agency, Galextur, which can organize island hopping, cruises, and diving with the on-site Dive Center Silberstein.

★ **Red Mangrove Hotel** (Darwin, tel. 593/5252-6564, www.redmangrove.com, $350-370 d, $550 suite) lives up to its name, as its 16 elegant rooms are nestled within a mangrove forest overlooking the bay. Remodeled rooms have top-quality furnishings and amenities including robes, a flat-screen TV, and spa toiletries. Breakfast is served in the elegant waterfront Almar restaurant, where you can frequently spot sea lions and marine iguanas resting on the dock. Free bicycle rental is an added plus.

Across the harbor and accessible by water taxi, the **Angermeyer Waterfront Inn** (tel. 9/472-4955, www.angermeyer-waterfront-inn.com, $274-374 d, $475 suite) feels a little like a secluded Mediterranean villa overlooking the bay. Lava rocks, driftwood, coral, and the hull of a boat incorporated into the building give it an eclectic maritime theme. Rooms are well-appointed, and all the premium rooms have great views. The on-site restaurant is a casual, breezy place to enjoy pasta, seafood, and homemade desserts.

The **Sol y Mar** (Darwin near Banco del Pacífico, tel. 5/252-6281, $285-300 d) has modern and plush rooms in town, all well-appointed with California king-size beds and balconies with ocean views. The sunny patio is an idyllic place for sunbathing, taking a dip in the pool, or soaking in the Jacuzzi. The on-site restaurant is open to the public for lunch and dinner; sushi and cocktails pair well with a view of the bay at sunset.

★ **Finch Bay Eco Hotel** (tel. 2/250-8810, ext. 2810, www.finchbayhotel.com, $509 s, $538 d, $752 suite) is the only beachfront hotel in Puerto Ayora, with a large pool and comfortable lounge area overlooking Playa de los Alemanes. Rooms are elegant and designed

for unwinding; there are plenty of hammocks but no TV. Notably, it is the most ecologically sound hotel in the archipelago. The hotel has its own freshwater system and its own sewage treatment plant, and solar panels heat most of the hot water naturally. Service is friendly and professional, and the staff can book diving and luxury day tours through Metropolitan Touring. It's a short walk to Las Grietas, and the hotel operates a free water taxi service across to town.

To escape town completely, head to the **Hotel Royal Palm Galápagos** (tel./fax 5/252-7408, www.royalpalmgalapagos.com, $450 bungalow, $550-$975 villas), a palatial spread with villas and suites commanding views of the lush, green highlands. It offers a gourmet restaurant, a piano bar, a pool, a spa, a gym, tennis courts, and walking paths. Note that most people stay here as part of a tour package with transportation; otherwise you will need a taxi to get into town.

Camping

There are no campsites within convenient walking distance of Puerto Ayora or accessible via public transportation. You will need to take a taxi to and from the campsite.

Camping in the national park is permitted in just a couple locations in the Galápagos, one of which is **El Garrapatero Beach,** a gorgeous beach a 30-minute drive from Puerto Ayora by taxi. There are a handful of campsites in a sheltered area just off the beach. Each has a picnic table and a small grill where you are allowed to cook with charcoal. There's a bathroom at the registration desk but no showers or other facilities. While the beach is busy during the day, it's spectacularly unpopular for camping due to the logistical difficulties of getting a camping permit).

It is much easier to camp in the highlands on private land. The ultra-luxury glamping resort **Galapagos Safari Camp** (Finca Palo Santo, Salasaca, tel. 2/204-0284, www.galapagossafaricamp.com, $548 s, $753 d) boasts stylish canvas tents with real beds and private bathrooms with hot water, an outdoor pool, and great views of the highlands. A taxi into town is approximately $10 each way, though most guests book the all-inclusive tour packages.

INFORMATION AND SERVICES

The **Cámara de Turismo** office (Darwin and 12 de Febrero, tel. 5/252-6206, www.galapagostour.org, 9am-5pm Mon.-Fri.) and the **Ministry of Tourism** office (Binford and 12 de Febrero, tel. 5/252-6174, 9am-5pm Mon.-Fri.) both have maps, brochures, and helpful staff. The Cámara de Turismo only has maps and information about Santa Cruz; go to the Ministry of Tourism for information on all the islands. The **Galápagos National Park Office** (tel. 5/252-6189 or 5/252-6511, www.galapagospark.org, 7am-12:30pm and 2pm-7pm Mon.-Fri.) is just before the Charles Darwin Research Station at the edge of town.

Banco del Pacífico on Darwin has an ATM. **Banco de Bolivariano** also has an ATM next to the supermarket opposite the ferry dock. Internet access is available around town, but it's slow.

The **hospital** (Baltra and Darwin, tel. 5/252-6103) has a 24-hour emergency room and is just up from the docks. The **police station** (tel. 5/252-6101) is behind the TAME airline office, down a side road off Avenida Darwin on the waterfront.

GETTING THERE AND AROUND
Airport

The main **airport** serving Santa Cruz Island, **Aeropuerto Seymour de Baltra** (airport code: GPS, www.ecogal.aero, tel. 5/253-4004) is actually located on Baltra, a small island just north of Santa Cruz. Getting to Puerto Ayora from the airport takes a few steps. First take one of the free **airport buses** located right after the luggage claim. The airport buses come frequently, take 15 minutes, and drop you off at the dock. From the dock, take a **ferry** across the channel to Santa Cruz island ($1); they run about every 15 minutes and take

10 minutes. Once you arrive at the dock on Santa Cruz, the easiest way to get to Puerto Ayora is by **taxi** (45 minutes, $25). Note that taxis almost always break the speed limit of 50 kilometers per hour and sometimes hit birds as a result.

A cheaper and more eco-friendly option for getting from the dock to Puerto Ayora is the **bus** ($2), which takes a little over an hour, though the schedule is sporadic; they leave at different times depending on when the flights land and when there are enough passengers, and they usually stop running by 10am. Going the opposite direction, buses leave Puerto Ayora for the dock 6:30am-8:30am. The bus stop in Puerto Ayora is in the *terminal terrestre* (bus station), a long walk from downtown or a $1.50 taxi. If you miss the last bus, then your only option is a taxi.

To change flights between the Galápagos and the mainland, you can head to one of the airline offices in town: **TAME** (Darwin and 12 de Febrero, tel. 5/252-6527), **AeroGal** (Rodríguez Lara and San Cristóbal, tel. 5/244-1950), and **LAN** (Darwin, www.lan.com.ec).

Interisland Ferries

Daily services connect Santa Cruz with San Cristóbal and Isabela. Ferries connecting Floreana and Santa Cruz run three to four times a week, but the schedule is sporadic, so check with the tourist agencies in town when making your plans. All routes cost $30 per person one-way and take about two hours. Tickets can be purchased at one of the kiosks by the dock or at any of the tour agencies in town.

Speedboats leave Puerto Ayora for Isabela and San Cristóbal at 7am and 2pm, and for Floreana at 8am. The reverse trip from Isabela to Puerto Ayora departs at 6am and 3pm; from San Cristóbal to Puerto Ayora, at 7am and 2pm; and from Floreana to Puerto Ayora, at 3pm.

Interisland Flights

If you're in a hurry or very prone to seasickness and can spare the extra cost, take an interisland flight with **Emetebe** (Los Colonos and Darwin, top floor, tel. 5/252-6177) or **FlyGalapagos** (tel. 5/301-6579, www.flygalapagos.net). Small eight-seat planes fly half-hour routes among San Cristóbal, Baltra, and Isabela several times per week. Fares start at $160 one-way, $240 round-trip or for any two flights (even different routes).

Around Puerto Ayora

White *camionetas* (pickup truck taxis) are available for hire around town and cost $1.50 for trips within the city limits, but the town is quite small so often it's easier to walk or rent a bike. You can also negotiate taxi prices to go into the highlands (usually $40 for a half day). **Water taxis** wait at the dock to shuttle passengers to boats waiting in the harbor ($0.80 pp by day, $1 pp at night) and across to the dock of Angermeyer Point to reach Playa de los Alemanes and Las Grietas.

Santa Cruz Highlands

The Galápagos's reputation for barren landscapes certainly doesn't apply to the highlands of Santa Cruz, and it's worth venturing inland and up 600 meters to experience a very different environment than the coast—misty forests and green pastures. Guided tours include Los Gemelos, the lava tunnels, and El Chato combined into a half-day tour ($40). Alternatively, you can visit many of the attractions on your own via bicycle or taxi.

★ TORTOISE RESERVES

The most famous draw of the highlands is the tortoise reserves on private land. Most tourism agencies describe this experience as "watching the giant tortoises graze in their natural habitat." However, it's best to think of it as watching the tortoises in a *more* natural environment compared to the enclosures at the tortoise breeding stations. The reality is that the reserves are former cattle ranches, where the native *escalesia* forests were cleared

El Chato Tortoise Reserve

and replaced with grass. Wild giant tortoises come and go at will between these private lands and the neighboring national park land, attracted to the reserves for the muddy ponds and delectable fruit from introduced trees. The reserves are quite similar, so most people just visit one.

About a 30-minute drive from Puerto Ayora is **El Chato Tortoise Reserve** (no phone, 8am-5pm daily, $5). You can wander around on your own and explore lava tunnels on-site. Don't miss the muddy pools where tortoises gather to cool off. There's a slightly dubious photo opportunity where visitors can wear the heavy shell of a dead tortoise. Free coffee and tea are included with entrance, and there's a restaurant on-site that sells decent *almuerzos.*

A similar but slightly less popular private ranch where you can see giant tortoises and lava tunnels is **Rancho Primicias** (no phone, 8am-5pm daily, $5), which borders El Chato.

A third option, **Cerro Mesa** (daily, $5), is on the east side of the island at higher el evation. You can spot giant tortoises here, though there aren't as many and there aren't great walking paths as at El Chato and Rancho Primicias. On the other hand, this site tends to have fewer tourists, and the lookout tower has a spectacular 360-degree view of Santa Cruz island. There is also a huge collapsed crater on-site, similar to Los Gemelos. Bring good hiking shoes; the trail to descend is steep.

LOS GEMELOS

A few kilometers up from Santa Rosa on either side of the road are 30-meter-deep craters called **Los Gemelos,** formed when caverns left empty by flowing lava collapsed on themselves. The view into the now verdant craters is impressive; Galápagos hawks, barn owls, and vermillion flycatchers flit through damp *Scalesia* forests. The trail bordering these craters is short; it doesn't take more than 15 minutes to visit.

LAVA TUNNELS

Lava tunnels are formed by the solidified outer skin of a molten lava flow. They are a popular stop combined with a visit to the tortoise reserve and Los Gemelos. Most people visit the popular tortoise reserves **El Chato** or **Rancho Primicias** and explore the lava tunnels on those reserves, which are included with the entrance fee. The largest lava tunnel at El Chato is extremely well-illuminated and popular with tour groups, although there are a couple very small tunnels where you need a flashlight. The tunnel at Rancho Primicias is also illuminated with artificial light, and it is longer, about 600 meters.

The most spectacular lava tunnels are the **Bellavista lava tunnels** ($3.50), which have a length of 2,200 meters, though only a 1-kilomter section is currently open for tourists. With a longer length, far fewer tourists, a more natural rocky path, and only minimal artificial lighting, these tunnels feel more like exploring a cave. The Bellavista tunnels are an easy walk from Bellavista, which is accessible by bus from Puerto Ayora ($0.50).

CERRO CROCKER AND PUNTUDO

Hiking in the highlands is definitely off the beaten path, and very rare on tour group itineraries. The trails are often muddy, much of the area has been impacted by invasive plants, and the views are obscured by fog. However, if you're looking for adventure, you can walk among lush endemic greenery, escape the crowds, and perhaps get a fleeting view of the Galápagos petrel in the morning. If you're very lucky and the weather is clear, you can also see the island from Cerro Crocker—the highest point on the island. The starting point is a trailhead north of the small town of **Bellavista,** north of Puerto Ayora. From the trailhead, it is about a two-kilometer walk north to **Media Luna,** or "half moon," a volcanic formation covered in native miconia trees. Continuing north past Media Luna, you will reach a fork in the road. To the right is **Cerro Crocker** at an elevation of 860 meters, five kilometers north of Media Luna. To the left is **Puntudo**, another, less popular peak. Hikers have become lost trying to hike directly between Cerro Crocker and Puntudo and there is no trail; you must backtrack to the fork and then take the left branch to get to Puntudo. Having a guide is advised but not required. If you don't go with a guide, take a friend or two and make sure to download an offline GPS map (maps.me is accurate). Fit walkers can do this hike in three hours; budget an extra couple hours if you plan to backtrack and visit Puntudo as well.

To get to the trailhead, take a taxi from Puerto Ayora ($10/ hour including waiting for you). You can also take the bus to the small town of Bellavista ($0.50) and walk three kilometers uphill along the dirt road to the trailhead. The walk to the trailhead has decent scenery, passing endemic escalesia trees, coffee farms, and the occasional cow, though it has significant elevation gain. You'll need to budget an extra two hours for the walk up and down the dirt road. A third alternative is to just ask for a taxi dropoff at the trailhead from town ($18) and then return downhill along the dirt road to Bellavista to catch the bus back to Puerto Ayora.

Santa Cruz Islands

EASTERN SANTA CRUZ ISLAND
El Garrapatero

El Garrapatero, 19 kilometers northeast of Puerto Ayora, is one of the most beautiful beaches in the archipelago. Located in a large, sheltered bay, it has calm turquoise waters. Though it's not as long as the beach at Tortuga Bay, you will often find fewer tourists due to the more remote location. The snorkeling is not great, but it is a nice place to relax, rent kayaks ($10 pp), and look for elusive flamingos at the inland lagoon. With a kayak rental, you can coast near the rocky, mangrove-lined shore by the remote stretches of beach on the opposite side of the bay. Note that you can't walk on the beach as it's a tortoise nesting area, but you can wade around in the shallows. It's also possible to swim to the stretches of beach on the opposite side of the bay with fins if you're a very strong swimmer (approximately 1 mile round-trip), though it's not recommended because the water is cloudy and there's not much to see. The beach is easy to visit independently; taxis from town charge $40 round-trip, including waiting for you at the beach, though you

can also get here by bike (see Biking). There is a bathroom at the registration office.

NORTHERN SANTA CRUZ ISLAND

Some day tours stop at Bachas Beach on their way to Seymour Norte or Bartolomé. **Black Turtle Cove** and **Cerro Dragón** are **accessible only by cruise.**

Bachas Beach

This beach is named for the remains of U.S. military barges wrecked during World War II. The remains are usually buried, though sometimes after a very high tide the rusty metal parts are visible jutting out of the sand. The white-sand beach is often covered in Sally Lightfoot crabs and is also a sea turtle nesting site, while the lagoons behind the beach are home to flamingos. The site is often included on cruise ship itineraries and on day tours combined with other sites such as Seymour Norte, due to its proximity to the dock on the north side of Santa Cruz. Despite its proximity to the dock, it is not possible to visit independently.

Black Turtle Cove

Just west of the canal between Santa Cruz and Baltra, this shallow mangrove lagoon extends far inland. There is no landing site, so visitors are restricted to a slow tour on a *panga* (small boat). Above water, there is abundant birdlife: herons, gulls, frigate birds, and boobies all nest in the tangled branches of red and white mangroves. Beneath the surface, golden and spotted eagle rays glide by, and green sea turtles are often seen mating September-February. You may also be lucky enough to see white-tipped reef sharks resting in the shallows. The only way to visit this site is via a cruise; it is often included at the beginning or end of cruises due to its proximity to the airport on Baltra.

Cerro Dragón (Dragon Hill)

This visitor site on the northwest side of the island has a dry or wet landing, depending on the tide. A lagoon is sometimes filled with flamingos, and a two-kilometer trail through a dry landscape of palo santo and opuntia cacti leads to the top of Cerro Dragón, which commands good views of the neighboring volcanic tuff cones. This is a good spot to see groups of land iguanas, which gave the hill its name. The only way to visit is via cruise.

Surrounding Islands

TOP EXPERIENCE

★ SANTA FÉ

This small island is midway between Santa Cruz and San Cristóbal, about two hours from each. There's a wet landing on the northeast side and trails through a forest of **opuntia cacti,** which grow up to 10 meters high. The trail is rocky in places, and you have to cross a steep ravine, so bring good walking shoes. The highlight is the yellowish **Santa Fé iguana,** endemic to the island, and you may be lucky enough to see Galápagos hawks in the forest. It is a popular cruise site and day-tour site. Day tours landing on the island start at $160, while artisanal fishing tours (about $100) are limited to the snorkeling sites around the island, where sea turtles, manta rays, white-tipped

The Santa Fé iguana is larger and paler than the species found on the other islands.

reef sharks, and sea lions can be seen in the shallow waters. Take care, as some of the sea lion bulls can be bad-tempered.

★ PLAZA SUR

Off the east coast of Santa Cruz are the two tiny Plaza Islands. You can only visit the south island, Plaza Sur, one of the smallest visitor sites in the archipelago at just two square kilometers.

The dry landing onto the docks usually includes a welcoming party of negligently stretched-out sea lions. A trail climbs through colorful landscape past a small colony of land iguanas to the far side of the island, where the cliffs teem with birdlife—red-billed tropic birds, frigates, and swallow-tailed gulls. There is less food on the Plaza Islands for the land iguanas compared to Seymour Norte Island, and consequently the **land iguanas** here are smaller and less brightly colored, and have evolved unique adaptations—such as attacking and eating birds to survive. The presence of both land and marine iguanas has led to a small hybrid colony, the offspring of both species mating, although sightings are rare. Like most hybrids, they are sterile. There is also a small sea lion bachelor colony, separated from the main colony, plotting their next challenge to the dominant males below. Note that swimming or snorkeling here is usually avoided due to the aggression of sea lion bulls. Like Seymour Norte, Plaza Sur is a busy visitor site, and prices start at $140 for a day tour.

the rocky trail on Plaza Island at dusk

★ SEYMOUR NORTE

A tiny island off the north coast of Santa Cruz, Seymour Norte is the best place to see large colonies of **blue-footed boobies** and magnificent **frigate birds.** You can decide for yourself which has the most interesting mating ritual: the boobies marching around displaying their blue feet, or the frigates inflating their red chests to the size of a basketball. Both present great photo opportunities. After you make a somewhat tricky dry landing on some rocks, you can hike the 2.5-kilometer trail that loops around the island and takes over an hour. At the end, you can appreciate the amazing sight of marine iguanas, sea lions, and red Sally Lightfoot crabs sharing the rocky beaches. Offshore there is a good swell, and sometimes you can see the sea lions body-surfing. There is excellent snorkeling along the cliffs of the island, where you can see sharks and tropical fish. This is a popular spot for cruises, and day tour prices start at $160.

PINZÓN

Pinzón, east of Santa Cruz, is one of the best snorkeling spots available via day tour from Puerto Ayora. The excellent snorkeling is the only attraction here; there is no landing site on the island. Visitors can see a huge variety of marine life, including sea lions, colorful fish, rays, sea turtles, and white-tipped sharks, in the shallow, calm water.

Artisanal fishing day tours cost $100-140. They include an attempt to catch fish and a relaxing visit to a nearby beach. Some also include a visit to **Daphne Major.**

DAPHNE MAJOR

Off the north coast of Santa Cruz, about 10 kilometers west of Seymour Norte, the two small Daphne Islands are not included on most itineraries, and access is restricted. The larger island, Daphne Major, is an important research site. This is where Peter and Rosemary Grant researched finches, documented in the Pulitzer Prize-winning book *The Beak of the Finch,* by Jonathon Weiner.

Day trips to bird-watch from the boat, snorkel, and fish off the coast of Daphne depart regularly from Puerto Ayora ($100-140). It's highly recommended to look for a tour that combines this site with the excellent snorkeling at **Pinzón**.

San Cristóbal

The most easterly island and the geologically oldest island in the Galápagos is San Cristóbal.

Its port **Puerto Baquerizo Moreno** is the capital and administrative center of the islands. It's not nearly as busy as Santa Cruz, and while Puerto Ayora has boomed in recent years, Baquerizo Moreno is a more modest tourism hub and very quiet off-season. Its quiet vibe belies a troubled history, however; in the late 19th century it was the site of a large penal colony, inland at the small town of El Progreso. These days San Cristóbal is a pleasant enough place, with excellent boat trips into the national park, excursions into the highlands, and walks to nearby beaches. However, unlike on Santa Cruz, you can't really fill more than five days here.

If you are staying on the island just a couple days, make sure to do the **360 tour,** which hits many of San Cristóbal's famous sites, including **León Dormido,** in one day. Then take a day trip to **Española,** a site that was previously accessible only by cruise, for its excellent bird-watching and to see the waved albatross. Spend your last day visiting the **Interpretation Center,** climbing to the viewpoint and snorkeling at **Cerro Tijeretas,** and seeing the huge sea lion colony at **La Lobería** in the afternoon. If you have extra time, you can fit in more snorkeling among sea lions at **Isla Lobos** or a trip to the highlands.

San Cristóbal has made significant progress in the archipelago's renewable energy drive. After an oil spill, wind turbines were installed in 2007. Over the next eight years these turbines provided 30 percent of the energy used by the town. This is part of the government's ambitious multi-pronged Zero Fossil Fuel on the Galapagos Islands initiative, which aims to eliminate fossil fuel usage by 2020.

Previous: sea lions at La Lobería; Punta Pitt's dramatic landscape. **Above:** the colorful underwater cliffs at Kicker Rock.

Look for ★ to find recommended
sights, activities, dining, and lodging.

Highlights

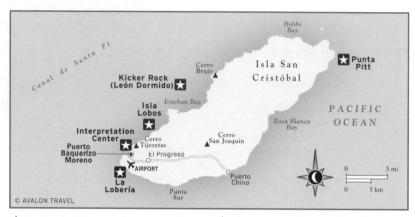

© AVALON TRAVEL

★ **Interpretation Center:** This is the best **museum** in the Galápagos to learn about the fascinating history of the islands and current environmental issues (page 83).

★ **La Lobería:** Don't miss the chance to walk among a huge **sea lion colony.** November to December is a great time to see the newborn pups playing in the sand (page 83).

★ **Isla Lobos:** Here you'll find excellent **snorkeling** among a colony of playful sea lions and colorful fish (page 91).

★ **Kicker Rock (León Dormido):** Dramatic cliffs shaped like a sleeping lion make this one of the most famous landmarks in the Galápagos. Visitors enjoy exceptional **snorkeling** with sharks, turtles, and fish (page 92).

★ **Punta Pitt:** Hike to a dramatic landscape where you can see all **three species of boobies** in one place (page 92).

San Cristóbal

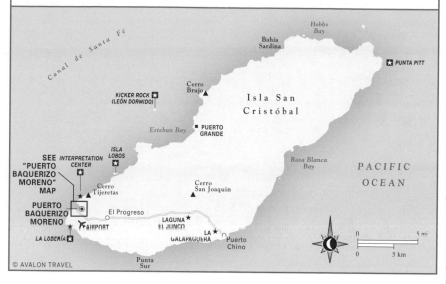

Puerto Baquerizo Moreno

The capital of the Galápagos Islands has a different feel from Puerto Ayora on Santa Cruz. It's smaller, cheaper, and not completely dependent on tourism—fishing and administration are also important employment sources in the town. The port has a very pleasant waterfront walkway where sea lions lounge lazily, and the beach just west of the center is the sleeping area for an entire colony—dozens of them congregate here at night. Note, however, that the omnipresence of sea lions is not without its drawbacks. The air has a permanently fishy smell, and there are few places to sit on the boardwalk that are not similarly smelly. Nonetheless, Baquerizo Moreno is a popular place to visit, with many sights within easy reach independently or on day tours. Española is widely regarded as one of the top three or four sites in the archipelago, and for many years it was only accessible by cruise. It is now a fantastic though pricey day tour from Puerto Baquerizo Moreno.

SIGHTS
West of Town

A 10-minute walk northeast of the center along Alsacio Northia is the small, popular **Playa Mann,** which gets busy on the weekend. Note that the water is not particularly clean. Opposite the beach is a branch of the University of San Francisco de Quito, and students are frequent visitors to the beach. There is also a small food stall that serves basic $8 *almuerzos.*

Playa Punta Carola, east past Playa Mann, is a beach area protected by a rocky outlet. Try snorkeling off the beach; you can sometimes spot sea turtles and sea lions. Go during high tide because of the rocky terrain.

Past Playa Punta Carola, the paved path curves to the right and you will see a large hill called **Cerro Tijeretas.** Cerro Tijeretas has two **viewpoints** with sweeping views of the cove below and neighboring beaches. *Tijeretas* means "scissors" in Spanish; the site is named

Puerto Baquerizo Moreno

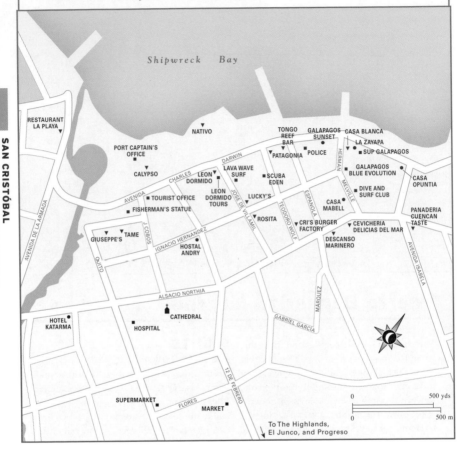

after the scissors-like tails of the frigate birds that inhabit the hill. Keep an eye out for frigate birds soaring above or perched in the trees, particularly in the morning. There is also a good swimming and **snorkeling spot** in a protected cove just below the hill, which is best at high tide. There is a wooden platform for entry into the water, but at low tide you will still need to scramble over the rocks.

Past Cerro Tijeretas lookout point, the path descends and turns into a rocky trail. There are some difficult sections with rocky scrambles over sharp, uneven lava rock. Though the path to **Playa Baquerizo** is only two

kilometers from this point, it frequently takes an hour to arrive from Cerro Tijeretas (Cerro Tijeretas is 30 minutes from town and 1 hour from Playa Baquerizo). Those who do make the trek out will be rewarded with the least crowded beach accessible from town. You can snorkel and swim here, too, though there's not much to see. Wear hiking shoes and be especially careful if it has rained recently, as slippery mud and sharp lava rocks are a dangerous combination.

You can easily visit all these sights on your own in less than a day. Starting in the morning, first visit the **Interpretation Center** to learn about history and environmental problems in the Galápagos. Walk to Playa Punta Carola for a refreshing dip and snorkel before continuing your trek up the hill to Cerro Tijeretas lookout. After watching the birds, start the strenuous hike out to Playa Baquerizo. You can eat lunch, relax, and cool off in the waves. Break up your hike back with a dip at the snorkeling point at Cerro Tijeretas.

★ Interpretation Center

Walk a little farther up from Playa Mann to reach the **Interpretation Center** (tel. 5/252-0358, 8am-5pm daily, free), which has detailed informational displays about the islands' history, geology, development, and current environmental problems. It's better than the smaller exhibition at the Charles Darwin Research Station in Puerto Ayora on Santa Cruz.

★ La Lobería

On the opposite end of town from Playa Mann is **La Lobería,** a rocky beach where there's a

large colony of **sea lions** lazing around. It's a 30-minute walk along an unmarked road near the airport, with not much to see but some dry cacti, so it's better to bike or take a taxi ($4) to the trailhead, which is only a quarter mile from La Lobería. Arrange a pickup time or walk (or bike) back. This is the only place on the island where you can walk among a sea lion colony, and there are usually dozens of these mammals stretched out on the beach and rocks. Snorkeling is common, though it is best at high tide to avoid swimming in shallow rocky areas, and visitors should beware of currents on the sides of the inlet. Though the trail from La Lobería is only about 0.6 mile, it is a difficult path across large, sometimes loose lava rocks. Wear good shoes.

TOURS
Highlands Tour

The half-day **highlands tour** ($40) visits La Galapaguera, Puerto Chino, El Junco, and occasionally Casa del Ceibo. You can save money by hiring a taxi to visit the same places ($10/hour).

Bay Tour

You can take a half-day **bay tour** ($60) near Puerto Baquerizo Moreno by either kayak or

frigate birds at the viewpoint Cerro Tijeretas

SUP. Glass-bottom boats and dinghies are no longer allowed in the bay because they disturb the wildlife.

Day Tours

Day tours visit León Dormido ($100) or Isla Lobos ($80) in combination with a nearby beach. Day tours to visit **Punta Pitt** ($150) don't leave every day; on these tours you disembark on the island and hike to the top, unlike the artisanal fishing tour to Punta Pitt.

The most expensive and most spectacular tour that leaves from Puerto Baquerizo Moreno is to see the waved albatross on **Española** ($200).

Artisanal Fishing Tours

One of the most popular tours is the **360 tour** ($140), which circumnavigates San Cristóbal and visits five sites in one day. It starts with snorkeling at the calm lagoons of Bahía Rosa Blanca, coasts by Punta Pitt to observe the birdlife on the coast (but you do not disembark), and has a rest stop at a beautiful white-sand beach, Bahía Sardinia. The tour then coasts by rock formations at Cerro Brujo to observe the scenery, and finishes with snorkeling at León Dormido. It includes a stop for fishing; if you're lucky, you may get fresh ceviche. Total navigation time is four hours, so avoid this tour if you get seasick easily.

Tour Operators and Agencies

Lava Wave Surf (tel. 5/252-1815, info@lavawavesurf.com) has surfboard rentals, surf classes, yoga classes, and guided bike tours of the highlands. They can also book almost any other tour on the island.

León Dormido Tours (Villamil at Darwin, tel. 99/445-1667, http://leondormidogalapagos.com.ec) is a popular tour agency that offers almost everything, including bike rentals, diving, ferry boat tickets, and day tours.

SUP Galapagos (Malecón at Melville, tel. 93/967-8592, reservas@galapagos.tours) is the only outfit in town that organizes stand-up paddleboarding tours of the bay.

Most tour agencies also sell dive tours, but for the best information, go directly to the dive operators.

Dive and Surf Club (Melville, tel. 8/087-7122 or 8/634-7256, www.divesurfclub.com) operates daily dive tours as well as discovery dives, PADI courses, and night dives.

Scuba Eden (Teodoro Wolf and Darwin, tel. 5/252-0666, http://scubaedengalapagos.

sea lion resting at La Loberia

com) operates daily snorkel and dive trips to Kicker Rock.

Galapagos Blue Evolution (Melville at Hernández, tel. 5/301-0264, http://galapagos-blueevolution.com.ec) is a dive operator that offers a full list of dive certifications, from open water to dive master.

RECREATION
Surfing

San Cristóbal has a strong surfing culture, and some of the agencies in town rent boards for $20 per day. Pass the military base at the east edge of town along Armada Nacional, and you will find some of the best surfing spots in the archipelago, **El Cañon** and **Tongo.** Note that these are rocky areas recommended only for experienced surfers, and there is no beach for sunbathing. You will need to show identification to walk through the military base on your way to these sites. Other surfing spots include **Punta Carola,** at the west edge of town, and **Manglecito** (accessible only by boat; look for an organized surf tour if you wish to go).

Biking

Tour agencies in town rent mountain bikes for $20 per day, or $10 for a half day. It's a fun option for visiting the highlands, and there is a protected bike lane that extends a decent way up toward the highlands. Be ready for a grueling day if you go all the way to Puerto Chino in the highlands and back.

Kayaking

Guided kayaking tours leave from the port and go either around the bay, along the coast, to the snorkeling spot at Tijeretas, or, in rare cases, take a longer kayaking trip all the way to Playa Ochoa. **Kayaking tours** cost $60 and don't leave every day if they don't have a minimum number of people signed up. Unfortunately, renting a kayak and going independently is no longer allowed due to tourists getting lost.

SUP

Stand-up paddleboarding tours have similar routes as the kayaking tours and cost approximately $60.

Diving

San Cristóbal has excellent diving, although there are fewer dive operators based here. There is a hyperbaric chamber at the Port Capitania. Prices for most trips are $140-160, although going to Punta Pitt or Española costs about $200-250.

There are open water dive certification courses for people who arrive without certification, and you can even get advanced level, rescue diver, and dive master training.

Tijeretas and the Caragua wreck is a trip particularly recommended for divers who need a refresher. Tijeretas is a relatively shallow site where they can review their skills among tropical fish. Caragua Wreck is where the boat that brought Manuel J. Cobos rests. Cobos is infamous for founding the sugarcane plantation on the island, terrorizing his workers, and later being murdered by them. The boat's skeleton forms an artificial underwater reef with schools of fish. There is a buoy rope between the wreck and the surface that you can climb down for greater control.

The most famous dive site on San Cristóbal is **Kicker Rock,** where divers frequently see hammerheads, sea lions, eagle rays, and stingrays. The site is suitable for all levels.

Dive trips to **Punta Pitt** are also possible, combining a short hike to see red-footed boobies with two immersions at Cerro Pitt (home to fish, sea turtles, and beautiful coral) and Bajo Pitt (home to Galápagos sharks, hammerheads, rays, and sea turtles). The drawbacks are the two-hour boat ride each way and the hefty price tag of $200.

A dive trip to **Española** visits the famous site of the waved albatross, Punta Suárez, and does two nearby immersions in Gardner Bay.

There are a couple more sites for advanced divers. **Islote 5 Fingers**, named for the five rocks that stick out of the water, is a good place to see schools of Galápagos sharks. **Roca Este** is a coral rock reef that hosts a wide variety of fish, Galápagos sharks, and rays. **Roca**

Ballena is similar to Roca Este but deeper, and it often has more sharks. The **Hitler Caves** are three large underwater caves with calm, well protected waters, bizarrely named after a local fisherman (of no relation to the Nazi party) who discovered them.

ENTERTAINMENT

Baquerizo Moreno comes alive at night, and you may be astonished at how many children and teenagers fill the waterfront on weekends. Nightlife options are restricted, though. There are various impromptu discos inland away from the center of town on the weekend. Just ask around or watch for flyers. For a quieter evening, have a cocktail or beer at the waterfront **Muyu** (Malecón inside Golden Bay Hotel) or **Calypso** (Darwin and Cobos, tel. 5/252-0154).

FOOD

Compared to Puerto Ayora, Baquerizo Moreno is rather lacking in variety. There are plenty of mom-and-pop restaurants serving passable if unspectacular Ecuadorian and fast food, as well as a couple upscale seafood restaurants. Some of the seafood restaurants also serve pizza and pasta, but you won't find many other options for international food.

Snacks

Panadería Cuencan Taste (Northia at Isabela, 5/301-0846, 2pm-9pm Mon.-Sat., rolls $0.25-0.50) is where the whole town buys their bread. There is a large variety of rolls, along with a few treats like empanadas, chocolate rolls, and cakes.

Ecuadorian and Seafood

Many informal restaurants serve breakfast, burgers, sandwiches, and snacks.

On the *malecón* are **Patagonia** (tel. 5/252-0017, breakfast, lunch, and dinner daily, $5-10) and **Tongo Reef Bar** (tel. 5/252-1852, breakfast, lunch, and dinner daily, $5-10). The food is just passable, and overpriced for the quality, but they are the only places in town that serve breakfast early enough to eat

before 7:30am day tours. For breakfast, there's American or continental breakfast as well as more local specialties such as the *bolon* (a fried plantain ball).

Farther north, **Casa Blanca Café** (Malecón and Melville, no phone, breakfast, lunch, and dinner daily, $5-12) overlooking the bay has similar typical food but in a more lively café atmosphere. The sandwiches are just adequate, but it is a popular spot for traditional snacks such as tamales or *humitas* (mashed corn filled with chicken, vegetables, or cheese) and cocktails, particularly at sunset.

One of the best cheap set meals in town is at **Lucky's** (Villamil and Hernández, no phone, 8am-9pm Mon.-Fri., 8am-2pm Sat.-Sun., $4), a hole-in-the-wall popular with locals that serves up an excellent-value two-course lunch and dinner, as well as simple breakfasts.

Cevicheria Delicias del Mar (Northia and Melville, no phone, 8:30am-3pm daily, $10-12) is where the locals go for ceviche and a beer or two. Pull up a plastic chair and choose between the basic fish ceviche or pricier mixed shrimp, oysters, and *canchalagua* (a local mollusk) ceviche. They all come with fried banana chips and popcorn.

Rosita (Villamil and Hernández, tel. 5/252-1581, noon-3pm and 5pm-10pm daily, entrées $15-20, *almuerzos* $6) is a popular restaurant among both tourists and locals. Outdoor seating, soccer jerseys, and flags of the world give it a fun, informal vibe. It has fish, shellfish, and meat dishes on the menu, prepared 10 different ways, but there is also a simpler set-meal lunch and dinner for $6.

The ★ **Descanso Marinero** (Northia and Melville, no phone, 8am-9pm daily, $15-20) has excellent food in large portions and a fun tropical atmosphere, complete with hanging lobster shells, surfboards, paper lanterns, and plenty of tropical greenery. Families sit in the larger tables in the center of the restaurant while couples prefer the rustic booths where tropical plants and straw create little hideaways. There is a wide variety of rice, chicken, shrimp, and fish dishes, but the specialties are the dishes *a la plancha*, which come on a sizzling iron skillet.

International

The best hamburger in town is at **Cri's Burger Factory** (Teodoro Wolf and Hernández, tel. 99/423-6770, 5pm-10pm daily, $7-12), a joint frequented by tourists and locals alike. The patties made with local beef are huge and grilled right out front, and the toppings are creative and heaping. The Hawaiian comes with pineapple chutney, while the Pepe has bacon, sweet corn, onion, and barbecue sauce. Pizza, hot dogs loaded with toppings, grill platters, and a couple salads round out the menu.

★ **Fresco's** (7:30am-6pm, breakfast $4, *almuerzos* $8 Mon.-Sun.) is a casual restaurant near Playa Mann with good breakfasts (avocado and egg toast), espresso drinks, and excellent international almuerzos. True to the restaurant's name, the food here is considerably fresher than at most places in town, and it's cooked to order. Note that they are open until 6pm but only serve espresso drinks and snacks after 3pm.

Giuseppe's (Darwin at Manuel Cobos, tel. 99/763-8540, 4:30-10:30pm daily, $10-20) has a wide range of Italian dishes, including pizza, pasta, seafood, and meat dishes.

Nativo (Malecón, no phone, 10am-10pm daily, $10-20) is a casual place for alfresco waterfront dining. There's an eclectic international menu of salads, seafood dishes, pizzas, wings, and drinks, made with mostly locally sourced ingredients. The prices are quite reasonable despite the location and a clientele that is almost all tourists.

Calypso (Darwin and Cobos, tel. 5/252-0154, 5:30pm-midnight daily, $10-15) is a friendly restaurant popular with tourists, with inviting decor and breezy outdoor tables right along the *malecón*. The varied menu has seafood, chicken, and burgers, but the specialty is gooey deep-dish pizza with traditional Italian toppings.

The top restaurant in Puerto Baquerizo Moreno is ★ **Muyu** (Malecón inside Golden

Bay Hotel, tel. 05/252-0069, 7-10am, noon-3pm, 5-10pm daily, entrées $20-35, tasting menu $65, menu bar menu $7). The farm- and sea-to-table concept means that all their food is sourced in the Galápagos, unlike most places where ingredients are imported from mainland Ecuador. The high-quality ingredients are well presented and served in a setting with panoramic windows overlooking the ocean. If the prices blow your budget, there's a less-sophisticated set of $7 meal-size bar bites that you can order at the seaside bar.

Self-Service

If you want to cook, there are numerous little convenience stores in town that have a very limited selection of fruit, vegetables, and meat. The **supermarket** is located at Quito and Flores, though it also lacks fresh produce.

The best selection of fruits and vegetables is at the **Municipal Market** (12 de Febrero and Flores, no phone, 6am-6pm Mon.-Fri, 4am-2pm Sat., 6am-noon Sun.), a farmers market on the outskirts of town, but note that during the week almost all the food for sale is imported from mainland Ecuador, meaning it is more expensive and less fresh. On Saturdays the local farms come to the market to sell local organic produce.

Fresh, locally caught seafood including lobster can be purchased at the **Muelle de Pescadores** (fishing dock) from about 7am until they run out. Lobster season (when fishers are allowed to catch and sell a limited quantity of lobster) is September 8 to January 8. The rest of the year is langostino season. (Langostino is very similar to lobster in taste and texture. The main difference is that the langostino lacks big front claws.)

ACCOMMODATIONS

Puerto Baquerizo Moreno has plenty of options for accommodation, particularly in the budget range. It lacks a large selection of mid-range and top-end hotels, which is not necessarily a bad thing because tour groups prefer to stay in Santa Cruz, keeping San Cristóbal quieter.

Lobster and Langostino

Locally caught lobster and langostino are perhaps some of the most delicious delicacies of the Galápagos. Langostino is known outside of the Galápagos as a "squat lobster" and has a similar taste, though it is slightly smaller. You can find lobster and langostino in local restaurants depending on the season. Lobster fishing is permitted from September to January, and langostino fishing is permitted the rest of the year. Or for a unique experience, buy and cook your own (though killing a lobster is not for the squeamish). You can purchase live lobster and langostino locally at the Muelle de Pescadores on San Cristóbal and at the fish market on Santa Cruz Island. A simple preparation is simply boiling and serving with butter and lime. Here is a more Ecuadorian recipe, courtesy of Byron Rivera Real, executive chef of Metropolitan Touring.

ECUADORIAN-STYLE LOBSTER IN COCONUT SAUCE

Ingredients

- 5 garlic cloves, minced

- 2 onions, diced

- 3 tablespoons achiote oil (this is oil flavored with annatto, very commonly sold in the Galápagos and Ecuador; if you are cooking in the United States, add annatto to the oil)

- 1 cup coconut milk

- ½ cup dry shredded coconut

- 1 tablespoon parsley

- 2 tablespoons cilantro

- 1 cup butter

- 3 teaspoons salt

- 3 green plantains (for *patacones*)

- 4 lobsters

- 1 hot pepper (fresh or dried)

- Fresh herbs for decoration

Preparation

- Sauté the garlic, onion, and pepper oil in a pan. Add the coconut milk and dried coconut, cover, and reduce. Add the parsley and cilantro and liquefy in a blender. Place the paste in a saucepan and mix with the butter, carefully melting the butter over a low flame. Add pepper to taste and save.

- In a separate saucepan, slice the plantains into chunks, then squish each chunk until it is thinner. Deep-fry the slices to make a side of *patacones*.

- Kill the lobsters by plunging the tip of a sharp knife straight down right behind the lobster's eyes. Open the lobster tails by cutting the membranes on both sides to take out the tail meat (for better control over the cooking). Salt and pepper the tails and cook them over a grill or in a saucepan for 3 minutes on each side over medium heat. Serve bathed in coconut sauce with *patacones* on the side. Decorate with fresh herbs.

- Chef's gourmet suggestion: To complete the main plate, add fresh fruit in citrus juice or a mint syrup for a fresh touch on the palate.

Under $50

Baquerizo Moreno has many informal, family-run *hostales*, which are converted family residences. Many have sprawled inland to rather inconvenient locations, and, despite the inconvenience, aren't really any cheaper than the locations in town. Budget *hostales* in Baquerizo Moreno typically have only Spanish-speaking staff, spotty Wi-Fi, and no breakfast (unless noted). Rooms have private bathrooms unless noted.

One of the best budget options is ★ **Casa de Laura** (Callejón 2 and Armada, tel. 5/252-0173, www.hostalcasadelaura.com, $20 pp). At the end of a quiet cul-de-sac, it is one of the most tranquil budget options in town. The *hostal* has hammocks and an inviting lounge, but the bright, air-conditioned rooms overlooking a beautiful tropical garden edged by lava rocks are the real reason to stay here. Some rooms even have a mini-fridge.

Another family-run option is **Casa de Huéspedes Milena** (Serrano at Northia, tel. 99/013-6604, milepibu11@hotmail.com, $25 pp), which has well-maintained, spacious guest rooms a little inland, but not as far inland as many other similar guesthouses.

More centrally located is the family-run **Hostal León Dormido** (Jose de Villamil and Malecón, tel. 5/252-0169, $25 s, $50 d), which has decent, though unfashionable, guest rooms with air-conditioning and TVs, a cozy lounge area, and a small coffee shop downstairs.

Travelers who want to cook head to the centrally located family house **Casa Mabell** (Melville and Northia, tel. 98/125-8617, $30 s, $40 d), one of the few *hostales* with a shared kitchen. The rooms are somewhat small but are more comfortable and modern than the other budget options in town. Rooms have air-conditioning and TV, and common areas have Wi-Fi.

$50-100

There are not too many hotels in the midrange in Puerto Baquerizo Moreno.

Hostal Andry (12 de Febrero at Ignacio Hernández, tel. 5/252-1652, hostal_andry@

outlook.es, $30 s, $60 d, breakfast not included) is a good value and centrally located. The rooms are simple and clean; ask for a room with a mini-fridge. There's an in-house tourist agency as well.

Hostal Galapagos (Playa de Oro, tel. 05/301-0947, www.hostal-galapagos.com, $50-60 s/d) has some of the least expensive beach-view rooms and is just next to the exclusive Golden Bay Hotel. Only the two rooms in front have views of the beach; the inland rooms are slightly cheaper. The detached, single-story rooms somewhat resemble *cabañas* (cabins) and are surrounded by cactus gardens. There are even hammocks out front, although the furnishings are on the plain and modern side. The included breakfast at **Fresco's** is excellent.

Just inland is the bright, whitewashed **Hostal Casa de Nelly** (Tijeretas and Manuel Agama, tel. 5/252-0112, saltosnelly@hotmail.com, $50 s, $70 d), a friendly *hostal* with nice terraces. The three-story building has cheerful, rustic rooms, a shared kitchen, and a couple hammocks for relaxing. Playa Mann is just a few blocks away.

La Zayapa (Darwin at Melville, tel. 99/643-9541, www.lazayapahotel.com, $60 s, $90 d) has comfortable, clean, modern rooms in a great location. The interior rooms lack views, but the exterior rooms have wide views of the bay.

Casa Blanca (Malecón and Melville, tel. 5/252-0392, www.casablancagalapagos.com, $70-120 d, $150 suite) on the waterfront is distinctive for its whitewashed Moorish architecture and bright blue cupolas. Inside, the rustic-chic guest rooms have hammocks, wide balconies with views of the harbor, and the most personality in this price range.

$100-200

Hotel Katarma (Northia and Esmeraldas, tel. 5/252-0300, $170 s, $200 d) is a boutique property with only 13 rooms and a beautiful courtyard where mosaic seahorses, fish, and a sphinx overlook a serpentine swimming pool. The rooms are plainer, without the artistic touches of the common areas, but are spacious. There is a sunny terrace and sauna. The only downside is the inland location for a hotel of this price.

Galápagos Sunset Hotel (Charles Darwin at Melville, tel. 5/252-0529, http://galapagossunset.com.ec, $138 d, $220 ocean-view suite) is a newly built, upscale boutique lodging on prime real estate on the *malecón*. Windows have panoramic views of the scene.

Casa Opuntia (Darwin, tel. 2/604-6800 in Quito, www.opuntiagalapagostours.com, $120-160 s, $150-185 d, $180-220 t) is one of the most well-known luxury options in San Cristóbal. The hotel has 13 elegant guest rooms, half of which overlook the harbor. The other rooms in the less-expensive extension overlook the pool, where visitors sun themselves during the day and swim up to the bar at night. The beautiful seaside restaurant is in a breezy open-air terrace with a cactus and lava-rock garden.

Over $200

The port has a few top-end hotels, but not as many as Puerto Ayora.

For an intimate experience, try the boutique hotel ★ **Casa Iguana Mar y Sol** (Alsacio Northia, tel. 5/252-1788, http://casaiguanamarysol.com, $135-285 d). The hotel has five suites, all with huge beds, separate sitting areas, and bay views. The largest are twice the size of the smallest and have a mini-kitchenette. The hotel is quite modern and was built in 2009. However, leopard-print bedding, artisanal touches, and rustic artwork remind you that you are in a tropical paradise.

Golden Bay Hotel & Spa (Playa del Oro, tel. 5/252-0069, www.goldenbay.com.ec, $305-410 d, $525 suite) is leaps and bounds ahead of the competition for poshest digs on San Cristóbal, with sumptuous beds, rainfall showers, an on-site spa, and, of course, the highest prices. The all-white interiors are soothing and designed to highlight the fantastic panoramic views of Playa del Oro through the floor-to-ceiling windows. A pool, a rooftop terrace with a hot tub, and the farm- and sea-to-table restaurant Muyu round out the amenities. If you really want to splurge, get a suite with a soaking tub.

Camping

Puerto Chino is the only spot in the national park where you can camp independently on San Cristóbal. This site is a beach on the other side of the island that is a popular spot for locals to sunbathe, and there is a small camping area just off the beach with no facilities. See page 39 for logistics of camping in the National Park. You'll also need a taxi drop-off and pickup, which usually cost $25 each way, although on Sundays only there is a bus.

The other two sites where camping is allowed by Galápagos National Park (**Manglecito** and **Puerto Grande**) are only accessible by organized tour. There is only one tour operator that runs organized camping and kayaking tours here (see **ROW Adventures** under Tours).

INFORMATION AND SERVICES

The **CAPTURGAL** tourist information office (Hernández, tel. 5/252-1124, 8am-noon and 2pm-5pm Mon.-Fri.) and the **municipal tourist office** (Darwin and 12 de Febrero, tel. 5/252-0119 or 5/252-0358, 8am-noon and 2pm-5pm Mon.-Fri.) have helpful maps and information.

Wi-Fi can be found at most hotels and cafés around town, though the speed is extremely slow.

Other services in town are the **post office,** at the western end of Darwin, past the municipal building; the **police station** (Darwin and Española, tel. 5/252-0101); and the town's main hospital, **Oscar Jandl Hospital** (Northia and Quito, tel. 5/252-0118), which has basic medical care and a 24-hour emergency room.

GETTING THERE AND AROUND

Airport

The **San Cristóbal Airport** (airport code: SCY) is at the west end of Avenida Alsacio

sea lion swimming at Isla Lobos

Cruz for San Cristóbal at 7am and 2pm. The reverse trip from San Cristóbal to Puerto Ayora leaves at 7am and 2pm.

Getting from San Cristóbal to Isabela in the same day is possible, though unpleasant, because it takes two ferries; take the morning ferry (7am) from San Cristóbal to Puerto Ayora, then the afternoon ferry (2pm) from Puerto Ayora to Isabela. For the reverse trip, take the morning ferry (6am) from Isabela to Puerto Ayora, then the afternoon ferry (2pm) from Puerto Ayora to San Cristóbal.

Getting from San Cristóbal to Floreana in the same day is not possible due to ferry schedules.

Interisland Flights

Small eight-seat planes fly half-hour routes among San Cristóbal, Baltra, and Isabela several times per week. Fares start at $156 one-way, $240 round-trip or for any two flights (even different routes). You can book interisland flights through either **Emetebe** (tel./fax 5/252-0615, www.emetebe.com.ec), or **FlyGalapagos** (tel. 5/301-6579, www.flygalapagos.net).

Around Town

Taxis are quite affordable and cost only $1 within Baquerizo Moreno. To visit sites in the highlands you can hire a taxi for about $10 per hour. **Buses** leave from the *malecón* half a dozen times daily for El Progreso in the highlands, or take a **taxi** (about $3).

Northia past the radio station. Take a taxi ($2) from the airport to town or walk (20 minutes).

Interisland Ferries

Traveling between islands is easy, with daily services on small launches connecting Santa Cruz with San Cristóbal and Isabela. All routes cost $30 per person one-way and take about two hours.

The ferries leave Puerto Ayora on Santa

Off the Coast

★ ISLA LOBOS

Isla Lobos is a tiny, rocky island 30 minutes north of Baquerizo Moreno by boat. Walking on the island is prohibited, so just jump straight in for excellent snorkeling with sea lions in the channel between the islet and the shore. Boobies and frigates can also be seen nesting here. Day trips cost $80 and combine

Isla Lobos with a nearby beach for sunbathing and swimming.

BAHÍA ROSA BLANCA

This peaceful bay is an excellent snorkeling spot. Its protected, crystalline waters turn interesting shades of turquoise depending on the sun, and visitors can snorkel among a wide variety of fish, white-tipped reef sharks, and sea turtles that take refuge here. The only way to visit this site is to take the 360 tour leaving from Puerto Baquerizo Moreno, which circumnavigates the island.

★ KICKER ROCK (LEÓN DORMIDO)

One of the Galápagos's most famous landmarks is **Kicker Rock,** also known as León Dormido (Sleeping Lion). Some people think it looks like a foot, while others see the shape of a lion. Whichever name you prefer, this is one of the best snorkeling and dive sites in the archipelago. The sheer-walled volcanic tuff cone has been eroded in half with a narrow channel between. This is a prime place to spot sharks—white-tipped reef sharks are commonly seen in and around the channel, while divers can go deeper to see awesome schools of hammerheads. Sea turtles and a wide range of rays are also common. Boats are not allowed in the channel, waiting at either end while you snorkel or dive. Snorkeling day trips cost $100 and stop at one of three beaches—**Cerro Brujo, Puerto Grande,** or **Manglecito,** depending on the day of the week, for more relaxed swimming, snorkeling, and sunbathing. **Cerro Brujo** is often said to be the most beautiful, with a long stretch of white sand capped by rocky cliffs, and cruises sometimes stop here for kayaking as well.

The famous Kicker Rock is also known as León Dormido (Sleeping Lion).

TOP EXPERIENCE

★ PUNTA PITT

On the northeast tip of San Cristóbal, the farthest site from the port is **Punta Pitt.** A wet landing is followed by a long and fairly strenuous hike uphill (two hours round-trip) past an olivine beach through thorny scrub and past tuff cones. The rewards are panoramic views and, more importantly, the only **red-footed booby** colony in the archipelago outside Genovesa, and the only spot where you can see all three booby species together. There are also populations of frigate birds, storm petrels, and swallow-tailed gulls.

Punta Pitt is common on cruise ship itineraries. There are day tours that visit from Baquerizo Moreno, although only a handful of agencies go here, and those that do charge a hefty premium ($150-200). There are also 360 tours, which do not disembark and hike up the hill but just coast by to observe the birds at a distance before sailing on.

San Cristóbal Highlands

Most of these sights can be visited on a guided tour ($40 pp), or you can save money by sharing a taxi (from $10/ hour). Enthusiastic bike riders can rent a bike in town (about $20/day) to get to these, but with a steep incline and 25 kilometers to the farthest point one-way, it is not a ride for the casual biker. Hiring a taxi to help somewhat is popular. One option is to be dropped off with a bike at the highest point (Laguna El Junco); you can bike downhill to La Galapaguera and Puerto Chino, and then bike back (you still have to climb the hill on the way back).

CASA DEL CEIBO

Avenida 12 de Febrero climbs north out of Baquerizo Moreno to **El Progreso,** a notorious former penal colony that's now a quiet farming village. There's not much to see, but for a unique experience, visit the **Casa del Ceibo** (near the main street, tel. 5/252-0248, www.lacasadelceibo.com, 9am-12:30pm and 1:30pm-5:30pm daily, $1.50), a small tree house in a huge kapok tree. The tree is a whopping eight meters wide and is claimed to be the world's widest of its kind. You can rappel up the side, relax in the hammocks, and drink the local coffee. A maximum of two people can stay overnight in the quirky tree house for $25 per person.

LAGUNA EL JUNCO

From El Progreso, the road continues north to the settlement of Soledad, near an overlook at the south end of the island, and east to Cerro Verde and Los Arroyos. About 10 kilometers east of Progreso on the way to Cerro Verde, a turnoff to the right goes along a steep dirt track to the **Laguna El Junco,** one of the few freshwater lakes in the Galápagos. At 700 meters above sea level, the collapsed caldera is fed by rainwater and shelters wading birds, frigates, the Chatham mockingbird, and seven species of Darwin's finches. It's also a good place to observe typical highland tree ferns. A narrow trail with spectacular panoramic views encircles the rim, and it's a leisurely 45 minutes to go all the way around. Note that this site can get very muddy in the rainy season (January-April).

a compacted-ash landscape at Punta Pitt

PUERTO CHINO

The road from Cerro Verde continues across the island to **Puerto Chino,** an isolated beach on the south coast that is frequented by local surfers. Swimming and snorkeling are not recommended due to the strong waves, but there is a *mirador* (viewpoint) toward the right side of the beach where blue-footed boobies can be seen. It's possible to camp here with permission from the national park office in the port, though you will need to bring your own equipment. If you're in San Cristóbal on Sunday, instead of an expensive taxi you can take a bus that goes from the mercado in Puerto Baquerizo Moreno to Puerto Chino and back ($2). Buses leave the market at 8am and 9am; to get back, the bus leaves the beach at 4pm.

LA GALAPAGUERA

A few kilometers inland from Puerto Chino is **La Galapaguera** (no phone, 6am-6pm daily, free), a giant tortoise reserve where San Cristóbal tortoises reside in 12 hectares of dry forest. Mature tortoises from San Cristóbal Island are kept in captivity to breed, and baby tortoises are protected from invasive species until they are five years old.

giant tortoises at the La Galapaguera

The baby tortoises are kept in raised enclosures, though the adults frequently wander across the stone walkway.

Isabela

Look for ★ to find recommended
sights, activities, dining, and lodging.

Highlights

★ **Tintoreras Bay:** Dramatic lichen-covered lava rocks, large populations of **marine iguanas,** and excellent snorkeling make this one of the most popular sites on Isabela (page 109).

★ **Los Túneles:** Lava-rock arches over a turquoise sea make a beautiful backdrop for watching **blue-footed boobies** nest and enormous **sea turtles** glide through the water (page 109).

★ **Sierra Negra and Volcán Chico:** The **best hike** in the Galápagos is a trip along the rim of this enormous active caldera (second largest in the world), followed by walking on the moonlike landscape of Volcán Chico (page 109).

★ **Tagus Cove:** Tagus Cove's claim to fame is a **short hike** to the beautiful blue-green Darwin Lake. On a clear day you see all the way to the other side of Isabela (page 111).

★ **Punta Vicente Roca:** The calm waters at this excellent snorkeling site are home to a large population of **sea turtles**. Around the corner, visitors can spot flightless **cormorants** and **fur seals** from a *panga* ride (page 111).

I sabela is by far the largest island in the Galápagos and, at nearly 4,600 square kilometers, accounts for half the archipelago's total landmass. At 100 kilometers long, it's four times the size of Santa Cruz, the next largest island.

One of the Galápagos's youngest islands, Isabela boasts a dramatic landscape dominated by six intermittently active volcanoes. From north to south, these are Wolf (1,646 meters) and Ecuador (610 meters), which both straddle the equator; Darwin (1,280 meters); Alcedo (1,097 meters); Sierra Negra (1,490 meters); and Cerro Azul (1,250 meters).

As the giant of the archipelago, it's only fitting that Isabela has one of the largest populations of giant tortoises, which feed on the abundant vegetation in the highlands. There are five separate subspecies here, one for each volcano (except tiny Volcán Ecuador). The slopes of Volcán Alcedo have the biggest population—more than 35 percent of all the tortoises in the archipelago.

The west coast of the island receives nutrient-rich, cool waters from both the Humboldt and Cromwell Currents. This is why the marine life is so abundant, with large populations of whales, dolphins, and flightless cormorants, which dive down into the cool waters in search of fish and no longer need their wings. Isabela also has the largest population of Galápagos penguins, although numbers fell dramatically as a result of the 1998 El Niño climate pattern.

Isabela's only port, **Puerto Villamil,** where most of the island's population of 2,000 lives, is slowly turning into a tourism hub, but on a much smaller scale than Puerto Ayora. There are plenty of visitor sites near the port as well as excursions inland to the volcanoes, but many of the best coastal sites are on the west side of Isabela, accessible only to cruises. Most cruises stick to the central and southern islands in the archipelago, and fewer than 25 percent make it out to Isabela due to the distance involved. Those that do are rewarded with some spectacular visitor sites.

Notable among the several visitor sites accessible to visitors staying in Puerto Villamil are the **Tortoise Breeding Center** (the

Previous: flamingo at Laguna Salinas; Los Túneles are dramatic lava rock formations above the sea. **Above:** a blue-footed booby at Los Túneles.

Isabela

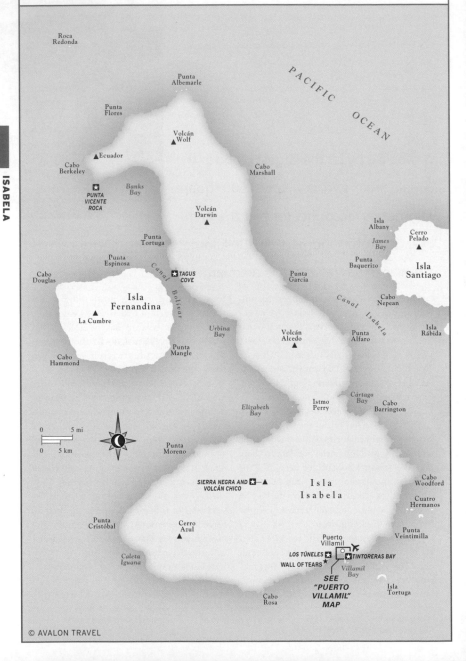

Roca
Redonda

Punta
Albemarle

PACIFIC OCEAN

Punta
Flores

Volcán
Wolf

▲Ecuador

Cabo
Marshall

Cabo
Berkeley

Banks
Bay

★
PUNTA
VICENTE
ROCA

Volcán
Darwin
▲

Isla
Albany

Cerro
Pelado
▲

James
Bay

Isla
Santiago

Punta
Tortuga

Punta
Espinosa

Punta
Baquerizo

Cabo
Douglas

Canal Bolívar

★ TAGUS
COVE

Punta
García

Cabo
Nepean

Isla
Fernandina

Canal Isabela

Isla
Rábida

La Cumbre ▲

Urbina
Bay

Volcán
Alcedo
▲

Punta
Alfaro

Cabo
Hammond

Punta
Mangle

Cártago
Bay

Cabo
Barrington

0   5 mi
0   5 km

Elizabeth
Bay

Istmo
Perry

Punta
Moreno

Isla
Isabela

Cabo
Woodford

SIERRA NEGRA AND ★—▲
VOLCÁN CHICO

Cuatro
Hermanos

Punta
Cristóbal

Cerro
Azul
▲

Punta
Veintimilla

Puerto
Villamil

Caleta
Iguana

LOS TÚNELES ★
WALL OF TEARS ★

★ TINTORERAS BAY

Villamil
Bay

SEE
"PUERTO
VILLAMIL"
MAP

Isla
Tortuga

Cabo
Rosa

© AVALON TRAVEL

largest in the archipelago) and the islets of **Las Tintoreras,** which offer great snorkeling with reef sharks, the stunning archways of **Los Túneles** and nearby snorkeling. In the highlands, one of the best hikes in the Galápagos is to **Sierra Negra,** Isabela's highest volcano, which boasts the second-largest active crater in the world. Marine sites accessible only to cruise boats include *panga* (dinghy) rides into the mangroves of **Punta Moreno** to see penguins and **Elizabeth Bay** to see flightless cormorants. **Urbina Bay** contains a fascinating raised coral reef, and **Tagus Cove** is notable for the graffiti left by generations of pirates as well as a hike to the deep-blue saline **Darwin Lake.**

HISTORY

Whalers and pirates began visiting Isabela in the 18th century, hunting in the waters off the west coast and stopping over to gather tortoises as food for long voyages. The names of many of these ships are still carved into the rocks at Tagus Cove.

In 1946, it was the humans' turn to endure hardships on the island, when a penal colony was built on Sierra Negra's southern slopes. The best evidence of the brutal regime is the lava-rock Muro de las Lágrimas (Wall of Tears), which still stands near Puerto Villamil, a thoroughly pointless construction sweated over by luckless convicts over many years. Food supplies were scarce in those days, and it was usually consumed by the guards, leaving many convicts to starve to death. The notorious jail was closed in 1959.

The tortoise population on Isabela has suffered considerably. The whalers used to hunt them, and more recently thousands of feral goats have eaten their vegetation; cows and donkeys trample their eggs. Volcanic eruptions and a human-caused fire that raged for five months in 1984 have also ravaged the landscapes. Things are improving, though, particularly after 100,000 goats were successfully eradicated between 1997 and 2006 by a huge government operation, mainly employing Australian hunters in helicopters. The tortoise breeding center on the island is one of the biggest in the archipelago, releasing hundreds of tortoises back into the wild.

ISABELA
PUERTO VILLAMIL

Puerto Villamil

About 2,000 people live in this small port on the southeast tip of Isabela. As well as fishing and a developing tourism industry, the locals have worked on all manner of projects—from sulfur mining in nearby Sierra Negra volcano to lime production and coffee farming. The town is quite charming and a far more laid-back base than the two larger ports in the archipelago. With a small selection of hotels and restaurants as well as nearby beaches, a lagoon, and highland hikes, Puerto Villamil has plenty to keep you busy for a few days. Bring cash, because there is no ATM on the island and credit cards are rarely accepted.

SIGHTS
Playa Grande
The town's main beach is a beautiful three-kilometer-long stretch of white sand ideal for a relaxed stroll, a swim, and watching the sunset. It starts in town, with a rickety wooden structure serving as a lookout point, and continues west, the beach becoming more and more pristine the farther you walk. Keep an eye out for blue-footed boobies, which are occasionally spotted here in huge feeding frenzies, diving in unison.

Concha de Perla
Concha de Perla is a great free place to go snorkeling on your own. Bring your own snorkel or rent one in town and simply walk

toward the dock from town for about 15 minutes. No guide, tour, or taxi is needed. The sheltered cove has calm water where fish, sea lions, and rays can be seen. The access path is a raised wooden pathway that goes through a tangle of mangroves to the dock.

TOURS
Highlands Tours
The classic must-see tour of Isabela's highlands is the hike to **Sierra Negra Volcano and Volcán Chico** ($40). Some of these tours include downhill bike riding back to town. A less popular trek available only via private tour is to the **sulfur mines** ($100 pp, minimum four people).

Bay Tours
The half-day **Tintoreras Bay tour** includes great snorkeling around the islet, a small walk along lava fields, and a visit to a channel where white-tipped reef sharks rest. The classic way to visit is by small dinghy ($40), though kayaking ($50) and SUP tours ($50) of the bay are also possible. Note that the kayaking and SUP tours don't disembark.

Artisanal Fishing Tours
The artisanal fishing tour to **Los Túneles** ($110) is widely regarded as the best tour available from Puerto Villamil. The tour to **Isla Tortuga** ($110) is less popular and does not leave every day. Both include a stop to attempt to catch fish for lunch.

Tour Operators and Agencies
GalaTourEx (Gil, tel. 5/252-9324, galatourex2017@hotmail.com) can help organize an overnight stay at Campo Duro EcoLodge for camping ($70), as well as tours ($48) to hike Sierra Negra combined with breakfast and a nice buffet lunch at Campo Duro (most other operators serve box lunches) and the on-site giant tortoise refuge.

Rosadelco Tour (Conocarpus at Pinzón, tel. 5/252-9237 or 99/494-9693, http://rosedelco.com.ec) is a reputable operator in town. They offer all the usual suspects—tours of Los Túneles, Sierra Negra volcano, Tintoreras, and snorkeling at Isla Tortuga.

Galapagos Bike & Surf (Escalesias at Tero Real, tel. 99/488-5473 or 5/252-9509, www.galapagosbikeandsurf.com) has surfing classes for $45, surfboard rentals for $25 full day or $15 half-day, and bike rentals for $20 for the day. They're also the only outfit in town that goes to Tintoreras by SUP rather than dinghy (tours $50 including snorkeling).

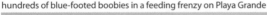

hundreds of blue-footed boobies in a feeding frenzy on Playa Grande

Puerto Villamil

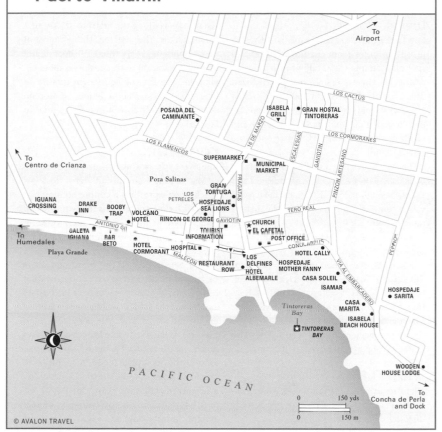

A couple times a week, they also offer tours of Sierra Negra that return by downhill biking.

RECREATION
Biking

Puerto Villamil is a fun place to ride a bike around town. You can get more easily to the spectacular far end of Playa Grande and see Los Humedales and the Wall of Tears independently. Hard-core bikers can ascend into the lush highland areas where the locals have farms, though it's quite steep. A less extreme ride is to rent a good mountain bike, get a taxi to drop you off at the trailhead, El Cura, for $25 and bike down.

Ask the travel agency where you rent the bike ($15/day) to call ahead and make a reservation at one of the excellent destination farm restaurants in the highlands for a nice lunch break. Note that this largely depends on luck; they primarily cater to tour groups and may not accept reservations for just one or two people unless they are already cooking that day. Of the highland restaurants where you can stop for lunch, **Campo Duro** is also a campground with a giant tortoise reserve, **Flor de Recuerdo** next door is an intimate, family-run farm that makes chicken on lava rocks, and **Hauser's** is an upscale, romantic restaurant with a well-appointed dining room. After lunch, stop at the volcanic caves **Cuevas de Sucre.**

Diving

Isla Tortuga is a great intermediate dive site just 30 minutes from the port. Divers can spot giant manta rays and hammerheads in relatively calm waters. There are advanced dive sites off the coast of Isabela—**Cuatro Hermanos** and **La Viuda**—but it is currently hard to find a day tour due to the popularity of Isla Tortuga and the lack of dive operators on the island.

There is currently only one dive operator on Isabela, **Isla Bella Tour** (Antonio Gil and Escalesias, tel. 5/252-9151, harrymoscoso@yahoo.com), which runs trips to Isla Tortuga most days for $150. Unlike at Puerto Ayora, however, there is no hyperbaric chamber on the island.

There is one other operator, **Natural Selection Tours** (Gil at Escalesias, tel. 96/837-6151, http://galapagosnaturalselection.com) that does discovery dives near Tintoreras, but the company does not go to the more spectacular Isla Tortuga. They also offer PADI open water dive certification.

NIGHTLIFE

Nightlife in Isabela is very low-key and limited to a handful of bars and a couple of seedy *discotecas* (dance clubs) inland.

The most popular place in town is the **Caleta Iguana Bar** (Gil, no phone, 7pm-midnight Mon.-Sat.), right at the Caleta Iguana *hostal,* with a chill bohemian vibe. The location right on the beach and the 5pm-7pm happy hour make it an excellent place to watch the sunset. Later you can test your state of sobriety by trying to walk on the slackline, or if that doesn't work, relax in the hammocks or by the beach bonfire.

A quieter place for a drink is next door at **Bar Beto** (Gil, no phone, 7pm-midnight Mon.-Sat.), a beach bar at the western edge of town. The cocktails are rather pricey, but the beer goes down well with the sea view.

FOOD

Restaurant options in Puerto Villamil are pretty limited. The highest concentration of restaurants is along the main road, Antonio Gil, and along the *malecón,* though most of the best options are elsewhere. Visitors should be aware that food in restaurants is more expensive than for the equivalent quality in Puerto Ayora and Puerto Baquerizo Moreno due to the higher cost of importing food to Isabela.

Ecuadorian

The **mercado municipal** (town market, 16 de Marzo, 7am-6pm daily, though it closes for lunch noon-2pm) has a couple nondescript stalls with the cheapest eats in town; you can find a passable breakfast or lunch for $5-6, and deep-fried empanadas for $1. Dinner isn't served, though.

The south side of the main square is **restaurant row,** with several popular casual restaurants that cater primarily to tourists and have a cute rustic ambience and similar menus and prices. The most popular item on the menu is the fixed-price breakfast ($6), and lunch and dinner for $8, though you can ask for only the main plate for $6. A couple serve pizza and pasta as well. The food is just passable—heaps of rice and beans, small portions of fish or chicken, microscopic sides of vegetables, watery soup, and sugary juice. The primary draw is the fun atmosphere and the fact that it is the cheapest food in town aside from the market.

Across from the main strip of restaurants, the inviting patio of **El Cafetal** (Fragatas and Gil, tel. 5/301-6775, www.elcafetalgalapagos.com.ec, 9am-1pm and 3pm-10pm daily, $15-25) is very well touristed. The small menu has pasta dishes, sandwiches, and a selection of seafood and cocktails. The vegetable and rice sides are nothing special, but it manages to justify its high prices with the nice ambience, skillful preparation, and large portions; the huge fish steak is particularly good.

★ **Coco Surf** (Gil at 16 de Marzo, tel. 5/252-9465 or 96/986-3340, cocosurfisabela@

hotmail.com, noon-2pm, 6pm-9pm Mon.-Sat, 6pm-9pm Sun., $12-25) is a casual restaurant with a focus on creative presentation and fresh ingredients primarily sourced from the islands. The *patacón pisao* is a smashed plantain topped with crispy rice, crab, chicken, or beef. The seafood fajita is also excellent; it comes heaped with fish, shrimp, octopus, and fresh veggies. The rustic patio seating is unassuming and easy to mistake for a cheap *almuerzo* (set-lunch) joint, but the quality of food here isn't much of a secret. The restaurant's popularity and small size mean you may want reservations around prime dinner time.

If you like a good dive, head inland to ★ **La Casa del Asado** (Av. Mercado Municipal at Cormoran, tel. 93/968-2481, 6:30pm-10pm daily, entrées $7-12, grill platters for two $20). It's a fun mix of outdoor patio seating, a huge sidewalk grill, tropical music, and a crowd of mostly locals. The most popular items are the big platters to share; the mixed seafood grill ($20), with fish, octopus, and shrimp plus sides for two, is highly recommended. There are also chicken and beef platters if you're sick of the seafood.

For a larger variety of meat, try the **Isabela Grill** (16 de Marzo and Los Jelies, tel. 5/252-9104, 10am-2pm and 5pm-10pm daily, $15-25), which offers everything from T-bone to filet mignon cooked over a charcoal grill, as well as chicken, pork, and seafood. Though the atmosphere is casual, it is one of the few indoor restaurants where you can hide from the mosquitoes.

International

Sun & Coffee (Gil at Petreles, tel. 5/252-9447, 7am-noon, 5pm-10pm daily, sandwiches and crepes $6-14, entrées $15-20) is a casual café-deli with fruit salads, large omelets and continental breakfasts, espresso drinks, crepes, ice cream, toasted sandwiches on homemade bread, and an assortment of seafood dishes. Grilled octopus in cacao sauce and the raw tuna *chabelas* (thin fried smashed plantain topped with fish) are some of the specialties. There's indoor seating with air-conditioning and a small patio outside.

The ★ **Booby Trap** (Gil, tel. 5/252-9500, 11am-3pm, 5pm-8:30pm Tues.-Sun., entrées $8-20, lobster $30) has it all—fresh, high-quality ingredients, large portions, great atmosphere, and reasonable prices. The menu is large, with several options for seafood and meat platters, tacos, pizzas, and burgers. For dinner, arrive at sunset time and enjoy the beach view from one of the charming wood-slab tables on the second floor. The raw tuna-avocado-octopus tartare and seared tuna tataki are particularly good.

Casa Marita Restaurant (Gil, tel. 5/252-9301, www.casamaritagalapagos.com, 7am-8:30pm daily, $15-25) boasts an elegant ambience and great views of the beach from the third floor of Casa Marita Hotel. The hotel is owned by a Peruvian/Italian couple, and many of the specialties in the restaurant—Peruvian ceviche and seafood pasta—come from their respective home countries. There are also the standard Ecuadorian seafood, meat, and chicken dishes with a good selection of sides.

The town's only gourmet restaurant overlooks the lagoons and is inside **Iguana Crossing** (Gil, tel. 5/252-9484, www.iguanacrossing.com.ec, 7am-9pm daily, $20-25). It serves local and international specialties, including standard grilled seafood as well as more imaginative dishes such as passion-fruit chicken and coconut lobster.

Self-Serve

If you stay in a *hostal* with a kitchen, it is possible to cook for yourself, though ingredients are more limited in variety compared to Puerto Ayora. You can buy fresh fruit and vegetables at the **municipal market** (16 de Marzo, 7am-6pm daily, though it closes for lunch noon-2pm). Next door is a small **supermarket** where you can find dry goods and staples.

ACCOMMODATIONS

There are fewer hotels in Puerto Villamil than Puerto Ayora, but there is quite a range from budget to luxury. For two people, below $40, prepare to sacrifice air-conditioning, location, or maintenance. The midrange of $50-100 has lots of perfectly clean and spacious rooms that are centrally located. If you're willing to spend $200 or more, there's a good number of luxury digs with fantastic views that will happily part you from your money.

Under $50

The cheapest place to stay is **Posada del Caminante** (near Cormorán, tel. 5/252-9407, https://posadadelcaminante.com, $18 s, $36 d, no breakfast) is about a 15-minute walk inland. Rooms are just adequate and are fan-only, but it's a good place for cooking as there's a shared kitchen and the lodging is a short walk to the municipal market. There are two wings to the hotel: the primary location and the secondary wing across the street. The best rooms for the same cost are on the upper floor of the secondary location (Posada del Caminante II).

A slightly nicer choice for travelers wanting to cook is **Hospedaje Sarita** (Pepino at Gil, tel. 5/301-6769, hospedaje.sarita@gmail.com, $30 d with fan, $50 suite with a/c and kitchen, no breakfast). All rooms are basic and have either an en-suite mini-kitchen or access to the shared kitchen. The suite with private kitchen and air-conditioning is a great value. Compared with Posada del Caminante, the rooms are nicer and the location is significantly closer to the beach, Concha de Perla, and the central square with restaurants and tourist agencies, though farther from the municipal market where you'll buy your groceries.

If you don't plan to cook, then **Hospedaje Mother Fanny** (Gil at Escalesias, tel. 97/997-9678, hospedajemotherfanny@yahoo.com, $25 s, $40 d, no breakfast) has the cheapest doubles with air-conditioning; rooms are small and nondescript though well located smack dab in the center of town.

The nicest budget rooms are at ★ **Casa Sea Lions** (Fragatas and 16 de Marzo, tel. 5/252-9198, www.hotelgrantortuga.com, $30 s, $50 d, no breakfast), which is run by Hostal Gran Tortuga next door. Compared to Hostal Gran Tortuga, Casa Sea Lions has similar cheerful, bright, slightly smaller rooms on the second floor, without breakfast, as well as a great central location.

Casa Soleil (Conocarpus at Malecón, tel. 9/940-3069 or 5/252-9121, oseegers@gmx.de, $40-45 s, $50-60 d, breakfast $5) is the best budget option directly on the beach. The friendly, family-run house has only three basic rooms. Owners speak English, German, and Spanish. The room upstairs is by far the best and well worth the extra dollars. Book direct for the best price.

$50-100

Hotels in this range all have air-conditioning, hot water, and Wi-Fi, and include breakfast.

A solid midrange option inland is the **Gran Tortuga** (Fragatas and 16 de Marzo, tel. 5/252-9198, www.hotelgrantortuga.com, $45 s, $67 d, $105 t), a small *hostal* with friendly service and bright, cheerful rooms with large, firm beds. The doubles are a good value, particularly on the second floor. There is a third-floor terrace strung with hammocks.

Another reliable choice is **Rincón de George** (16 de Marzo and Gil, tel. 5/252-9214, rincondegeorge@gmail.com, $55 s, $70 d, $105 t), with comfortably furnished guest rooms with firm beds, hot water, and TV. The owner of Rincón de George is a registered tour guide. Continental breakfast is served on the fourth-floor terrace, and there's a very nice kitchen for cooking.

A good option farther inland is **Gran Hostal Tintorera** (Escalesias at Cormoran, tel. 5/252-9248, http://galapagostintorera.com, $40 s, $70 d). Compared to the previous two options, you can get a slightly larger room and an idyllic courtyard with fruit trees and hammocks. The trade-off is an additional four-block walk inland.

Hotel Cally (Gil at Piquero, tel. 5/252-9072,

http://hotelcallygalapagos.com, $60 s, $90 d, $140 t) is a medium-size hotel with immaculate, if generic, rooms with large beds in a new building close to the beach and downtown. There are also noisier but equally clean rooms on the first floor for $35 per person.

The ★ **Wooden House Lodge** (Gil, tel. 5/252-9235, www.thewoodenhouse.com.ec, $45 s, $90 d) is a cute cabin-style lodge on the east side of town. Notably, it is the closest hotel to the snorkeling at Concha de Perla. Comfortable rooms with wood interiors and a quaint exterior make it quite cozy. The dipping pool isn't very inviting, but you'll probably go snorkeling instead, anyway. It is a 10-minute walk into town.

Tanned beach-bum types choose **Caleta Iguana** (Gil, tel. 5/252-9405, www.iguana-cove.com, $30-100 d), also known as the Casa Rosada. The *hostal* boasts its own surf camp and tour agency as well as a fantastic location on the beach. Choose among options from basic, fan-only rooms facing the road ($30, no breakfast) to ocean-view rooms with air-con ditioning and breakfast for $100. Rooms are run-down for the price, but nonetheless popular for the social atmosphere and location. The on-site bar is the most popular in town, which can make the rooms noisy at night.

The beachfront **Drake Inn** (Gil, tel. 5/301-6986, www.drakeinngalapagos.com, $98-130 d, $178 two-bedroom suite) has perhaps the most character in town, with cheerful, breezy rooms and a fun nautical theme. You can peer out a port window, admire a large statue of Poseidon, or relax in the aqua-colored lounge. There are two sunny terraces; visitors can pick between soaking away their cares in the sea-view Jacuzzi or enjoying the view from the third-floor terrace, which overlooks the beach on one side and the lagoons on the other.

$100-200

Puerto Villamil is beginning to cater to luxury land-based tours, and some top-end hotels have opened.

Run by an expat from the United States, the **Isabela Beach House** (Gil at Pepino, tel. 5/252-9303, theisabelabeachhouse@gmail.com, $132 d, $160 d with ocean view, $200 t) is a beachfront house that prides itself on friendly, personalized service. The cute, simple rooms are purposely beachy, with plenty of fish and seashells to go around. Breakfast ($10 pp) is served on tables on the beach.

At the east end of town on a quiet strip of beach is the artsy **Casa Marita** (Gil, tel. 5/252-9301, www.casamaritagalapagos.com, $115-125 d, $170-220 suite), a 20-room beach house with uniquely decorated guest rooms and suites, each housing eclectic art and furniture handpicked by the Peruvian and Italian owners. Each room has a mini-fridge but no TV. You won't miss the TV, however, when you can watch the sunset from beachside lounge chairs and hammocks. The elegant upstairs restaurant has Italian, Peruvian, and Ecuadorian specialties. The cheaper extension wing across the street is more mundane and doesn't have any views.

Opened in 2017, the modern ★ **Hotel Cormorant** (Av. Antonio Gil Y Calle Los Pinquinos, tel. 5/252-9192, $160 interior view, $180 ocean view, $250 suite) impresses with panoramic views of the ocean, polished wood, and accents of lava rock. The charming courtyard hosts blue-footed boobies and frigate birds painted across the polished concrete floors. Solar panels provide hot water, and breakfast is served across the street at the Sun & Coffee restaurant. The interior-view rooms don't have the lovely views and they're not as impressive as the ocean view rooms or suites.

Over $200

Right downtown, the **Hotel Albemarle** (Malecón, tel. 5/252-9489, www.hotelalbemarle.com, $165 d pool view, $235 d ocean view) has 17 rooms, 12 with spectacular ocean views. The other rooms face a central courtyard, where you can bathe in the dipping pool among tropical greenery. All rooms are well-appointed with high ceilings and modern coastal decor.

The **Isamar** (Gil, tel. 593/99 555-3718, isamargalapagos.com/en/home, $148 d, $266 d

Iguanamen Sing the Blues

If you hear blues music in the Galápagos, there is a good chance that it is the local group Iguanamen from Isabela Island. Residents of Isabela are particularly fond of the music—and the acoustic twangy beats seem to go well with the chill vibe of the town. The group's most famous member was the late "Gringo Juan," an American named Juan Volkes, who was rumored to be hiding from the law and who passed away in 2008. They released three albums: *Iguanaamerica, Super Criollo Blues y Más*, and *Iguanamen de Galápagos*.

While some songs, such as "Ain't No Sunshine," are covers, there are quite a few original numbers, including songs titled "Santa Cruz Blues" and "Isabela." The lyrics of the latter song don't do much to dispel the rumors:

> Going to Isabela never coming back.
> Going to burn my bridges, cover up my tracks.
> Cause in Isabela, life is mighty fine.
> In Isabela, oh the sun is gonna shine.

with ocean view) is an upscale lodge of just eight rooms on a prime beachfront location. Rooms are large and modern, with tidy white linens, security boxes, and sofa chairs. Rooms are arranged in single-story rows; the few best ones have unobstructed views of Isabela's long, sandy beach. The deck has lounge chairs overlooking the beach.

Swanky **Iguana Crossing** (Gil, tel. 5/252-9484, www.iguanacrossing.com.ec, $288 d, $457 suite) overlooks the beach on the quiet west side of town. There are 14 elegant guest rooms, each with stylish decor, flat-screen TV, mini-fridge, and views of the ocean. The deck has a small pool and enormous lounge-chair-beds. The third-floor terrace is even more spectacular, with more couches, a Jacuzzi, and a 360-degree view of both the beach and the lagoons. The on-site restaurant serves gourmet local and international specialties.

Camping

Camping in the national park is permitted at **El Cura** (the entry point to Sierra Negra) and **Las Minas de Azufre** (Sulfur Mines) with prior permission from the national park, but unfortunately independent camping is not allowed; you must be accompanied by a guide. El Cura is accessible by car, whereas Las Minas de Azufre is a hike-in and camp spot. Tour agencies in town can provide tents and arrange the required guide, permits with

the national park, food, and transportation. None of the agencies, however, organizes regular group tours that solo travelers can easily join. Only private tours are offered, and the costs are steep (roughly $1,000 for a group).

It is much easier to camp on private land at **Campo Duro** (road to Sierra Negra, tel. 098/545-3045, www.galapagoscampoduro-ecolodge.com.ec, $10-25 pp). The camping site is in the lush green highlands (a $7 taxi ride from town) and has on-site bathrooms, showers, an organic garden, a tortoise refuge, and a restaurant. If you bring your own tent and sleeping bag, the cost is $10 per person; otherwise, they will provide everything for $25 per person.

If money is no object, glamping at the **Scalesia Lodge** (tel. 593 3/250-9504, www.scalesialodge.com, $331 s, $442 d) in Isabela's lush green highlands is a completely different camping experience, inspired more by the luxury safari camps in Africa. Due to the difficulties in getting to and from the lodge, most visitors here opt for the all-inclusive packages and island-hopping packages.

INFORMATION AND SERVICES

There is no bank or ATM on Isabela; some top-end hotels accept credit cards, but you are strongly advised to bring enough cash for the duration of your stay.

The local **iTur** tourist office (16 de Marzo

and Las Fragatas, tel. 5/301-6648, 9am-5pm Mon.-Fri.) is two blocks inland. The **national park office** (Gil and Piqueros, tel. 5/252-9178, 7am-12:30pm, 2pm-7pm Mon.-Fri.) is one block from the main plaza.

GETTING THERE AND AROUND

Airport and Interisland Flights

The **General Villamil Airport** (airport code: IBB) is just north of town, a short taxi ride away. It only serves interisland flights to San Cristóbal and Baltra; you cannot fly directly to Isabela from mainland Ecuador.

Small eight-seat planes fly half-hour routes among San Cristóbal, Baltra, and Isabela several times per week. Fares start at $160 one way, $240 round-trip or for any two flights (even different routes). Interisland flights can be booked through **Emetebe** (tel./fax 5/252-0615, www.emetebe.com.ec), or **FlyGalápagos** (tel. 5/301-6579, www.flygalapagos.net).

Interisland Ferries

Interisland **ferries** leave for Puerto Ayora (2-2.5 hours, $30 pp one-way) daily at 6am and 3pm from the main dock. The reverse trip leaves Puerto Ayora for Isabela at 7am and 2pm. It is possible (though tiring) to take the morning ferry, arrive in Puerto Ayora, and take the afternoon ferry for San Cristóbal the same day, but there are no direct routes. Water taxis from the ferry to the dock charge $1 per person. The dock charges a $10 tax per person when you land ($5 for Ecuadorian residents).

Around Town

Buses leave only once a day at the crack of dawn for the highlands, and you need a guide to visit the volcano Sierra Negra anyway, so you're better off exploring on a guided tour.

Taxis can be picked up near the main plaza and will take you around town for $1 and to nearby visitor sites for $10 per hour.

Bicycles can be rented in town for $3 an hour and are the most popular way to explore Los Humedales.

Near Puerto Villamil

LOS HUMEDALES AND CENTRO DE CRIANZA

The most famous sight in Los Humedales (The Wetlands) is the Wall of Tears, a reminder of Isabela's history—but there are also beaches, lookout points, a tortoise breeding center, and tons of lagoons. The farthest point is six kilometers west of town, so you can visit on a guided tour with a van ($25 pp) for a half-day tour. If you have all day, you can rent a bike ($3/hour) or hike. The route to the Wall of Tears and the wetlands is easy—mostly flat and quite pleasant along the beach, though it is a long distance, and the last section to the Wall of Tears is uphill along a hot, exposed road. To visit the Centro de Crianza requires a long walk along an exposed trail that branches off the main trail. Hence, riding a bike is a more popular way to see the

wetlands than hiking. The bike ride can be sweaty on sunny days, but you can take a dip at one of the beaches to cool off. Another option is to get a taxi to drop you off at the Wall of Tears ($5) and walk or bike back to town.

Before leaving Puerto Villamil, check out **Laguna Salinas**, a lagoon at the west end of town where flamingos can sometimes be spotted. There isn't much to see otherwise, but it's right on the edge of town so it's worth a quick check.

Centro de Crianza

Go 1.6 kilometers inland from the main road, following the signs, and you will reach the **Centro de Crianza (Tortoise Breeding Center).** Parallel to the main road, there is a hiking path that passes by several lagoons where you may be able to spot flamingos.

There are some 850 tortoises separated into eight enclosures, all from Isabela Island, as well as an information center documenting the life cycle of these fascinating creatures and an excellent program to boost the populations of Isabela's five subspecies. After visiting the breeding center, you will have to backtrack to the coast to visit the rest of the sights in Los Humedales. Note that this breeding center is quite similar to Charles Darwin Research Station on Santa Cruz and La Galapaguera on San Cristóbal; most people need only visit one.

Lagoons and Beaches

At the western edge of town is a set of lagoons with sizable populations of flamingos that flock here to mate. **Poza de los Diablos (Devil's Pool)** is actually the largest lagoon in the entire archipelago. Wooden walkways take you past the lagoons before joining a trail through a forest. The **Pozas Verdes** are smaller lagoons filled with greenish water and surrounded by cactus. Afterward, see if you can find the **Poza Escondida (Hidden Lagoon)** at the end of a short trail.

It's easy to miss the turnoff to the tiny, sandy cove known as **Playita (Small Beach),** which has a small strip of sand, rocks with marine iguanas, and a calming view of the sea.

Next, there is a forked path off the main trail. To the left you will find **Playa del Amor,** a small but beautiful beach with a large population of marine iguanas. To the right is the **Túnel del Estero**—a short walk to see a small, rocky tunnel and a view of the sea.

The **Camino de Tortuga** is a short trail lined on either side by lush, green majagua trees and leading to a calm mangrove-lined inlet where you can wade in the water to cool off.

Wall of Tears and Mirador Orchilla

Bike another 30 minutes uphill from the Playa del Amor (or walk another hour), and you will reach the last two stops in Los Humedales. **Mirador Orchilla** is a wooden stairway and lookout point with an excellent panoramic view of the island. **Muro de las Lágrimas (Wall of Tears)** is just a wall, 100 meters long and 7 meters high, but the brutal story behind it is interesting. It was built by convicts from a penal colony in the 1940s and served no real purpose except punishment, which only adds to the tragedy of the men who suffered and died building it. There is a set of steps up to an impressive view of the wall and the surrounding landscape. If you are lucky, you might spot

Los Túneles

wild giant tortoises here that have been repatriated from the breeding center.

★ TINTORERAS BAY

Just off the coast of the dock at Puerto Villamil is the best spot for snorkeling, a set of islets called **Las Tintoreras,** named after the reef sharks that frequent them. The islets are visited by a small *panga* (dinghy) ride, during which you can spot penguins, sea lions, and blue-footed boobies on the rocks. After disembarking on a dry landing, you take a short trail over otherworldly, rocky terrain, where whitish-green lichens top flat fields of craggy, black volcanic rocks. Along the trail, Sally Lightfoot crabs scuttle and marine iguanas nest. At the end of the trail is a channel where white-tipped sharks can be observed resting from above. The tour also includes snorkeling in clear, shallow water where rays, sea lions, and lots of fish can be observed. Day tours cost $40 per person.

TOP EXPERIENCE

★ LOS TÚNELES

Take a 45-minute boat ride south of town to the amazing rock formations of **Los Túneles,**

also known as Cabo Rosa and El Finado. Boats navigate mazes of rocks, where stone archways form the namesake tunnels over the ocean. The tour includes a short walk on the rocky terrain; you can see blue-footed boobies perched at the foot of endemic opuntia cactus trees while majestic sea turtles glide through the water below. After the walk, tours include excellent snorkeling in the vicinity, where there are many sea turtles resting. Day tours cost $110 per person.

ISLA TORTUGA

Crescent-shaped **Isla Tortuga** is about an hour boat ride away from the port and is best known as a diving site. Nonetheless, snorkeling tours also come here to attempt to spot the same Galápagos sharks, hammerheads, and manta rays that divers often spot in deep water at the cleaning station. The tradeoff is that the currents here can make for difficult snorkeling. Some tours also combine Isla Tortuga with a visit Cuatro Hermanos, another islet farther afield. Day tours cost $110 and do not run every day.

Isabela Highlands

TOP EXPERIENCE

★ SIERRA NEGRA AND VOLCÁN CHICO

The best excursion to take from Puerto Villamil, and perhaps the most impressive geologic sight in the entire archipelago, is the hike up to the active Sierra Negra, Isabela's oldest volcano. The last eruption was in 2005 and took geologists by surprise.

The more popular trek is to the crater of Sierra Negra and Volcán Chico. After you hike about an hour, your toils will be rewarded with fantastic views of the **Sierra Negra crater,** which is 10 kilometers in

diameter. You then descend for about an hour and a half to **Volcán Chico,** a fissure of lava cones northwest of the main crater. On this side, there is less mist and rain, offering spectacular views over the north of Isabela and across to Fernandina. This trek takes five hours walking at a brisk pace with minimal breaks. Alternatively, it is possible to just go to the edge of the crater and back at a leisurely pace in two hours. Some tours include visits to nearby **Mirador de Mango,** a lookout spot with a 360-degree view of the island, and the **Cuevas de Sucre,** a nearby lava tunnel not unlike the lava tunnels on Santa Cruz. Still others combine a trip to the crater with lunch and a visit to the tortoise reserve at **Campo Duro Ecolodge**. There are also tours that combine a trip to the volcano with **downhill biking** back to town. Standard day tours cost $35 per person; lunch at Campo Duro and downhill biking cost more.

The longer and far less popular trek is to **Las Minas de Azufre** (Sulfur Mines). It takes seven hours in total and is tougher, particularly in the rainy season, when it gets very muddy. The hike culminates in a dramatic descent into the yellow hills of the sulfur mines, which spew out choking gas (hold your breath!). Because this tour is less popular, tour agencies only offer private tours. Try to find other travelers who want to go and then approach a tour agency together. The cost will depend on the number of people. For a group of four people, you would pay around $90-100 per person. Even more expensive and less popular are camping tours here.

Nautilus (Gil and Las Fragatas, tel. 5/252-9076, www.nautilustour.com) charges $40 per person for the Sierra Negra and Volcán Chico trek.

the colorful volcanic landscape at Volcán Chico

Northern and Western Isabela Island

Some of Isabela's best sites are along the western side of the island. All of the following visitor sites are off-limits to land-based visitors and are **only accessible to cruise tours.**

PUNTA MORENO

This visitor site is often the first point on Isabela for boats approaching from the south. It is reachable via a *panga* ride along the sea cliffs and into a grove of mangroves where penguins and great blue herons are often seen. After a dry landing, a two-kilometer hike inland along a pahoehoe lava flow lined by cacti leads to a handful of brackish ponds frequented in season by flamingos and white-cheeked pintails. There are impressive views of three of Isabela's volcanoes. Wear comfortable shoes because the lava rocks are difficult

to negotiate in places, and note that it's quite a strenuous hike; take plenty of water and sunblock.

ELIZABETH BAY

North of Punta Moreno, Elizabeth Bay has no landing site, so it can only be explored by *panga*. There are small populations of flightless cormorants and marine iguanas in the bay. The marine iguanas here are comparatively big, munching themselves to a healthy size on the abundant supplies of algae. Farther in is a set of shallow lagoons where you can see rays, turtles, and, occasionally, white-tipped sharks. The *panga* then heads out to some rocky islets called Las Marielas, where there is a small colony of nesting penguins.

URBINA BAY

This bay was created by remarkable geologic activity in 1954. A volcanic eruption lifted a chunk of seabed, including a coral reef, six meters above the water's surface. After a wet landing on the beach, you can enjoy the somewhat surreal experience of seeing coral littered with bones and the shells of marine life. The short loop trail is easy and takes less than two hours. Land iguanas can be observed, and if you are lucky you might also spot a giant tortoise or two; the juveniles are repatriated from the breeding center and stay until they reach sexual maturity, and the females come to Urbina Bay from Volcán Alcedo to nest. Along the shoreline, flightless cormorants, blue-footed boobies, and penguins can often be seen, and there are rays and sea turtles in the bay.

★ TAGUS COVE

Tagus Cove is the best place to see how humans have left their mark—literally—on the Galápagos Islands. The rocks above this popular anchorage in the Bolívar Channel are covered in graffiti. It's a strange but interesting sight, with the oldest readable record from whalers dating to 1836.

The two-kilometer hike from the cove to the interior is quite strenuous but worth the effort. A dry landing leads to a trail through a steep gully to a wooden staircase and then along a gravel track. At the top is an impressive view over the deep blue **Darwin Lake.** This eroded crater is 12 meters deep, and the waters have a high salt content, so it's largely lifeless. Scientists have concluded that seawater seeped in through the porous lava rocks beneath the surface. The small round pebbles covering the trails began as raindrops that collected airborne volcanic ash and hardened before hitting the ground. The trail leads to the lower lava slopes of Volcán Darwin, and there are spectacular views over the entire island of Isabela.

After the hike, there is a *panga* ride, and you can cool off with excellent snorkeling along the rocky northern shore. Highlights include sea turtles, Galápagos penguins, flightless cormorants, marine iguanas, and sea lions.

TOP EXPERIENCE

★ PUNTA VICENTE ROCA

Punta Vicente Roca is easily the best spot for snorkeling with sea turtles in the archipelago.

the view above Darwin Lake at Tagus Cove

The snorkeling site is in a protective cove at the base of Volcán Ecuador, where they can be spotted resting in the calm waters by the dozens, along with flightless cormorants, penguins, and fish. Snorkeling is often followed by a *panga* ride along spectacular cliffs and a cave formed out of tuff (compacted ash), and to a rocky area where fur seals make their home.

OTHER SITES

There are various other sites on Isabela, most of which have restricted access. Just north of Tagus Cove is **Punta Tortuga,** a beach surrounded by mangroves, and one of the few spots to see the mangrove finch. At Isabela's northern tip, **Punta Albemarle** was a U.S. radar base in World War II. There is no landing site, but there is plenty of birdlife to see from the boat, including flightless cormorants and penguins.

On the east side of Isabela, there is a landing site at **Punta García,** one of the few places on this side where flightless cormorants can be seen. This is the beginning for the trail up to **Volcán Alcedo,** famous for its seven-kilometer-wide crater and the largest population of wild giant tortoises on the islands. This particular species of giant tortoise is endemic

Punta Vicente Roca is the best place to find sea turtles in the archipelago.

to Volcán Alcedo and is the most "giant" of all the giant tortoises. Unfortunately the site is now closed to tourists, and only scientists can visit.

Floreana

Look for ★ to find recommended
sights, activities, dining, and lodging.

Highlights

★ **Playa Negra:** This **black-sand beach** is right in town but is a surprisingly tranquil spot to relax and cool off (page 118).

★ **La Lobería:** A short, scenic walk leads along the beach to a **lookout point,** where you'll find snorkeling with sea turtles and spectacular sunsets (page 119).

★ **Mirador de la Baronesa:** It was the former favorite lookout of the "baroness" of the Galápagos. Now visitors can **kayak** past beautiful rocky black lava, mangroves, penguins, boobies, and sea lions (page 127).

★ **Devil's Crown:** An eroded **volcanic crater** forms the jagged shape of a crown in the sea off the coast of Floreana. Snorkelers swim in the middle with a variety of marine life (page 128).

★ **Enderby and Champion Island:** Off the coast of Floreana, snorkelers swim along rock cliffs that host a diverse range of **fish and sea lions** (page 128).

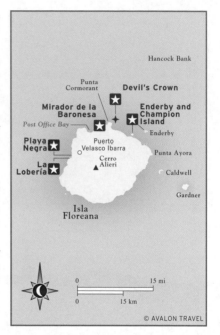

Floreana is the smallest of the inhabited islands, with an area of just 67 square miles and a tiny population of only 130 people.

Southern cruises stop here for the tranquil, mangrove-lined coast, the chance to mail a postcard at the quirky post barrel, and the excellent snorkeling on the nearby islets. People come on day tours to take in a bit of Floreana's mysterious history, dip their toes in black-sand beaches, and swim with sea turtles. Visitors stay on the island to get away from it all, and to experience Galápagos life at its slowest.

The tiny port of **Puerto Velasco Ibarra** feels like a scene from the past. The people meander slowly up dirt roads, stopping to smile and greet each other as they pass. Everyone knows everyone. It is the only town in the Galápagos where tourism takes a back seat to farming and fishing.

Floreana's best sites include the beautiful beaches **Playa Negra** and **La Lobería;** the peaceful, mangrove-lined coast of **Mirador de la Baronesa;** and outstanding snorkeling spots at the submerged volcanic cone of **Devil's Crown,** along with **Enderby** and **Champion Island.**

HISTORY

As the lush hills of Floreana come into view, it's difficult to believe that such a serene island could have such a troubled history. The population of the island today stands at a tiny 130 people, but Floreana was actually the first island in the archipelago to be populated.

Early History

Floreana Island was originally called Charles Island after King Charles II of England. In the 18th century, whalers and pirates were drawn to a rare spring water supply in the hills as well as fresh meat in the form of the island's giant tortoises. Rats, cats, and goats were introduced to Floreana, causing untold damage and decimating the tortoise population. The whalers would spend so long at sea that they decided to set up a post office on the island as the only means of communicating with their families. You can still see evidence of the early settlers in carvings in the rocks of caves in the highlands.

In 1807, Floreana had its first permanent

Previous: Devil's Crown; Red vesuvium. **Above:** Floreana's marine iguanas are nicknamed "Christmas lizards."

Floreana

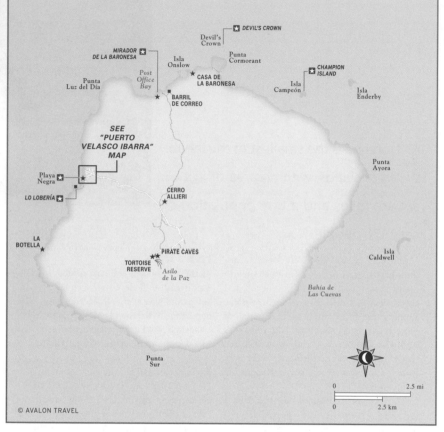

DEVIL'S CROWN

Devil's
Crown

MIRADOR
DE LA BARONESA

Isla
Onslow

Punta
Cormorant

CHAMPION
ISLAND

Post
Office
Bay

CASA DE
LA BARONESA

Punta
Luz del Día

Isla
Campeón

Isla
Enderby

BARRIL
DE CORREO

SEE
"PUERTO
VELASCO IBARRA"
MAP

Punta
Ayora

Playa
Negra

LO LOBERÍA

CERRO
ALLIERI

LA
BOTELLA

PIRATE CAVES

Isla
Caldwell

TORTOISE
RESERVE

Asilo
de la Paz

Bahía de
Las Cuevas

Punta
Sur

0   2.5 mi

0   2.5 km

© AVALON TRAVEL

resident, Irishman Patrick Watkins. He was marooned here and lived for two years by growing vegetables. Eventually, he stole a ship's longboat, took a small crew, but arrived alone in Guayaquil weeks later. Nobody knows what became of his crew.

After Ecuador's independence in 1830, Floreana was named after the country's first president, Juan José Flores, and it became a penal colony. Soon afterward, in 1841, Herman Melville, author of *Moby-Dick,* visited the island and wrote about its history, increasing worldwide interest.

The Galápagos Affair

By the early 20th century, the world had woken up to the wonders of the Galápagos, and it was only a matter of time before Europeans were attracted to escape to a place depicted in books and newspapers as a slice of Pacific paradise. A certain Friedrich Ritter, an eccentric German doctor with a love of nudism, was so enchanted that in 1929 he set off for Floreana with his mistress, Dore Strauch, a former patient crippled by multiple sclerosis. Not a man to do things by halves, he foresaw a problem with the lack of dental facilities on the islands and removed all his teeth before traveling, replacing them with metal dentures.

The couple arrived in Floreana and lived a quiet life of gardening. When Ritter sent dispatches of their experiences back to Germany, however, others inevitably thought it would be a good idea to join them. Visitors came and went, but most were deterred by the challenges of setting up life on such a remote island. The Wittmer family was different, though—father Heinz, pregnant wife Margret, and their sickly 12-year-old son, Harry, arrived in 1932. Margret wrote of the "Herculean task" that confronted them in building a life on Floreana, and their second son, Rolf, was born in a cave. Ritter, however, infamously unsociable, was none too pleased with the new arrivals and steadfastly refused to help them, keeping his food supplies to himself.

Shortly afterward, an Austrian woman in her early forties stepped off a boat wearing riding breeches and carrying a pearl-handled revolver. She called herself Baroness Eloise Wagner von Bosquet and was accompanied by two men—Robert Philipson, whom she referred to initially as her husband, and her lover, Rudolf Lorenz. As soon as she arrived, the baroness began causing trouble. She seemed to regard the island as her own and began rifling through the post. She bathed naked in the island's only drinking water supply and began appropriating supplies that the other islanders had ordered. The "baroness" also made no secret of her desire to open a luxury hotel on Floreana and charmed the governor of the islands into giving her 10 square kilometers of land for the construction. United by their dislike of the baroness, Dr. Ritter and the Wittmer family developed closer contacts, and Ritter made formal complaints about her to the Ecuadorian government, but to no avail. By this time, the residents on the island were well known to the world's media, and luxury yachts began stopping off to see what all the fuss was about.

Meanwhile, the love triangle started to go pear-shaped. Lorenz, initially the baroness's favorite, was jilted and demoted to servant, and the baroness took up with Philipson while eagerly pursuing other men who visited Floreana. Lorenz, humiliated by his treatment and bearing scars from beatings, told residents that the baroness's title was bogus, her marriage a sham, and that she had previously worked as a nightclub dancer and even a spy.

Events took a turn for the worse in March 1934 when the island experienced a severe drought. According to the Wittmers, the baroness announced abruptly that she was leaving for Tahiti with Philipson, as if it were a day trip rather than a 5,000-kilometer voyage. No boat was sighted and nobody saw her leave the island, but she and Philipson were never seen again. Suspiciously, they had left behind their luggage and prized possessions. Dore Strauch later recalled hearing a blood-curdling scream in the middle of the night. Lorenz's behavior became increasingly erratic after the baroness's disappearance, while Dr. Ritter seemed strangely calm.

To this day, what happened to the baroness remains a mystery. If she was indeed murdered, Lorenz is generally agreed to be the prime suspect, while Dr. Ritter didn't entirely escape suspicion. Neither of them lasted long enough to defend themselves, though: In July Lorenz finally raised enough money to take a boat to San Cristóbal with a Norwegian captain named Nuggerud, but they never made it. Four months later, their bodies washed up on remote Marchena in the north, and evidence suggested that they had died of dehydration. Ritter's demise in November 1934 was equally mysterious. According to Dore Strauch, she accidentally poisoned her chickens by feeding them spoiled pork meat, due to food shortages. Not wanting to waste the chicken meat, she killed them and boiled them, thinking that this would destroy the poison. Despite being a vegetarian, Ritter apparently ate it and fell gravely ill from food poisoning. He died a few days later, allegedly cursing his lover with his dying breath.

Dore Strauch returned to Germany and wrote a book titled *Satan Came to Eden.* She died in 1942. The Wittmers continued to live on the island; Heinz and Margret's son Rolf opened a successful tour company, and later the family opened a small hotel. Both of these still operate. Margret wrote a book that included the events of the 1930s, titled *Floreana: A Woman's Pilgrimage to the Galápagos*. She lived to age 95, dying in 2000. The story of these people later was turned into a documentary film, *The Galapagos Affair: Satan Came to Eden*, in 2013.

Floreana Today

Nowadays, Floreana is a comparatively quiet island. While the archipelago's three other ports have developed apace with thousands of inhabitants, Puerto Velasco Ibarra has a population of fewer than 130. Floreana is the only island that has actually shrunk or remained stable in population over the past years, as many of its younger people move to other islands in search of work opportunities. The vast majority of the visitors to the island come either on cruise ships or on day trips from Santa Cruz. Of the invasive species, goats have been eradicated, but rats are far more difficult to remove, and the endemic mockingbird is just one species that is now endangered as a result. The tortoise population, which was hunted to extinction on Floreana in the 19th century, has been boosted by breeding programs. There are day trips to Floreana from Santa Cruz most days, though relatively few visitors stay on the island. A community tourism project launched in 2015; the goal is to make Floreana the premier ecotourism destination in the Galápagos.

Puerto Velasco Ibarra

This tiny port lives in comparative isolation from the rest of the islands. There are no banks, no markets or convenience stores, and no cell-phone coverage, and the only mail service is through the Post Office Bay barrel.

Tour agencies in Santa Cruz only have one commissionable product to sell on Floreana (the day tour) and frequently discourage staying on Floreana because "it's boring" and "you can see everything on a day tour." Don't believe it. If you root for the underdog, seek out off-the-beaten-path experiences, and don't mind roughing it a bit, Floreana may very well be your favorite island. Staying on Floreana can be a unique glimpse into life in the Galápagos before the tourism boom, providing a chance to experience beautiful sites with far fewer tourists.

If you do stay on the island, it's easy to spend two nights filled with activities. On the first day, take in the highlands and the excellent community-run kayaking tour to La Botella. Do a tour of Post Office Bay the second day and visit Sendero Los Pulpos at sunset. On the third day, relax at La Lobería, then take the afternoon ferry back. In the near future, with the launch of bicycle tours of highland farms, it will be easy to fill another day. Then again, to get into the true spirit of Floreana, you can always just relax on the beach for a day. Do come well prepared (food options are limited, and there is no bank or ATM), and bring bug spray since Puerto Velasco Ibarra has the worst mosquito population of any of the ports.

SIGHTS
★ Playa Negra

This beautiful black-sand beach is directly in front of Hotel Wittmer but is open to the public. Tour groups often spend a couple hours here in the afternoon after returning from the highlands, but at other times it is surprisingly peaceful, and you may even find it empty if you are lucky. Sunbathing on the shore is idyllic, and swimming and snorkeling off the beach are also good, though there is not nearly as much marine life as at La Lobería nearby.

Puerto Velasco Ibarra

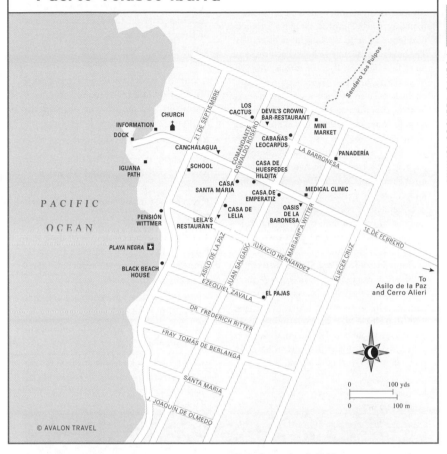

CHURCH
INFORMATION
DOCK
CANCHALAGUA
21 DE SEPTIEMBRE
LOS CACTUS
DEVIL'S CROWN BAR-RESTAURANT
CABAÑAS LEOCARPUS
COMANDANTE OSWALDO ROSERO
MINI MARKET
LA BARRONESA
PANADERÍA
IGUANA PATH
SCHOOL
CASA SANTA MARÍA
CASA DE HUESPEDES HILDITA
CASA DE EMPERATIZ
MEDICAL CLINIC
PACIFIC OCEAN
PENSIÓN WITTMER
LEILA'S RESTAURANT
CASA DE LELIA
OASIS DE LA BARONESA
MARGARITA WITTER
IC DE FEBRERO
PLAYA NEGRA
ASILO DE LA PAZ
JUAN SALGADO
IGNACIO HERNANDEZ
ELIECER CRUZ
BLACK BEACH HOUSE
EZEQUIEL ZAVALA
EL PAJAS
To Asilo de la Paz and Cerro Alieri
DR. FREDERICH RITTER
FRAY TOMÁS DE BERLANGA
SANTA MARIA
J. JOAQUIN DE OLMEDO

Sendero Los Pulpos

0   100 yds
0   100 m

© AVALON TRAVEL

★ La Lobería

If you come on a day tour, you will head to this snorkeling spot after visiting the port and the interior of the island. There is a small population of sea lions, but the primary attraction is snorkeling among the marine turtles that come here to feed. Hotel-based visitors can walk south from town along a scenic 900-meter walking path, mostly through gravel and sand. The path overlooks the ocean and crosses through black lava and dry cactus forest. This is also the most spectacular site near Puerto Velasco Ibarra to watch the sunset.

Sendero Los Pulpos

This trail was recently opened by Galápagos National Park and is infrequently visited; neither cruises nor day tours stop here. The primary attraction is getting out of town by yourself and walking across rugged lava formations, though at the end of the trail there is a rocky stretch of ocean and a small lagoon where you might spot flamingos if you're lucky. The trail takes 40 minutes each way; wear good shoes and go at sunset for the views.

TOURS

A **day tour** from Puerto Ayora to Floreana costs approximately $80 and is the most common way to visit Floreana, though it's not recommended due to the long time in transit. The boat takes about two hours each way and takes in Asilo de la Paz, the tortoise reserve, Playa Negra, and La Lobería. Tourism based on Floreana is in its nascent stages. There are no dive operators on the island; no naturalist guides live here either. If you are staying on the island, you can visit many of the sites yourself or, if you prefer, tag along with the day trip ($20) from Puerto Ayora by showing up at the dock at around 10am when the day tour arrives.

Other activities aren't included on the day tour and can only be done by staying on the island and booking through **CECFLOR** (Centro Comunitario Floreana) and its affiliated tour operator **Floreana Post Office Tours** (tel. 5/253-5055, reservas.postofficetours@gmail.com), which is the sole tour operator on the island. Plan in advance or bring friends because tours don't leave every day, and they require a minimum of four people. Though these tours are available, at this writing prices have not yet been set by CECFLOR.

- A guided **hike to Post Office Bay and Mirador de la Baronesa** (three hours to arrive; includes snorkeling and a speedboat back to port). Note that some visitors walk on their own from the port; this is against national park rules and may result in a hefty fine.

- A tour to **kayak to Post Office Bay and Mirador de la Baronesa.** You need to be reasonably in shape to do this one; each direction is 1:30-1:45 in kayak.

- **Kayak rentals** for exploring the bay

- A kayaking trip to **La Botella** ($45 per person/2 person minimum), an excellent snorkeling spot. Kayaking along the coast is part of the fun and takes 40 minutes each way.

In the near term, bicycles are on their way to Floreana, and the following tours are scheduled to launch in the near future. Contact CECFLOR for confirmation and rates.

- **Bicycle rentals** for exploring the dirt roads of the highlands

- **Bicycle tours** through the local farms in the highlands

In the future, the larger vision of the project includes **camping tours** at the beautiful and

La Lobería

Community Tourism

Floreana has been a day tour destination from Santa Cruz for years. The residents of Floreana call it "lightning tourism" because big tour groups "strike" the island for an instant and then are gone. While visitors may eat lunch at a restaurant in town, the residents see little of the profits. Floreana residents don't want the large-scale development and numbers of tourists that visit the other ports. Puerto Ayora may not seem hectic to you, but if you compare its throngs of souvenir shops, luxury hotels, spas, and touts to Floreana's sleepy dirt roads and population of 130, it might as well be New York City. The challenge has been to maintain the uniqueness of Floreana's slow pace of life while creating economic opportunities for the locals.

To that end, Floreana has worked with the national park and several conservation organizations to develop an entirely different model of tourism. The goal is to serve a limited number of tourists and ensure that the profits flow equitably into the community. Unlike Santa Cruz where multiple tour operators tout their services every time you walk down the street, Floreana has only one. The single community tourism operator **CECFLOR** (Centro Comunitario Floreana) directs the flow of group tours to hostels and restaurants and is the only company authorized to operate day tours to the beautiful Post Office Bay, Mirador de la Baronesa, and La Botella. As an independent traveler, consider yourself lucky; you can choose where to stay and eat. In contrast, when large tour groups arrive, people are assigned to stay in community-run guest houses and eat in community-run restaurants on a rotation schedule. A percentage of the proceeds goes back to CECFLOR for its operating costs, to support the local school and other projects to benefit the community.

A key difference you may notice is that all of CECFLOR's tours are run by local community guides. There are no naturalist guides living on Floreana, so the national park has authorized CECFLOR to send tourists to protected areas with locals instead. Unlike naturalist guides, community guides are locals who have other jobs outside of tourism; these tours are a source of extra income. Their English may be quite limited and they don't have the training that naturalist guides go through, but they do know the sites well and can point out animal species to you.

As an outsider, it may seem unfair that you aren't allowed to walk on your own to Post Office Bay and Mirador de la Baronesa, but Floreana residents can go alone. Keep in mind, however, that many residents of Floreana are older; they lived on the island before the national park came into existence in 1959. For years the national park only allowed visits with a naturalist guide, but since no naturalist guides live on Floreana, it effectively prevented anyone from going unless they were on cruise ships. Under the new rules, residents can finally return to their favorite childhood haunts.

remote **Mirador de la Baronesa** and tours to **Devil's Crown** (currently accessible only via cruise), but it's not certain whether these will obtain approval.

FOOD

If you come on a day tour, your lunch will included. For the independent traveler, food options are very limited. All the restaurants are informal and have outdoor patio seating; there are no international or upscale establishments. Restaurant hours are unpredictable, as most do not cook or stay open if there are no customers. It is recommended that you stop by a restaurant and let them know you are

coming two hours in advance. Prices are the same at all the restaurants: $7 for breakfast, $12 for lunch, and $15 for dinner.

On the main strip, the **Canchalagua** (12 de Febrero, no phone, lunch, coffee, and dinner daily) is the town's only coffee shop and café. The specialty of the owner, Cookie, is *canchalagua* pizza and burgers—made with a local mollusk. Despite the nondescript atmosphere, visitors love the Canchalagua for the friendly service and home-cooked food.

Farther up the main road, try the **Devil's Crown Bar-Restaurant** (12 de Febrero, no phone, breakfast, lunch, and dinner daily, set

Dance Aerobics

If you want to hang out with the locals in the Galápagos, there is no place better than the daily community exercise classes. In all the port towns you can burn off that fried fish to *bailoterapia*—dance aerobics done to the blaring rhythms of salsa, merengue, reggaeton, and cumbia. The instructions are yelled in Spanish and the moves are faster than a swimming sea lion, but it is easy enough to mimic the dance instructors on stage. If you're off beat, you certainly won't be alone. Most of the people seem to be moving in opposite directions at the same time; the only rules are to get low, shake your hips, and sweat profusely.

The classes take place in public spaces and are free for the community. It is part of a larger Ecuadorian government program called *"Ecuador Ejercitate!"* or "Ecuador Exercise!" to help people stay healthy and combat obesity. As part of the program, free exercise classes are held Monday-Friday in parks across Ecuador. The program was founded in 2012, with a $6.5 million investment to initiate classes in 278 locations all over Ecuador.

Schedules change once in a while, so ask a local to double-check the time and then head to one of the following locations:

- **Puerto Velasco Ibarra, Floreana:** high school off the main road (12 de Febrero, classes 6pm-7pm)

- **Puerto Ayora, Santa Cruz:** Coliseum (San Cristóbal and Calle No. 6, classes 7:30am-8:30am, 7:30pm-8:30pm)

- **Puerto Baquerizo Moreno, San Cristóbal:** Estadio (stadium) (Serrano and Flores, classes 7pm-8pm)

menu). The atmosphere is nothing special, but the fried fish is delicious.

At the end of the main road is the **Oasis de la Baronesa** (12 de Febrero, tel. 5/253-5006, lunch and dinner daily). They serve standard fare of fish, rice, and a small salad, with a soup for a starter.

Off the main strip, **Leila's Restaurant** (Juan Salgado, tel. 5/253-5041, breakfast and lunch daily) is one of the most popular restaurants with tour groups. The food is about the same as the other restaurants on the island—fixed menus with soup and rice with fish or chicken, but the atmosphere is decidedly pleasant, with long wooden tables, plants, and hammocks.

The restaurant inside **Hostal Wittmer** (Playa Negra, tel. 5/253-5033, erikagarciawittmer@hotmail.com) is the nicest place in town, as well as the only restaurant with views of the beach and the only indoor restaurant where you can escape the bugs at night.

ACCOMMODATIONS

There are only 10 options for accommodation on the island, with capacity for about 100 guests, and none is as luxurious as you will find on the other three inhabited islands. They do all come with hot water, and there's Wi-Fi throughout the town.

Hostels and Hotels

Both Black Beach House and Hotel Wittmer have the unique aspect of living history; they are run by the descendants of the Wittmer family, some of the earliest inhabitants of the Galápagos Islands, whose lives have been well documented in several books and a film. Hotel Wittmer and Floreana Lava Lodge cater primarily to large tour groups.

★ **Black Beach House** (Playa Negra, tel. 5/252-0648 or 98/475-5473, ingridgarciawittmer@hotmail.com, $30 pp) is a two-room house built out of brick with a fantastic location right on the beach and friendly personal service. The rooms are spacious, and there's a pleasant living room with views of the beach and hammocks outside. The fully equipped kitchen is a huge benefit since eating out on Floreana is more expensive and less convenient than on any other island. If you plan to cook, the safest bet is to purchase all your food from Santa Cruz.

The beachfront **Hotel Wittmer** (Playa Negra, tel. 5/253-5033, erikagarciawittmer@hotmail.com, $30 pp) is a *hostal* with a sense of history; the sitting room has a small exhibit on the history of Floreana and the Wittmer family. The second-floor rooms have some of the best views on the islands. The guest rooms and bungalows are simple but comfortable, with hot water and ceiling fans; some have mini-fridges as well. There are no room keys, but there is a safe-deposit box for valuables. The *hostal* is primarily occupied by organized tour groups.

The most expensive place in town is the **Floreana Lava Lodge** (road to La Lobería, tel. 5/253-5022, malourdes.soria@hotmail.com, $138 s, $153 d or t, breakfast included), a collection of 10 oceanfront pine cabins in a private area tucked a little away from town and overlooking the ocean. It is one of the few places in town with air-conditioning. Rooms, though quite compact, are fully equipped with reading lamps, hair dryers, and safe-deposit boxes;

the triples have bunk beds. The lodge is mainly occupied by organized tour groups. The kayaks and stand-up paddleboards at the lodge are only for guests on all-inclusive packages.

Community Tourism Guesthouses

In addition to the regular *hostales*, Floreana also has seven mom-and-pop guesthouses that are affiliated with the community tourism project. These houses currently offer the same price of $35 per person, though there is a surprising variation in quality and amenities. The following list is ordered roughly in order of quality, best options first. Unless noted, these guesthouses do not include breakfast or air-conditioning. Note that there are plans to continue investing in renovating the guesthouses; prices may potentially increase.

None of these guesthouses use online booking platforms; make your reservation through the direct emails provided below or through CECFLOR with a special request for the guesthouse of your choice.

Casa Santa Maria (Ignacio Hernández, tel. 5/253-5022, malourdes.soria@hotmail.com, $35 pp), run by the seasoned owners of the Floreana Lava Lodge, boasts six relatively modern rooms with mini-fridge, safe-deposit

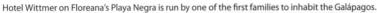

Hotel Wittmer on Floreana's Playa Negra is run by one of the first families to inhabit the Galápagos.

box, and hot water; it's a block inland. Ask for a room on the third floor.

Casa de Emperatriz (12 de Febrero, tel. 5/253-5014, orquideasalgado@hotmail.com, $35 pp) has three rather dingy rooms a couple blocks inland by the main road, but it is the only budget option on the island with air-conditioning. Some rooms also have mini-fridges.

Casa de Lelia (Ignacio Hernández and Oswaldo Rosero, tel. 5/253-5041, leliaflorimarc8@gmail.com, $35 pp), a block inland, has pleasant rooms with remodeled bathrooms, hammocks, and hot water; some rooms have mini-fridges.

Los Cactus (Oswaldo and La Baronesa, tel. 5/253-5011, loscactus.gps@gmail.com, $35 pp), is slightly inland near the dock. There are four basic, modern-style guest rooms; the two on the second floor have limited views of the bay. There is a kitchen that guests are sometimes allowed to use, but it's best to ask.

Casa El Pajas (Wittmer at Zavala, tel. 5/253-5002, hospedaje.elpajas@gmail.com, $35 pp) has an attractive tiki-style log cabin vibe but is located a little farther inland than the other options. There is also a breezy second-floor sitting area and a couple hammocks.

Cabañas Leocarpus (12 de Febrero, tel. 5/253-5054, veritoemi2006@gmail.com, $35 pp) on the main street has a similar rustic vibe. The guest rooms on the second floor have a very distant view to the sea. Each has one double bed and one single bed.

Casa de Huéspedes Hildita (12 de Febrero and Juan Salgado, tel. 5/253-5079, $35 pp) has five guest rooms built around an empty gravel courtyard. Be aware, however, that while water is a precious resource on the entire island, this *hostal* has the strictest water usage policy.

INFORMATION AND SERVICES

There are very few services on Floreana. Bring all the cash you need because there's no ATM or bank. Bring clean clothes because there's no launderette.

Renewable Energy Gone Nutty

While the residents of Santa Cruz and San Cristóbal are primarily investing in solar and wind alternative energy, the island of Floreana has an alternative approach. If you want to know what powers the lights in Velasco Ibarra, head up off the main road. Two large generators make a hum that can be heard a block away. Rather than using fossil fuels, however, they are running completely off piñon oil. Piñon is a nut grown in the Manabí province of Ecuador and processed into a thick biodiesel. The nut oil now provides electricity for Floreana 24 hours a day.

There are no supermarkets to buy food or snacks, and the one **minimarket** is frequently closed. If you are desperate for a snack, there is a small *panadería* (bakery) by the power station at the east edge of town that sells loaves of bread, rolls, and soft drinks. If you stay the night, it is highly recommended to bring snacks from Puerto Ayora. You can bring food including fruit and vegetables as long as it does not contain seeds (apples, bananas, pineapples, and pears are permitted; passion fruit is not).

You can drink the tap water if you boil it first, though many *hostales* have large dispensers of drinking water.

The **CECFLOR** office is by the main dock and is the only source of tourist information on the island. Like most businesses in Floreana, it is open from morning to late afternoon, though hours are sporadic.

There is no hospital, but there is a small **medical clinic** along the main road for minor cuts and bruises.

There are no Internet cafés or phone cabins for making international calls. If you need to use the Internet, there is a free public Wi-Fi network that reaches most of the town.

Walk among giant tortoises in the tortoise enclosure in the Floreana highlands.

GETTING THERE AND AROUND
Interisland Ferries

There is no airport on Floreana, so the only way to get there is either on a cruise or a speedboat from Puerto Ayora on Santa Cruz.

Ferries don't leave every day, so ask for the ferry schedule before making your plans and booking accommodation. Ferries ($30) depart Puerto Ayora at 8am and arrive around 10am. The return trip leaves Floreana at approximately 2:30pm and arrives in Santa Cruz at 4:30pm.

Organized island-hopping tour groups occasionally charter speedboats directly between Floreana and Isabela or San Cristóbal, but there are no public ferries. If you run into such a group, you can try your luck finding the captain or guide and buying your way on board, but don't plan on it; most like to keep their exclusive group tours exclusive.

Around Puerto Velasco Ibarra

There aren't any **taxis** in Puerto Velasco Ibarra as in the other ports, because the town is so small.

The local *chiva* ($1), a rustic open-air bus, is the only form of public transportation, and it leaves just two times a day at 6am and 3pm. It leaves port from the main road (12 de Febrero) and goes to the highlands, stopping at local farms to drop off locals and stopping at Asilo de la Paz if there are tourists. It picks people up and returns to port after an hour and a half.

Floreana Highlands

Away from the dry port of Velasco Ibarra, Floreana is beautifully lush and green in the highlands.

ASILO DE LA PAZ

Head inland from port eight kilometers into the boundaries of the national park and you will reach the visitor site Asilo de la Paz, a lush green area in the hills where you can explore a tortoise reserve, a freshwater spring, and even pirate caves, all in close proximity along a well-marked path. First is the **tortoise reserve,** where you can walk right among

the animals on a dirt path. Unlike the tortoise reserves on the other islands, this one has no breeding center. The tortoises here used to be the pets of the islanders before the national park prohibited it and moved the animals to this reserve. Next, follow the path past the tortoise reserve and you will find a tiny **freshwater spring** through the fence, where water trickles over rocks into a reservoir. It is not much to look at, but it is a fascinating indicator of the history of Floreana, since this tiny spring used to supply the entire island. Around the corner is a stone carving of a face, reminiscent of moai on Easter Island, but don't get too excited about ancient civilizations as this was done by the Wittmer family kids. Last are the **pirate caves**. These small shelters were carved out of the hill by pirates centuries ago and were later used as the temporary home of the island's earliest inhabitants (the Wittmers) when they first arrived on the island. There aren't any remnants of the early inhabitants, but it's fun to crawl inside a cave and let your imagination run wild.

This site is often included on day tours, though visiting it independently is also possible if you can wake up in time for the 6am *chiva* to the highlands ($1, 45 minutes). The *chiva* returns to port after an hour and a half, so it is possible to catch it after your visit to get back, but it will be a very rushed visit. For a more leisurely visit, take the *chiva* to Asilo de la Paz and then walk back afterward, downhill eight kilometers, stopping to take in Cerro Alieri on your way back. There is another *chiva* at 3pm, but it's not recommended because if you miss the *chiva*, you may be walking back as it is getting dark. It is possible to walk there and back (16 kilometers roundtrip) if you start early. Keep in mind, though, that getting there is significantly harder because it is uphill. The path is hilly and the weather is unpredictable, so bring a jacket and good walking shoes.

CERRO ALIERI

Cerro Alieri is a hill about halfway between town and Asilo de la Paz. The trailhead is well marked on the left-hand side on the main road to Asilo de la Paz. Visitors ascend a steep path and staircase for about 20 minutes and are rewarded with fantastic views of both sides of the island, from Puerto Velasco Ibarra and Post Office Bay to the green hills of the highlands. Darwin's finches can also be spotted along the trail. The walk from town to the trailhead isn't terribly interesting, but it only takes an hour each way (head inland away from port along the main road). It is also possible to eliminate the walk by taking the 6am or 3pm *chiva* ($1); ask to be dropped off at the trailhead and then picked up on the *chiva*'s way back down. A third option for visiting is to take the *chiva* to Asilo de la Paz, walk down to Cerro Alieri (1.5 hours), and then return to town walking (one hour).

The Coast and Surrounding Islets

The coast and surrounding islets of Floreana have some of the best snorkeling sites in the archipelago. Only **La Botella, Post Office Bay, and Mirador de la Baronesa are accessible by day tour** from Puerto Velasco Ibarra. The rest are **currently only accessible by cruise.**

Diving at Punta Cormorant, Enderby, and Champion Island is possible via a day trip from Puerto Ayora on Santa Cruz Island, but ironically cannot be done as a day trip from Puerto Velasco Ibarra since there are no dive agencies there.

LA BOTELLA

Beyond La Lobería is a protected bay with great snorkeling with marine turtles, fish, and the occasional rays. Farther from town and with calmer waters, it has considerably more to see than La Lobería. The beach is a sea turtle nesting ground. Despite its proximity to port, this site is not reachable on foot as there is no trail, and the only way to arrive is by kayak tour.

POST OFFICE BAY

Post Office Bay is one of the quirkiest sites in the Galápagos. You wouldn't imagine that a mailbox would be of much appeal, but it has an interesting history and is also a bit

Underwater Photography Tips

- Get close to your subject if possible; water quickly washes out light, and you will end up with very fuzzy images otherwise.

- Holding your breath and swimming underwater to take a picture usually results in more interesting angles and better lighting.

- To stay underwater longer, try equalizing the pressure in your ears and using a frog kick rather than a scissors kick.

- Take photos of animals near the surface at an upward angle and create a visual "horizon" with the surface of the water.

- Use a fast shutter speed and turn on burst mode if your camera has it—it will help you get a shot of the fish or sea lions facing the camera.

- Stay calm around sea turtles and fish; sudden movements will scare them away before you can take any pictures.

- Be careful not to kick up sand with your fins; cloudy water will ruin your pictures and those of your group.

playful sea lion at Champion Island

of lighthearted fun. Back in 1793, whalers began the practice of leaving mail in a barrel for homeward-bound ships to collect. Crews would then hand-deliver the letters to their destination in a remarkable act of camaraderie. These days the tradition has been carried on, mainly by tourists. Leave a postcard for a fellow national to collect, and take one home with you. Tradition dictates that you should deliver it in person, but paying the postage is probably preferable these days to turning up on a stranger's doorstep. The barrel has evolved into a wooden box on a pole surrounded by an assortment of junk.

A visit to the bay begins with a wet landing directly onto the brown-sand beach. Just a few meters beyond the barrel is a lava tunnel, and you often need to wade through water to reach it. There are also the rusted remains of a Norwegian fish operation dating back to the 1920s, as well as a football field used by crews who may invite you to a game. Be aware that there are sizable populations of introduced wasps, and their sting is painful, so take care. A more scenic end to the visit is a *panga* (dinghy) ride past a sea lion colony, where you can also spot sea turtles and occasionally penguins.

★ MIRADOR DE LA BARONESA

Mirador de la Baronesa (Baroness's Lookout) was where the baroness of Floreana Island would often sit and watch for passing ships. Nowadays, cruise ships often stop at this idyllic mangrove-lined lagoon for snorkeling, kayaking, or a *panga* ride to spot the blue-footed boobies, sea lions, and occasionally penguins sitting on the rocky shores, which are covered in black lava and endemic cacti.

PUNTA CORMORANT

Visiting this site on the north side of Floreana starts with a wet landing onto a beach colored green by olivine minerals, which are silicates of magnesium and iron. A 720-meter trail leads up to a saltwater lagoon. Along the trail, Floreana's comparatively lush surroundings can be appreciated. The lagoon is a good spot to see flamingos and other wading birds, such as white-cheeked pintails, stilts, and gallinules. The lagoon is surrounded by gray, seemingly lifeless palo santo trees. Among the vegetation is abundant birdlife, including yellow warblers and flycatchers. Beyond is a beautiful beach, nicknamed "Flour Beach" for its incredibly fine white sand. Stingrays and spotted eagle rays are common near the beach, and sea turtles nest here November-February. There are signs to keep out of their nesting areas, but you may be lucky enough to see the turtles swimming. Note that snorkeling and swimming are not allowed. The only drawback of this site is its perplexing name—there are no flightless cormorants here.

Diving at Punta Cormorant is possible via a day trip from Puerto Ayora on Santa Cruz Island. Day tours cost up to $200 per person for two dives per day.

★ DEVIL'S CROWN

Offshore from Post Office Bay, the jagged peaks of this submerged volcanic cone poke out of the water and supply its name, Corona del Diablo (Devil's Crown). The nooks and crannies of this marine site offer some of the best snorkeling in the islands, either outside the ring or in the shallow inner chamber, which is reached through a side opening. There is a rich variety of tropical fish—parrot fish, angelfish, and damselfish—and you can occasionally see sea lions and sharks. Note that the current can be quite strong on the seaward side, so pay close attention to your guide. It is currently accessible only by cruise.

Devil's Crown is home to schools of surgeonfish.

★ ENDERBY AND CHAMPION ISLAND

These two sites are very popular with snorkelers and divers. Enderby is an eroded tuff cone where you can snorkel with playful sea lions, and Champion Island is a small offshore crater, a popular nesting site for boobies. Landing is not allowed, but the snorkeling and diving are great, with the chance to see many species of sharks, fish, and sea turtles. Snorkeling at these sites is currently only possible from cruise ships. Diving at these sites is available via a day trip from Puerto Ayora on Santa Cruz Island. Day tours cost up to $200 per person for two dives.

Remote Uninhabited Islands

Look for ★ to find recommended sights, activities, dining, and lodging.

Highlights

★ **Bartolomé Island:** This jagged rock jutting out of the sea is the most frequently photographed sight in the Galápagos (page 135).

★ **Punta Espinosa on Fernandina:** Flightless cormorants stretch their stubby wings against a backdrop of swirling pahoehoe lava at the only spot on Fernandina open to visitors (page 138).

★ **Punta Suárez on Española:** Punta Suárez is most famous as the only site to see the rare **waved albatross,** which nest here from April to November (page 139).

★ **Genovesa:** This island in the far north of the archipelago is home to the largest colony of **red-footed boobies** in the world (page 139).

★ **Diving at Wolf and Darwin Islands:** Whale sharks, schooling hammerheads, and giant manta rays make these dive sites world-famous (page 140).

© AVALON TRAVEL

The uninhabited islands are the most pristine, least visited, and most fascinating places in the Galápagos Islands. With the exception of Española, Bartolomé, and Sullivan Bay, the only way to arrive is by cruise.

Fernandina, Española, and **Genovesa** are perhaps the most famous spots for wildlife-watching in the archipelago, and visitors sometimes choose cruises just based on which of these sites they include.

Española and Genovesa are birding paradises. Española is the only place in the world to view the waved albatross. Whether you see the enormous creatures nuzzling beaks in their mating ritual or landing at the "albatross airport," it is sure to be a highlight of your trip. Genovesa is home to the largest colony of red-footed boobies in the world. They inhabit a beach and cliffs surrounding an enormous submerged crater, along with a slew of other native birds. Fernandina is the most volcanically active island, where flightless cormorants stretch out their vestigial wings between trips into the water, and enormous marine iguanas fight over territory on the rocks. From June to September migrating whales frequently swim through the channel between Fernandina and Isabela and stop just long enough to awe the passing cruise ships.

The small uninhabited islands close to Santa Cruz—Seymour Norte, Santa Fé, the Plazas, Pinzón, and Daphne—are covered in the Santa Cruz chapter.

Previous: Bartolomé is famous for its volcanic landscapes; waved albatross at Punta Suárez. **Above:** sea lion on the beach on Española.

Remote Uninhabited Islands

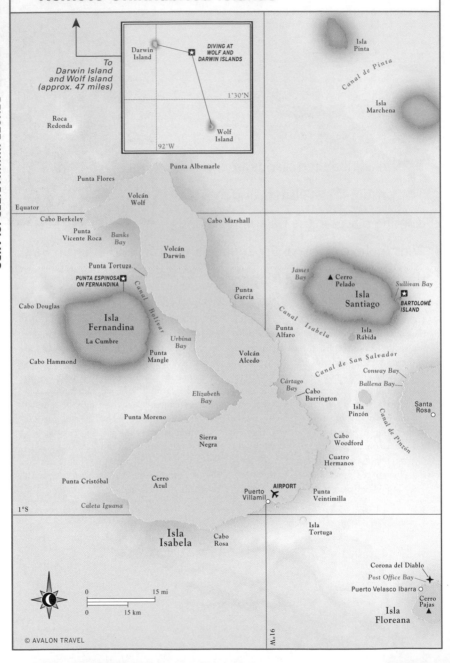

To
Darwin Island
and Wolf Island
(approx. 47 miles)

Darwin
Island

DIVING AT
WOLF AND
DARWIN ISLANDS

1°30'N

92°W

Wolf
Island

Isla
Pinta

Canal de Pinta

Isla
Marchena

Roca
Redonda

Punta Albemarle

Punta Flores

Volcán
Wolf

Equator

Cabo Berkeley

Cabo Marshall

Punta
Vicente Roca

Banks
Bay

Volcán
Darwin

Punta Tortuga

PUNTA ESPINOSA
ON FERNANDINA

Canal Bolívar

Cabo Douglas

Isla
Fernandina

Punta
Garcia

La Cumbre

Urbina
Bay

Cabo Hammond

Punta
Mangle

Volcán
Alcedo

Elizabeth
Bay

Cártago
Bay

Punta Moreno

Sierra
Negra

Cabo
Barrington

James
Bay

Cerro
Pelado

Sullivan Bay

Isla
Santiago

BARTOLOMÉ
ISLAND

Punta
Alfaro

Canal Isabela

Isla
Rábida

Canal de San Salvador

Conway Bay

Ballena Bay

Isla
Pinzón

Canal de Pinzón

Santa
Rosa

Cabo
Woodford

Cuatro
Hermanos

Punta Cristóbal

Cerro
Azul

Puerto
Villamil

AIRPORT

Punta
Veintimilla

1°S

Caleta Iguana

Isla
Tortuga

Isla
Isabela

Cabo
Rosa

Corona del Diablo

Post Office Bay

Puerto Velasco Ibarra

Cerro
Pajas

Isla
Floreana

0   15 mi

0   15 km

Mo16

© AVALON TRAVEL

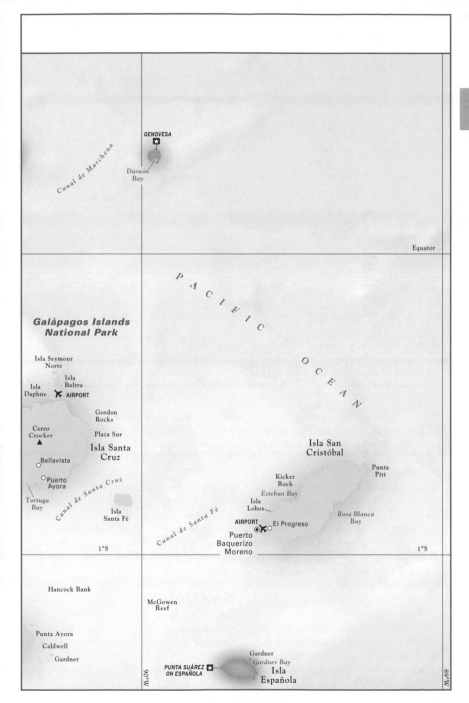

GENOVESA

Canal de Marchena

Darwin Bay

Equator

PACIFIC

Galápagos Islands National Park

OCEAN

Isla Seymour Norte

Isla Daphne

Isla Baltra

✈ AIRPORT

Gordon Rocks

Cerro Crocker ▲

Plaza Sur

Isla Santa Cruz

Bellavista

Puerto Ayora

Canal de Santa Cruz

Tortuga Bay

Isla Santa Fé

Isla San Cristóbal

Kicker Rock

Esteban Bay

Isla Lobos

Canal de Santa Fé

AIRPORT ✈

El Progreso

Punta Pitt

Rosa Blanca Bay

Puerto Baquerizo Moreno

1°S

1°S

Hancock Bank

McGowen Reef

Punta Ayora

Caldwell

Gardner

PUNTA SUÁREZ ON ESPAÑOLA

Gardner

Gardner Bay

Isla Española

90°W

89°W

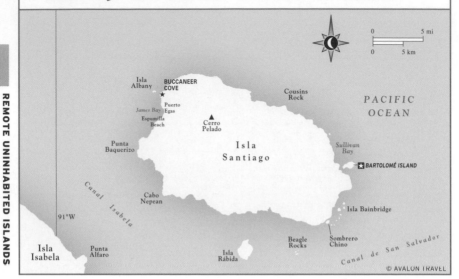

Santiago and Central Uninhabited Islands

Isla Albany · BUCCANEER COVE ★ · Puerto Egas · James Bay · Espumilla Beach · Cerro Pelado · Punta Baquerizo · Isla Santiago · Cousins Rock · PACIFIC OCEAN · Sullivan Bay · BARTOLOMÉ ISLAND · Canal Isabela · Cabo Nepean · 91°W · Isla Bainbridge · Isla Isabela · Punta Alfaro · Isla Rábida · Beagle Rocks · Sombrero Chino · Canal de San Salvador · © AVALON TRAVEL

0   5 mi
0   5 km

Santiago and the Central Uninhabited Islands

Stepping onto the Galápagos's fourth-largest island, also known as San Salvador, is rather like stepping back to the beginning of time. The effects of a long history of volcanic eruptions are everywhere on this island: Blackened lava dominates the landscape, and small plants and cacti are the first signs of life sprouting from the ashes. In recent years destruction of a different kind has occurred on the island. Feral goats, introduced in the 1880s, grew to number over 100,000 in less than a century. A large-scale effort by the National Park Service and Charles Darwin Research Station successfully eradicated the goats by 2006.

The most popular sites on and near Santiago include the black lava trails of **Sullivan Bay;** the colonies of sea lions, fur seals, and marine iguanas at **James Bay;** the famous **Pinnacle Rock** off Bartolomé, the most photographed site in the archipelago; and the red-sand beach on **Rábida.** There are good diving spots at **Bartolomé, Cousins Rock,** and **Beagle Rocks.**

Only Sullivan Bay on Santiago and Bartolomé can be visited as a day trip from Puerto Ayora on Santa Cruz Island. (Diving at Bartolomé, Cousins Rock, and Beagle Rocks is also possible via a day trip from Puerto Ayora.) The other sites cannot be visited on day trips at present and must be seen as part of a cruise tour.

SANTIAGO
Sullivan Bay

One of the most popular sites on the island is this bay on the east side. An eruption in 1897 left the area covered in mesmerizing patterns of black lava, known as pahoehoe (a Hawaiian word for rope) because of its tendency to buckle when it cools. The lava's glassy, almost ceramic feel comes from its high silicate content. The walk over the 1.5-kilometer loop takes about 1.5 hours and is very uneven—it's a natural trail—so bring good walking shoes.

Buccaneer Cove

A freshwater source made this cove a haven for pirates in the 17th and 18th centuries. A few years back, divers found evidence in the form of ceramic jars on the seabed, still intact and filled with wine and marmalade. There is no landing spot, but cruises either take *panga* boats or allow passengers to kayak along the coast to appreciate the steep cliffs and dark-red volcanic sand beach.

James Bay

On the west side of Santiago, a very popular visitor site is **Puerto Egas,** named after the owner of a salt mine that operated on the island in the 1960s. There is a wet landing onto the long black-lava shoreline, home to a small colony of sea lions and large populations of marine iguanas.

A two-kilometer, three-hour loop trail leads inland past the rusted remains of the salt mine and a rather makeshift soccer field built by cruise crews. Look to the skies and you may be lucky enough to see Galápagos hawks, circling in search of prey in the form of Galápagos doves and mockingbirds. Farther down the trail are the famous fur-seal grottoes, where the ocean fills a series of pools and underwater caverns occupied by seals, sea lions, and bright-red Sally Lightfoot crabs. There are great snorkeling opportunities here.

At the north end of James Bay, five kilometers from Puerto Egas, is **Espumilla Beach,** another good spot for snorkeling and swimming. Visitors make a wet landing onto a beach where sea turtles can sometimes be spotted; they come ashore at night to lay their eggs. A short trail (two kilometers round-trip) leads inland through the mangroves to a lagoon populated by Galápagos flamingos, herons, and other wading birds.

TOP EXPERIENCE

★ BARTOLOMÉ ISLAND

This tiny island off the southeast coast of Santiago is one of the most photographed sights in the archipelago. A wooden staircase leads 114 meters up to a summit with a breathtaking view—and for once, this is no exaggeration. In the foreground the mangroves are flanked on either side by twin

the iconic Pinnacle Rock on Bartolomé

Volcano Vocab

The Galápagos Islands are home to some of the most stunning volcanic landscapes in the world. Here are just a few of the formations you can see and the associated vocabulary:

- **Caldera**—a cauldron-shaped formation created by the collapse of a magma chamber in a volcano. The top of Volcán Sierra Negra on Isabela is an example of a caldera. These are often confused with craters.

- **Crater**—a cauldron-shaped formation created when magma erupts and gases and lava eject. Darwin Bay on Genovesa is an example.

- **Shield volcano**—a volcano built from fluid lava flows, usually wide and with a low profile. Santiago is a shield volcano, as are Fernandina and Sierra Negra.

- **Tuff**—compacted volcanic ash. Punta Pitt on San Cristóbal is a good example of a tuff formation.

- **Hornitos**—hollow structures in the lava where high pressure causes the lava to ooze and splatter out ("little ovens" in Spanish). There are many hornitos on Bartolomé and on Volcán Chico on Isabela.

- **Pahoehoe lava**—lava that appears rippled or buckled, formed when liquid lava flows over and around an obstruction. Sullivan Bay is the most famous example in the Galápagos.

- **Aa lava**—rough lava made of jagged fragments, almost impossible to walk on and formed by a viscous flow of lava. See if you can spot both pahoehoe and aa lava at Puerto Egas on Santiago.

half-moon beaches. Rising up behind is the famous 40-meter-high **Pinnacle Rock**, a jagged volcanic formation that has endured years of erosion as well as the U.S. Air Force using it for target practice during World War II. The blackened lava fields of Santiago in the background complete a perfect photograph.

A dry landing is followed by a 30-minute round-trip hike to take in the view. It's a steep but short climb. Afterward, you take a short boat ride to the two beaches, where there is excellent snorkeling with a small colony of sea lions as well as the occasional chance to see Galápagos penguins. Out of the water, a trail winds through the mangroves to the beach on the other side (500 meters each way). Swimming is not allowed on this side, but look closely and you may glimpse stingrays, white-tipped sharks, and sea turtles that come ashore at night to lay their eggs. In the mangroves, bird-watchers should keep their eyes open for Galápagos hawks, herons, and oystercatchers.

Bartolomé is included on many cruise itineraries, but as a day trip it has become more expensive and will set you back $180 per person with tour operators in Puerto Ayora. Some day trips combine Bartolomé with Sullivan Bay, whereas others visit Bachas Beach (on the north side of Santa Cruz) instead. It is also possible to dive here on a day tour from Puerto Ayora ($200).

RÁBIDA ISLAND

About five kilometers south of Santiago, this small island, also known as Jervis, is the exact geographic center of the Galápagos archipelago. There's a wet landing onto a rust-colored beach filled with dozens of sea lions stretched out; this is a great spot to walk among a colony and listen to their snorts and snoring. It's also an excellent place for snorkeling, but note that the male sea lion population is quite large (it's mainly a bachelor colony), so take care. The beach is also one of the best places in the archipelago to see brown pelicans nesting.

Chicks have a high mortality rate, so don't be surprised to stumble across numerous corpses. Still, there are plenty of live ones filling the skies and crying to their parents, who are busy dive-bombing the ocean in search of the family lunch.

Aside from the beach, there is a 1.1-kilometer loop trail through the palo santo forest and along a brackish lagoon. On the trail, look for Galápagos hawks perched watchfully on tree branches as well as Galápagos flamingos and yellow-crowned night herons stabbing at fish and shrimp in the salt ponds.

SOMBRERO CHINO

This tiny island off the southeast tip of Santiago, just south of Bartolomé, is a volcanic cone with the rough shape of a "Chinese hat" (hence the name). Most cruise tours simply pass it to admire the shape, because landing access is restricted to boats carrying 12 people or fewer. Sombrero Chino has a small sea lion colony, marine iguanas, excellent snorkeling, and a short 700-meter trail across the island that takes half an hour and commands impressive views.

Fernandina

West of Isabela is the archipelago's youngest and most volcanically active island, **Fernandina.** There is one visitor site at **Punta Espinosa,** which has a large population of nesting flightless cormorants, the largest colony of marine iguanas in the archipelago, and a large sea lion colony.

Fernandina is special even by Galápagos standards. The westernmost island in the archipelago is one of the few that have escaped invasion by introduced species, and the island's pristine ecosystem has been preserved. This island is also less visited than most of the others due to its remote location, and it retains the air of a land that time forgot.

At under one million years old, Fernandina is the youngest volcanic island in the archipelago and also the most active. The volcano, La Cumbre, has erupted several times in recent years, most spectacularly in 1968, when the caldera collapsed more than 300 meters, and most recently in April 2009.

the red beaches on Rábida

★ PUNTA ESPINOSA

Fernandina has just one visitor site, **Punta Espinosa,** on the island's northeast corner across from Isabela's Tagus Cove, but it's arguably one of the best sites in the archipelago. A dry landing among the mangroves leads 250 meters to a sandy point partly covered by lava from recent flows, both the rippled glass-like surface of pahoehoe lava and the rough, rocky lava. Nearby is the dramatic sight of the largest colony of marine iguanas in the archipelago sunning themselves on the rocks. The marine iguanas on Fernandina are the largest in the archipelago, due to the abundance of food from the cold currents in this side of the archipelago. In the afternoon you may be able to see the largest males head-butting as they fight over territory.

Next you pass a large sea lion colony with the sound of barking bulls filling the air. This is also one of the biggest nesting sites of flightless cormorants. Watch out for males returning from fishing to bring lunch to their mate, who sits in a tangled nest of seaweed and twigs near the water's edge.

After retracing your steps, you can take a longer 750-meter trail leading over jagged lava spotted with lava cacti (bring good shoes). Brilliant vermilion flycatchers often sit in the mangrove branches. At low tide a pool offers

A flightless cormorant stretches its vestigial wings on Fernandina.

excellent bird-watching. The tour usually ends with a *panga* ride out into the strait, where schools of dolphins are often seen. There is excellent snorkeling at several locations around Punta Espinosa, offering chances to see penguins, marine iguanas, flightless cormorants, and sea turtles.

Española

The southernmost island in the Galápagos is also the oldest in the archipelago, at nearly 3.5 million years, compared with Fernandina in the northwest, which is less than one million years old. The waved albatross that nest here April-November are the island's main draw. Witness these enormous birds taking off and landing, and enjoy their amusing mating dance. Española is accessible via cruise or as a pricey day tour ($200) from Puerto Baquerizo Moreno on San Cristóbal.

GARDNER BAY

On the northeast side of Española, this beautiful crescent beach is reached by a wet landing. There are no hikes, so the main draw is the excellent snorkeling. Highlights include frolicking with playful sea lions (there's a colony here) as well as spotting stingrays or occasional white-tipped sharks. The beach is an important nesting site for marine turtles, so you might be lucky enough to see them. **Turtle Rock,** a short *panga* ride offshore, is another good snorkeling spot with a rich variety of bright tropical fish, such as moorish idols, damselfish, and parrot fish.

On the beach, you can walk among the sea lion colony, but try to give the males a wide berth. At the east end, there are marine iguanas and Sally Lightfoot crabs, and you can often see the endemic hood mockingbirds.

TOP EXPERIENCE

★ PUNTA SUÁREZ

On the western tip of Española, Punta Suárez is one of the top visitor sites in the Galápagos. A dry landing leads to a trail toward the cliffs on the south side of the point. Unique to Española is a subspecies of **marine iguanas** nicknamed "Christmas iguanas" that are splotched with bright red and green colors around the end of the year. Along the way there are cliffs where Nazca boobies or blue-footed boobies nest, depending on the time of year. Watch your step, as these tame birds remain utterly unconcerned by your presence and sit in the middle of the trail.

The best is yet to come. If you visit between April and November, farther along the trail is the biggest breeding site of **waved albatross** in the world; this site is even nicknamed the "albatross airport." Some 15,000 couples congregate on the island, and it's quite a sight to witness these massive birds with their 2.5-meter wingspans taking off from the cliffs. Seeing them land is also impressive but rather less elegant, as they often fall over, being unsteady on their feet after long flights. The highlight is their entertaining courtship, as the couple dance around each other in a synchronized circular walk, clacking and calling skyward. In November, there are fewer adults, but the babies can be seen waddling about with fluffy gray feathers.

This site is teeming with birdlife, and aside from the boobies and albatross, you can see Galápagos hawks, Galápagos doves, swallow-tailed gulls, oystercatchers, red-billed tropic birds, and finches. The views of the cliffs below are equally impressive, with waves crashing into rocks and water spurting high into the air through blowholes. The rocks are often covered in marine iguanas sunning themselves; these iguanas are more colorful than those found on other islands, with turquoise tinges to their backs and legs, perhaps the result of eating algae endemic to Española.

The entire trail is about three kilometers round-trip and takes about two hours.

Genovesa and the Far North

Genovesa, Darwin, and Wolf are the most remote islands that can be visited in the archipelago, and most boats need to travel overnight. Each has its unique attractions: Genovesa is known for its birds, particularly red-footed boobies at **Darwin Bay Beach** and **Prince Philip's Steps;** and Darwin and Wolf rank among the best dive sites in the world.

TOP EXPERIENCE

★ GENOVESA

Genovesa, also known as Tower Island or even **Booby Island**, is famed for its abundant birdlife, notably the world's largest colony of red-footed boobies, but it takes some getting to—about eight hours by boat overnight, so stock up on seasickness tablets. The bay is actually a large submerged volcanic crater. Interestingly, there are no land reptiles on Genovesa, only a small population of marine iguanas.

Darwin Bay Beach

After a tricky entrance into the bay, where you pass rocks decorated with graffiti from visiting ships, there is a wet landing onto the beach. A short trail (approximately 1.5

kilometers round-trip) leads inland to the mangroves filled with the nests of red-footed boobies and frigate birds. Masked boobies and swallow-tailed gulls also nest here, and you may spot storm petrels and short-eared owls.

The end of the trail leads over rough rocks next to a series of tidal pools, where you can see yellow-crowned night herons half-asleep by day. At high tide, you may be wading through this part of the trail. Other species to watch for include mockingbirds, Galápagos doves, and Darwin's finches. The opuntia cacti you see on the trail are noticeably softer than on other islands. Scientists believe this is because the plants don't need to defend themselves against giant tortoises (there has never been a tortoise population on the island).

Visitors can also snorkel off the beach or along the rocky coastline and spot a wide variety of tropical fish and the occasional shark.

Prince Philip's Steps

Named in honor of a royal visit in the 1960s and also known as El Barranco, this site is near the tip of Darwin Bay's eastern arm. A *panga* ride along the bottom of the cliffs provides glimpses of red-billed tropic birds landing in their crevice nests and a large population of frigate birds. If you're lucky, you may glimpse elusive fur seals. Ashore, a steep-railed stairway leads to a dramatic trail along the top of the cliffs (1.5 kilometers round-trip). Masked and red-footed boobies nest here with frigate birds lurking nearby, ready to scavenge. It's also a good area to see Galápagos doves and sharp-beaked ground finches, also known as "vampire finches" because they peck away at boobies' tails. Storm petrels are also seen in large numbers, and occasionally you may spot the Galápagos owl. The *panga* ride and hike combined take about two hours.

★ WOLF AND DARWIN ISLANDS

These tiny islands, about 215 kilometers northwest of the main island group, are hidden jewels visited only by diving tours. It takes a full night to get here, but the rewards are rich indeed—these islands rank among the best dives in the world. You might even recognize **Darwin's Arch**—a striking stone formation just east of Darwin Island—from magazine articles. The waters around Wolf and Darwin attract whale sharks June-November. Other shark species commonly seen are hammerheads, Galápagos sharks, and reef sharks. Manta rays, dolphins, and turtles abound.

red-footed boobies on Genovesa

Who Was Lonesome George?

If you visit the Charles Darwin Research Station on Santa Cruz, you may find an enclosure left conspicuously empty. This is where Lonesome George, last of the Pinta Island tortoises, lived the last years of his life. During those years, Lonesome George was known as the rarest animal in the world.

By the 1970s, scientists thought that the tortoise was already extinct on Pinta Island. Fishers had introduced feral goats just decades before, wanting a source of fresh meat. The goat population had exploded, destroying the local vegetation and tortoise habitat. A scientist visiting the island to study snails was surprised to find Lonesome George in 1971 and reported the discovery to the national park. Rangers soon moved Lonesome George to the Charles Darwin Research Station. Scientists searched far and wide for a breeding partner, both on Pinta Island and in zoos around the world. There was even a $10,000 reward for a suitable mate.

Efforts to find another Pinta Island tortoise failed. Scientists placed females from other tortoise species in the enclosure with Lonesome George. They hoped that Lonesome George and the female tortoises would produce hybrid offspring, but all the eggs were infertile. He died in 2012 of old age. His body was preserved and shown at the American Museum of Natural History in New York. After his passing, Lonesome George's body was meticulously preserved and shown in museums around the world before returning to his permanent home at Charles Darwin Research Station.

After Lonesome George's death, researchers from Yale were astonished to find hybrid tortoises on Volcán Wolf at the northern tip of Isabela. Genetic analysis showed that the tortoises had partial ancestry from Pinta Island tortoises. They hypothesized that whalers transported the tortoises—taking them from Pinta and tossing them overboard if they were no longer needed for food. Unfortunately, later expeditions to find hybrid Pinta tortoises to bring back to the Charles Darwin Research Station for captive breeding have been unsuccessful.

REMOTE UNINHABITED ISLANDS
GENOVESA AND THE FAR NORTH

MARCHENA AND PINTA ISLANDS

Midway between Wolf and Genovesa in the far north of the archipelago, these two medium-size islands are closed to visitors, although diving is possible in the waters off the coast of Marchena. Pinta is famous as the original home of the tortoise known as Lonesome George, and giant tortoises are currently being repopulated on the island. Marchena has a 343-meter-high volcano at its center that last erupted in 1991.

Gateway Cities

International visitors fly into either Quito or Guayaquil and must spend at least the night before catching a morning flight to the Galápagos Islands.

Quito is the country's capital and is known for its well-preserved colonial architecture, impressive cathedrals, and beautiful mountain backdrop. It has become one of Ecuador's most popular tourist destinations in its own right, with enough sights to keep you busy for weeks. It is highly recommended to fly into Quito if you have extra days for sightseeing before or after the Galápagos Islands.

Guayaquil is the country's largest city by population and the main port for trade. Though it pales next to Quito in terms of tourist attractions, it is the most convenient point of departure for the Galápagos Islands, due to the proximity of its airport to downtown and because flights from Quito to the Galápagos stop in Guayaquil anyway.

Previous: the famous La Compañía church; Sunday street performers in Old Town Quito. **Above:** the fruit at the Municipal market in Quito.

Look for ★ to find recommended sights, activities, dining, and lodging.

Highlights

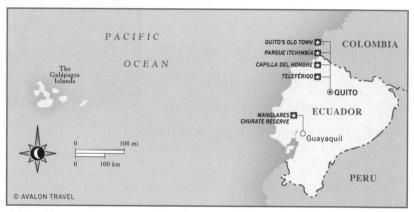

★ **Manglares Churute Reserve:** Take a canoe through dense mangrove forests home to nesting ospreys, elegant herons, and showy spoonbills, and visit nearby cacao farms near Guayaquil (page 150).

★ **Quito's Old Town:** Tourists mix with locals throughout a historic neighborhood of cobblestone streets, traditional workshops, and impressive cathedrals (page 162).

★ **Parque Itchimbía:** This beautiful park in Quito offers spectacular views of the city without the crowds (page 163).

★ **Capilla del Hombre:** Visit this Quito museum to learn about the life of Ecuador's most famous artist, Oswaldo Guayasamín, whose works are known throughout South America and beyond (page 165).

★ **TelefériQo:** This cable car ascends to dizzying heights over Quito on the slopes of Volcán Pichincha. Avid hikers can even take the cable car up and summit the volcano (page 165).

Guayaquil

While Quito is Ecuador's capital and cultural center, the largest city and economic center is actually Guayaquil. Many tourists pass through Guayaquil because of its convenience as a departure point to the Galápagos Islands. The great majority, however, spend as little time there as possible due to the city's reputation for crime, heat, and smog. It's pretty easy to have a terrible time in Guayaquil, wandering the dirty sidewalks of downtown amid the heat, bus exhaust, and mosquitoes.

However, if you know where you're going and don't mind the heat, it can be a pleasant place to spend a couple days concentrating on the redeveloped areas in Guayaquil and the natural areas nearby. Just outside Guayaquil, the lush mangroves and tropical dry forests of Manglares Churute Reserve are an off-the-beaten-path destination for bird-watching. The reserve also offers a glimpse into an entirely different ecosystem. On Isla Santay, you can take bike rides on long, winding paths built atop a mangrove forest. At night, the waterside walkways of Malecón 2000 and Malecón Salado are pleasant places to stroll,

with tropical gardens, fountains, light shows, and South America's largest Ferris wheel.

SAFETY

Crime is a serious issue in Guayaquil. **Muggings** and *secuestros exprés* (express kidnappings) are common, although mainly rich Ecuadorians are targeted. Take taxis at night and never take unmarked cabs. Avoid aimless wandering at any time of day—go directly from place to place, and stay on the main streets in the center.

Scopolamine drugging is a problem in Ecuador's major cities. The hypnotic drug has been used in robberies and sexual assaults, leaving the victim unable to remember the incident. Avoid strangers offering food, drink, and cigarettes, and keep an eye on your drink.

SIGHTS AND TOURS

Guayaquil does not have a lot of tourist attractions, so it is not recommended to spend more than a night or two here. Extra vacation days are usually better spent in the Galápagos or Quito. If you have a full day and your budget

view from the top of Cerro Santa Ana in Guayaquil

Guayaquil and the Southern Coast

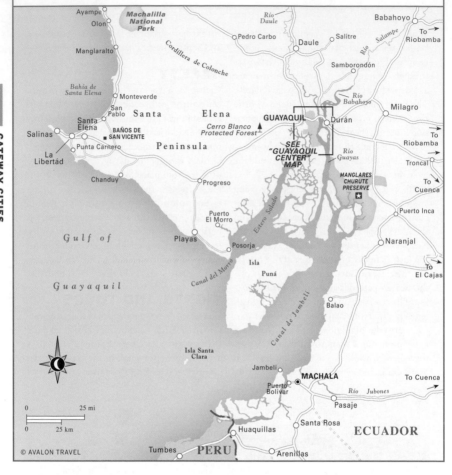

allows, visit the pricey but fantastic Manglares Churute Reserve and the nearby cacao plantations. Otherwise, take a bike ride through Isla Santay. At night, go to Urdesa for dinner, then wander either the Malecón 2000 and Las Peñas or Malecón Salado.

Malecón 2000

Guayaquil's waterfront is the pride of the city and symbol of its redevelopment. In the late 1990s, Mayor León Febres Cordero launched **Malecón 2000** (no phone, www.

malecon2000.org, 7am-midnight daily, free), a hugely ambitious project that completely overhauled the run-down area along the Río Guayas. This three-kilometer promenade now has historic monuments, sculptures, museums, botanical gardens, fountains, and restaurants. The view of the brown river and unshaded concrete walkway is underwhelming, but the cool breezes and the watchful eye of security guards make Malecón 2000 a relaxing place to stroll at night.

The best starting point is **La Plaza Cívica**

Guayaquil Center

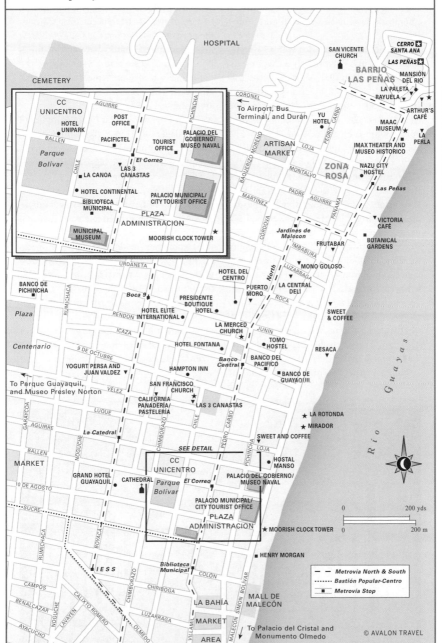

HOSPITAL

SAN VICENTE CHURCH

CERRO ✚ SANTA ANA

LAS PEÑAS ✚

BARRIO LAS PEÑAS

MANSIÓN DEL RIO

CEMETERY

LA PALETA

RAYUELA

CORONEL

To Airport, Bus Terminal, and Durán

YU HOTEL

ARTHUR'S CAFÉ

CC UNICENTRO

AGUIRRE

POST OFFICE

MAAC MUSEUM

LA PERLA

HOTEL UNIPARK

PACIFICTEL

PALACIO DEL GOBIERNO/ MUSEO NAVAL

ARTISAN MARKET

IMAX THEATER AND MUSEO HISTORICO

BALLEN

TOURIST OFFICE

LOJA

Parque Bolívar

CHILE

El Correo

ZONA ROSA

NAZU CITY HOSTEL

LA CANOA

LAS 3 CANASTAS

MONTALVO

HOTEL CONTINENTAL

PALACIO MUNICIPAL/ CITY TOURIST OFFICE

PADRE

AGUIRRE

Las Peñas

BIBLIOTECA MUNICIPAL

PLAZA ADMINISTRACION

MARTINEZ

PANAMA

VICTORIA CAFÉ

MUNICIPAL MUSEUM

MOORISH CLOCK TOWER

CORDOVA

Jardines de Malecon

IMBABURA

FRUTABAR

BOTANICAL GARDENS

URDANETA

North

LUZARRAGA

MONO GOLOSO

BANCO DE PICHINCHA

RUMICHACA

Boca 9

HOTEL DEL CENTRO

PUERTO MORO

ROCA

LA CENTRAL DELI

PRESIDENTE BOUTIQUE HOTEL

SWEET & COFFEE

Plaza

RENDON

HOTEL ELITE INTERNATIONAL

ICAZA

LA MERCED CHURCH

JUNIN

Centenario

9 DE OCTUBRE

HOTEL FONTANA

TOMO HOSTEL

RESACA

YOGURT PERSA AND JUAN VALDEZ

HAMPTON INN

Banco Central

BANCO DEL PACIFICO

To Parque Guayaquil, and Museo Presley Norton

VELEZ

SAN FRANCISCO CHURCH

BANCO DE GUAYAQUIL

LUQUE

CALIFORNIA PANADERIA/ PASTELERIA

LAS 3 CANASTAS

LA ROTONDA

GARAYCOA

AGUIRRE

La Catedral

CHIMBORAZO

CHILE

PEDRO CARBO

MIRADOR

BALLEN

NOGUCHE

SEE DETAIL

SWEET AND COFFEE

LOJA

MARKET

GRAND HOTEL GUAYAQUIL

CATHEDRAL

CC UNICENTRO

Parque Bolívar

El Correo

PALACIO DEL GOBIERNO/ MUSEO NAVAL

HOSTAL MANSO

10 DE AGOSTO

PALACIO MUNICIPAL/ CITY TOURIST OFFICE

SUCRE

BOYACA

PLAZA ADMINISTRACION

MOORISH CLOCK TOWER

RUMICHACA

HENRY MORGAN

IESS

Biblioteca Municipal

COLON

Metrovía North & South

Bastión Popular-Centro

CAMPOS

CHIRIBOGA

Metrovía Stop

BENALCAZAR

CALIXTO ROMERO

NOGUCHE

LAVAYEN

LA BAHÍA

SIMON BOLIVAR

MALL DE MALECÓN

AYACUCHO

LUZARRAGA

OLMEDO

VILLAMIL

MARKET AREA

MALECON

To Palacio del Cristal and Monumento Olmedo

0   200 yds

0   200 m

Río Guayas

PICHINCHA

BAQUERIZO MORENO

PEDRO CARBO

© AVALON TRAVEL

at the end of 9 de Octubre. A highlight is *La Rotonda,* a statue depicting a famous meeting of South America's two most prominent liberators, José de San Martín and Simón Bolívar.

South of La Plaza Cívica is the 23-meter **Moorish Clock Tower.** This is the latest incarnation, built in 1931, of a clock tower that dates back to the 18th century. Just down from the clock tower is the *Henry Morgan* (tel. 4/251-7228, www.barcomorgan.com, 4pm-7:30pm Tues.-Thurs, 4pm-11:30pm Fri., 1pm-10:30pm Sat., 1pm-7:30 Sun., $7, open bar $20), a replica of the famous Welsh pirate's 17th-century ship. A one-hour trip is a great way to see Guayaquil from the river, and trips leave every hour. Tuesday and Wednesday are family night, whereas the weekend is a party crowd. Next is **Plaza Olmedo** with its contemplative monument of José Joaquín de Olmedo (1780-1847), the first mayor of Guayaquil. Beyond that are **La Plaza de la Integración** and a small **artisans market.**

North of *La Rotonda* is a large children's playground leading to a nice set of **botanical gardens** (no phone, open daily, free). The gardens are one of the highlights of Malecón 2000, though they are closed off after dark.

North of the botanical gardens is the **Museo Guayaquil en la Historia** (tel. 4/256-3078, 4pm-6pm Mon.-Fri., 9am-6pm Sat.-Sun., $2.50), which tells a fascinating history of the city from prehistoric times to the present in 14 dioramas. It's one of the few museums in Guayaquil where everything is in English, so it's worth a visit. Above the museum is one of South America's few **IMAX cinemas,** with a 180-degree screen; all shows are in dubbed in Spanish.

Toward the water is **La Perla Guayaquil** (laperladeguayaquil.com, 10am-10pm Mon.-Thurs., 10am-midnight Fri.-Sat., $3.50 weekdays, $5 weekends), the biggest Ferris wheel in South America. From one side you can see downtown Guayaquil; descending, you have a great view of Las Peñas. The wheel moves slowly, so the entrance fee covers just one 12-minute turn.

The north end of Malecón 2000 culminates in the impressive **Museo Antropológico y de Arte Contemporáneo (MAAC)** (Malecón and Loja, tel. 4/230-9400, www. museos.gob.ec/redmuseos/maac, 9am-5pm Tues.-Fri., 10am-4pm Sat.-Sun., $1.50, free Sun.), which has an exhibition on ancient history, a huge collection of pre-Columbian ceramics, and a modern art exhibition.

Numa Pompilio Llona is a quaint colonial street in Las Peñas.

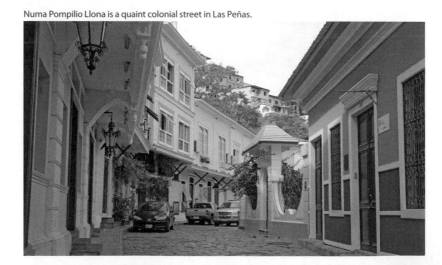

Visitors walk among the urban iguanas of Parque de las Iguanas.

Casa de la Cultura

Casa de la Cultura (9 de Octubre 1200 and Pedro Moncayo, tel. 4/230-0500, 10am-6pm Tues.-Fri., 9am-3pm Sat., $1) is a museum with an impressive collection of art and archaeology located in **Plaza Centenario.**

Parque Histórico

Across the bridge in the wealthy district of Entre Ríos, the eight-hectare **Parque Histórico** (Entre Ríos, tel. 4/283-3807, www. parquehistorico.gob.ec, 9am-5pm Wed.-Sun., free) is a fun, cheap trip out of town if you have time to kill. The park is divided into three zones: The wildlife zone was created out of the natural mangroves of the Río Daule, though the enclosures are more reminiscent of a zoo. The traditions zone has reconstructed some of Guayaquil's lost colonial buildings. Inside one of the colonial buildings is **Casa Julián,** an expensive restaurant that is part of **Hotel Oro Verde.** Comedy shows and boisterous music are also free in the plaza on weekends. There are buses to Entre Ríos from the terminal, or get a taxi from downtown ($4-5).

Isla Santay

Take a relaxing bike ride along raised wooden paths through the verdant coastal forests of **Isla Santay** (www.islasantay.info, 6am-5pm daily, free, $4 bike rental). The island was originally inhabited by fishers who lived in isolation in small huts among the swamps. In recent years the government undertook an ambitious project to improve their quality of life by building a bridge and launching the island as a tourist attraction. Now there is a small eco-village where a restaurant serves typical plates for $3-4, a couple shops sell souvenirs, and a pen holds native crocodiles. In previous years, you could take the Metrovía to station Barrio Centenario and walk four blocks to the bridge to the island. However, in 2017 a boat crashed into the bridge, making it necessary to take a taxi to Duran and then ferry to the island ($5). Bridge reconstruction is currently in progress.

pink spoonbills in Manglares Churute Reserve

★ Manglares Churute Reserve

Most of Ecuador's mainland mangrove and coastal forests have been decimated in favor of shrimp farming. Manglares Churute, an hour outside of Guayaquil, is one of the few areas where you can experience this unique ecosystem. The reserve encompasses 49 hectares. The Sendero de Monos Aulladores is a relatively flat trail going through tropical dry forest where you occasionally spy howling monkeys and birds high in the trees, and a waterfall in wet season. Sendero de Cerro Mate, right at the registry office, is a steep two-hour hike ascending a hill in a similar forested area. Sendero La Flora is a short, 300-meter trail that leads to the dock where visitors take a motorized canoe through the mangrove-lined estuaries. This canoe ride is the highlight of the area, and bird sightings include hundreds of native and migratory species such as ospreys, hornbills, and herons. Unfortunately, it is impossible to visit this highlight independently, as the trailhead is miles from the registry area. Even with a private vehicle, the fishers who drive the canoes tend to be out fishing without coordination with the tour operators. Tour prices ($125-250) depend on how many people are in the group, and most are booked as private, small-group tours. Hence, plan well in advance if you're traveling alone. Swarming mosquitoes inhabit the tropical forests and are far worse than on the Galápagos, so cover up accordingly. Sendero de Cerro Mate is the only part of the reserve that can be visited independently via a bus from the Terminal Terrestre (take the bus toward Naranjal and ask to stop at the reserve; look for the registration desk at km 15 on the highway; one hour, $1.50).

Tours

Tour operators in Guayaquil often specialize in Galápagos tours, although some also offer guided city tours and tours of the areas surrounding Guayaquil.

Viasam Tours (tel. 9/9200-1612, http://viasam.com.ec) is an agency with a wide variety of offerings—from Galápagos cruises and island hopping to day tours in Guayaquil. Day tours include city tours downtown, Manglares Churute Reserve, neighboring cacao farms and fruit plantations, and dolphin watching at the small town of Puerto Morro.

Hacienda Agroturística Lara (tel. 9/6868-5890, kerlymartinezgutierrez.92@gmail.com) is the principal operator of Manglares Churute tours and can offer birdwatching in the reserve and neighboring lagoon. They also own and operate a nearby cacao farm.

Turibus (tel. 4/232-7384, www.turibus.com.ec, 10am-8pm daily, $8 pp) doubledecker tourist buses make the rounds of the Malecón 2000, Las Peñas, and the major parks and plazas. Hop-on hop-off tours leave from the Plaza Olmedo at the south end of Malecón 2000 every hour on the hour.

ENTERTAINMENT AND EVENTS
Nightlife

Guayaquil's nightlife rivals Quito's, and the locals, of course, will tell you that it beats the capital hands down. As in Quito, bars are usually empty before 9pm, and the night gets going toward midnight on weekends. The in places change regularly, so for the latest information, visit www.farras.com or www.guayaquilcaliente.com.

The breezy staircase of **Cerro Santa Ana** makes it a pleasant area to visit at night, with countless small bars frequented by a young crowd of locals. It's also far safer than alternative nightspots in the city, with regular police patrols. The typical bar on the staircase is nondescript, pumps reggaeton and electronica beats, and sells beer by the keg.

Hidden away from the main drag on the staircase, around the corner to the right and up cobbled Numa Pompilio Llona in **Las Peñas,** are unique bars with a bohemian vibe. First is **Rayuela** (Numa Pompilio Llona 206, tel. 99/930-9318, 5pm-2am Mon.-Sat., 9am-4pm Sun.), a dark, candlelit café-bar filled with groups of locals chatting over cocktails to chill rock music. Next is one of Guayaquil's most interesting bars, **La Paleta** (Numa Pompilio Llona 174, tel. 4/232-0930, 8am-2am Tues.-Sat., $15 minimum consumption). The city's creative crowd comes here to enjoy the eclectic, colorful decor, low ceilings, cozy nooks and crannies, and wide-ranging menu of cocktails and tapas. It epitomizes the arty atmosphere of the district, and if you're not in Guayaquil for long, this is one place you shouldn't miss. Last is **Arthur's** (Numa Pompilio Llona 127, tel. 4/231-2230, 7pm-midnight Mon.-Thurs., 7pm-2am Fri.-Sat.), a two-story restaurant-bar with live music on weekends. Locals head here to enjoy snacks, take in the beautiful view of the river, and chat on the breezy open-air patio.

Theaters

The best theatrical performances are at the **Teatro Centro de Arte** (Vía a la Costa, km 4.5, tel. 4/200-3699, www.teatrocentrodearte.org) north of the center (take a taxi). **Centro Cultural Sarao** (Ciudadela Kennedy, tel.

4/229-5118) also has dance and theater performances Friday-Saturday.

FOOD

Downtown Guayaquil and **Malecón 2000** are not great places to wander for food. The majority of the options are cheap chain fast food, food courts, and holes-in-the-wall offering $2-3 *almuerzos* (set lunches) of variable quality. There are a few midrange restaurants scattered throughout downtown and expensive business-oriented restaurants hidden inside hotels. The Malecón's food courts on the north end and near the IMAX offer greasy, uninspired food for $4-6.

In contrast, the **Urdesa** district northeast of downtown (a $4 taxi ride) has many good restaurants and far more international options than downtown, making it easy to wander into something delicious.

At the **Malecón Salado,** the **patio de mariscos** is an open-air plaza with several informal seafood stalls with a wide range of options. You can also find generic chain coffee from **Juan Valdez** and **Sweet & Coffee** in many places around the city. These are reliable places for an air-conditioned break and clean bathrooms.

Downtown and Malecón 2000

★ **El Mono Goloso** (Luzarraga 202 at Panama, tel. 9/9802-1567, 8am-6:30pm Mon.-Fri, 11am-5pm Sat., expresso drinks, pastries, and bread $1-3) is a tiny French-style bakery with Guayaquil's only house-made sourdough bread, as well as baguettes, croissants, eclairs, tartlets, and espresso drinks. For best results, time your visit to their baking schedule; pastries come fresh out of the oven in the morning, the baguettes at 11am, and the sourdough at noon. There's no air-conditioning.

★ **La Central Deli** (Panama at Luzarraga, tel. 9/8098-1579, 8:30am-6:30pm Mon.-Sat., sandwiches and salads $4-7) is a cute, succulent-adorned fast-casual place with a fantastic variety of large salads (try the Greek with kale, chickpea, feta, and quinoa) and sandwiches, made on fresh baguettes from

El Mono Goloso, the bakery across the street. The *banh mi* is particularly good. There's no air-conditioning.

Yogurt Persa (Boyaca at 9 de Octubre, inside the Juan Valdez, no phone, 8am-7pm Mon.-Thurs., 8am-10pm Fri., 9am-10pm Sat., 8am-7pm Sun., drink combos $2-3) is a fast-food spot with tropical-fruit-flavored, ice-blended yogurt drinks and *pan de yuca* (savory bread made out of yucca starch and cheese). Ask for the yogurt *natural, sin azúcar* (natural, no sugar) if you don't have a sweet tooth.

Las 3 Canastas (Vélez and Chile, no phone, breakfast, lunch, and dinner daily, $1-4) hits the mark; wash down empanadas, *humitas* (corn cakes), and other snacks with a huge variety of juices and shakes containing fruit you may never have heard of. There's a sister café at Pedro Carbo and Clemente Ballén.

Victoria Café (Jardines Botánicos, Malecón, tel. 98/147-5302, lunch and dinner daily, entrées $7-15) serves meat, chicken, and fish dishes in the cool, shaded atmosphere of the botanical gardens on the *malecón*. The food quality and value are just average, but the atmosphere is nice.

La Canoa (Chile between 10 de Agosto and Ballén, tel. 4/232-9270, breakfast, lunch, and dinner daily, entrées $9-12), attached to the Hotel Continental, is informal and offers reasonably priced Ecuadorian dishes such as goat or chicken stew, though the breakfast buffet ($15) is overpriced for the quality.

La Resaca (Malecón 2000 at Junín, tel. 099/942-3390, 11am-midnight Mon.-Wed., 11am-2am Thurs.-Sat., 11am-11pm Sun., $5-12) is the boat-shaped restaurant right on the Malecón. It attracts primarily tourists with well-prepared Ecuadorian food as well as hamburgers and sandwiches. The $3.50 *almuerzo* is a lunch bargain if you like lots of rice and a little meat. Its main seating area has panoramic windows overlooking the bay.

For an upscale experience, try **Puerto Moro** (Córdova at Junín, tel. 4/230-0407, www.puertomoro.com, 2pm-10pm Mon.-Sat.,

$15-25). The signature dish is *arroz moro* (rice with lentils and fresh cheese), served alongside grilled meat, chicken, and seafood. You can actually see the huge portions of meat on the grill through a Plexiglas window into the kitchen area.

El Caracol Azul (9 de Octubre 1918 at Los Ríos, tel. 4/228-0461, http://elcaracolazul.ec, lunch and dinner Mon.-Sat., entrées $10-20) is a frequently recommended restaurant for seafood. Though you are likely to be one of several tourists here, their reputation for high-quality seafood and good service is well-deserved. Try the salmon in tarragon or shrimp in coconut.

Urdesa

Urdesa's restaurants are conveniently located on a central avenue. This list is from south to north.

The **Red Crab** (Victor Emilio Estrada and Laureles, tel. 4/288-7632, www.redcrab.com. ec, lunch and dinner daily, entrées $15-20) is an upscale place with quality seafood—crab, shrimp, and lobster—cooked every way imaginable. If in doubt, try the coconut sauce.

Frutabar (Victor Emilio Estrada at Las Monjas, tel. 4/230-0743, www.frutabar.com, 8am-midnight daily, entrées $5-10) is a dimly-lit, tropical tiki bar-restaurant that feels like a beachside shack. The front patio faces the loud main street. Order a huge fruit smoothie, a creative hamburger, or a large salad and head to the back room, where the chill music, tropical murals, and rustic wood furniture might make you forget where you are. There is also a location downtown at Malecón 2000 and Martínez.

A slice of Italy in Ecuador, **L'Italiano Ristorante** (Victor Emilio Estrada at Las Monjas, tel. 4/502-3111, http://litaliano.com. ec, $9-18) serves up authentic antipasti, pasta, pizza, lasagna, and tiramisu in an intimate, upscale space.

★ **Camelliastea** (Victor Emilio Estrada at Ficus, tel. 4/503-4031, 10:30am-8:30pm Mon.-Thurs., 10:30am-11pm Fri., 11am-9pm Sat. tea $3, entrées $7-12, desserts $5) is Guayaquil's best teahouse. Whether you are vegan, lactose-intolerant, paleo, gluten-free, or no-sugar, Camelliastea has you covered. Customizable teas come in infinite combinations given the creative flavors (grapefruit-ginger, guayusa, rose), milk bases (coconut, almond, cashew, rice), and boba. There are also creative salads, acai bowls, smoothies, sandwiches, and entrées like lasagna, veggie burgers and spiralized zuchini "pasta." For dessert, try the guiltless avocado, cacao, almond flour, stevia, and raspberry cake.

Juice Club (Victor Emilio Estrada at Ebanos, tel. 9/8661-4983, 7am-11pm daily, $3-5) is a fast-casual, air-conditioned place to start a health kick, with large, reasonably priced green salads, cold-pressed green and detox juices, superfood smoothies, fruit salads, and acai bowls. Try to make your food greener than the Astroturf that covers the walls and floor. There is also a location downtown at 9 de Octubre at Machala.

For sushi, try **Saitama** (Urdesa Central, Diagonal 417 at Victor Emilio Estrada, tel. 4/288-6725, noon-11pm Mon.-Fri., 6:30pm-11pm Sat., $8-15), a small, family-run restaurant with bright decor and huge rolls and high-quality fish. The friendly service and huge tuna rolls have garnered this restaurant a loyal local following.

ACCOMMODATIONS

Most visitors stay in **downtown Guayaquil,** which is conveniently located for sightseeing, although the area is rather unattractive and noisy, so ask for a back room or a higher floor. Walking around to find a room is relatively easy, though it's not pleasant in the heat. Visitors passing through town can find hotels near the airport, although the quick taxi ride downtown ($5) makes staying downtown almost equally easy. Many of the cheap *hostales* have tiny or no signs on the door—look for the street number. Breakfast is included unless noted otherwise. Most of Guayaquil's mid-range to high-end hotels cater to people traveling on business, so don't expect hotels with a lot of personality or charm. A hip alternative is to stay in **Urdesa,** which is cleaner than downtown and where most of the international restaurants are.

An unfortunate note about staying in dorms in Guayaquil is that sleep quality is far worse than staying in dorms in Quito. Since many travelers only crash for one night, there's a constant shuffle of departures late at night and early in the morning, as well as a less social atmosphere.

Under $50

The most popular hostel downtown is **Tomo Hostel** (Victor Manuel Rendon 212 at Panama, tel. 4/256-2683, $18 dorm, $49-55 s, $77 d, $98-110 t, $102 q, breakfast and towels extra), located just a block away from the Malecón. The hostel has comfortable mixed dorms with individual outlets and shelves, plus a sunny patio with hanging wicker cocoons. The biggest downside is penny-pinching policies that detract from the experience; there's no air-conditioning in the rooms until 8pm, and each dorm room is filled to capacity before empty dorm rooms are used. There's food storage but no cooking allowed in the kitchen. Common areas are fan-only.

Edgy, bohemian **Nazu City Hostel** (Juan Montalvo #102 at Av. Malecón, tel. 9/9911-51587, http://nazucityhostel.com, $14 dorm, $41-49 d, $72 t, $96 q, breakfast and towels included) isn't afraid to be funky with murals, Astroturf, and recycled pallet furniture. Dorms are average quality, though air-conditioning is available in the rooms whenever, you can cook in the shared kitchen, there's even a small on-site gym and table tennis. Tip for female travelers: Request a bunk in the three-bed, women-only dorm because it's the same price as the mixed five-bed and eight-bed dorm rooms. Common areas are fan-only.

Hotel Elite International (Baquerizo Moreno 902 at Junín, tel. 4/256-5385, $28 s, $30 d) is an aspirationally named budget hotel that is neither elite nor international. The rooms look frumpy and the street noise can be loud, but overall the hotel has some of the cheapest clean, private rooms in downtown.

Amenities include Wi-Fi and cable TV, though they don't serve breakfast.

Hotel La Fontana (P. Icaza 404 at Córdova, tel. 4/230-7230, www.lafontana-ecuador.com, $35-40 s, $40-45 d, $60 t) is a mundane but non-objectionable hotel that caters primarily to businesspeople. Guest rooms are modern, with air-conditioning, private baths with hot water, cable TV, and telephones. The lobby on the second floor has a breezy sitting area, sleek decor, and a sunny patio.

A solid budget choice for couples is **Hotel del Centro** (Junín 412 at Córdova, tel. 4/256-2114, hotel-delcentro@hotmail.com, $40 s, $44 d). Service is minimal, with the receptionist behind a glass window. It's hard to find complaints about the bright, modern rooms and firm beds at this price point, though, and the location is very central.

$50-100

Presidente Boutique Hotel (Junín 407 at Córdova, tel. 4/503-7000, http://presidente-boutique.com, $75 d) is a well-located, immaculate, business-oriented hotel that borders on classy, with well-appointed rooms that are better decorated than most, with several textures of neutrals.

Yu SmartHotel (Rocafuerte at Loja, tel. 4/259-7850, www.yuhotels.com, $59 d) is an architect's futuristic vision of how to maximize sleep quality per dollar. Rooms have California king beds with impossibly white sheets and duvets. The beds are so large that they fill the small rooms, leaving just enough space for a small desk, flat-screen TV, and modern bathroom. Don't expect any superfluous amenities like pools or gyms at this minimalist establishment. There is, however, a tiny Astroturf terrace and dining area where continental breakfast and snacks are served.

If the drab streets of downtown don't appeal to you, escape to ★ **Cedros Inn** (Cedros Sur 107 at Estrada, tel. 4/504-5754, www.cedrosinn.com, $60 d, $100 suite) in Urdesa. The stylish boutique hotel was built in a renovated colonial-style house with a tiny dipping pool and lounge chairs. Urdesa is possibly Guayaquil's best neighborhood for browsing international and Ecuadorian restaurants and bars, and it's far cleaner than downtown. Though all the downtown tourist attractions will be a bus or taxi ride away, you can "live like a local" in Urdesa. For a splurge, get a suite with a Jacuzzi.

Over $100

With a couple exceptions, most of the luxury hotels in Guayaquil are plush and modern, though a little generic and business-oriented.

Hotel Continental (Chile 512 at 10 de Agosto, tel. 4/232-9270, www.hotelcontinental.com.ec, $140 d, $194 suite) overlooks Iguana Park. Its standard rooms are modern and very comfortable if unremarkable, but the suites are fantastic, with a spacious living room and everything recently remodeled. It has three restaurants on-site: the Canoa for casual though pricey Ecuadorian, the more upscale El Fortín, and El Astillero, a cocktail bar with a view.

On the other side of Parque de las Iguanas is the elegant **Unipark Hotel** (Ballén 406 at Chile, tel. 4/232-7100, U.S. tel. 800/447-7462, www.uniparkhotel.com, $75-120 s or d). Guests can pick from three classes of rooms: The standard and business class rooms are plush, if a bit generic, and the more expensive signature rooms were recently remodeled and have views of the park. On-site restaurants include the casual Unicafe and the upstairs Unibar, which specializes in sushi and has great views of the park. There's also a gym with a hot tub and a sauna.

If you're looking for amenities galore and great service, **Hotel Oro Verde** (9 de Octubre and Moreno, tel. 4/232-7999, www.oroverdehotels.com, $140-200 s or d, buffet breakfast and airport transfers included) is easily the top hotel in Guayaquil. The downtown location boasts 192 guest rooms and 62 suites with air-conditioning, satellite TV, and video players. There's also a deli, a casino, three gourmet restaurants, a piano bar, and a fitness center. There's also a second location in Parque Histórico that is more secluded. The high-end decor may feel a little predictable, but Hotel Oro Verde continues to be recognized as one of Ecuador's most award-winning hotels.

★ **Mansión del Río Boutique** (Numa Pompilio Llona 120, tel. 4/256-6044, www.mansiondelrio-ec.com, $150-200 d) was originally the residence of a wealthy British family, and it is now Guayaquil's only hotel with a sense of history. Though the rooms have modern amenities such as Wi-Fi and cable TV, many of the furnishings are original, with chandeliers dripping in crystal, ornate carved wood, and museum-worthy paintings.

In addition, Guayaquil has several international chain hotels. The **Hampton Inn** (www.hamptoninn.com) is in a central location downtown. Of hotels near the airport, the **Holiday Inn Airport Hotel** (www.holidayinn.com) is the closest (it's within walking distance), and the **Hilton Colón Guayaquil** (www.hilton.com) is the most luxurious.

INFORMATION AND SERVICES

The **city tourism office** (Ballén and Pichincha, tel. 4/252-4100, www.guayaquil.gov.ec, 9am-5pm Mon.-Fri.), opposite the Palacio Municipal, stocks general information about the city and the area. There's also a small visitor information center in a train car north of La Rotonda on the *malecón*.

Head to Pichincha and Icaza, near the *malecón*, to find **Banco de Guayaquil** and **Banco Pichincha,** both of which have ATMs and offer credit-card cash advances. **Banco del Pacífico** has an ATM nearby on Icaza and Pichincha.

There are a couple large, air-conditioned malls with good-size chain food courts in Guayaquil: **Mall del Sol** and **Mall del Marino.** They are too generic for tourist shopping or as restaurant destinations, but useful if you need to buy something; a taxi from downtown is $4.

If you need to reach the national **police,** dial 101. The closest police station to downtown is the **Unidad de Policía Comunitaria** at Rendon and Panama. There are several **hospitals** in Guayaquil: the U.S. Consulate recommends **Clínica Kennedy** (Av. San Jorge between la Novena and la Décima, tel. 4/228-6963, www.hospikennedy.med.ec) and **Hospital Alcívar** (Idelfonso Coronel and Mendel, tel. 4/372-0100, www.hospitalalcivar.com).

GETTING THERE AND AROUND

Air

Guayaquil's award-winning **José J. Olmedo International Airport** (airport code GYE, Las Américas, tel. 4/216-9000, www.tagsa.aero) is five kilometers north of the city center. It has flights to a wide range of North American, South American, and some European destinations, as well as to national destinations such as the Galápagos Islands. Taxis from downtown cost $5 and take about 10 minutes. You can also exit the airport, cross the street using the pedestrian bridge, and find a **Metrovía** light-rail service to downtown ($0.25).

Bus and Light Rail

The poor traffic situation downtown means that **local buses** ($0.25) are not really worth it for short distances. Even then, buses are slow and often jam-packed, and pickpockets can be a problem. Bus number 52 goes from the *malecón* to Urdesa and number 2 goes to the airport.

The **Metrovía** light-rail service (tel. 4/213-0402, www.metrovia-gye.com.ec, $0.25) is cleaner and faster, though still very crowded. The line runs south from Hospital Luis Vernaza to La Catedral, the most convenient stop for the downtown sights, and then farther south. It returns north from Biblioteca Municipal to Las Peñas and north to the bus terminal. Note that pickpockets are also a problem on Metrovía, so don't carry valuables, and be vigilant.

Taxi

Taxi drivers in Guayaquil are notorious for driving badly and overcharging foreigners. Few of them use meters, so negotiate the price in advance. It's worth asking at your hotel for the approximate price and then telling the driver, rather than waiting for them to give you an inflated price. As a guide, short journeys around downtown should be about $3, trips from downtown to Urdesa and other northern districts $4, and transfers to the airport $5. Never take unmarked cabs, and if possible, ask your hotel to call you a taxi from a reputable company. Reliable firms include **Movisat** (tel. 4/259-3333), **Fastline** (tel. 4/282-3333), and **Solservice** (tel. 4/287-1195). If you have data service on your phone (through international roaming or a local SIM card), using **Uber** is convenient, secure, and less expensive than a taxi.

Quito

Ecuador's capital is a city that scales many heights, not least in terms of altitude. The second-highest capital in the world after Bolivia's La Paz, Quito (population 1.8 million) sits at 2,850 meters above sea level in a valley hemmed in by mountains, including the twin peaks of Volcán Pichincha. Quito's dramatic geographical position gives the city a long, thin shape: spread out over 50 kilometers long but just 8 kilometers wide.

Quito is best known for the wealth of colonial architecture in the Old Town: churches, monasteries, and museums set among stately plazas and cobbled streets. The New Town is quite a contrast, with plenty of international restaurants, hotels, and tourism services, but it also has some interesting museums. The city

Plaza Grande is the heart of colonial Old Town.

also has several breathtaking viewpoints to appreciate its dramatic location. Quito's altitude can leave you feeling breathless and lightheaded, so take things slowly, eat light food, avoid alcohol, and take a rest if you feel dizzy.

SAFETY

The biggest problems in Quito are **pickpocketing** and **purse-snatching.** Pickpocketing is rampant on the bus and light-rail systems and in popular tourist spots downtown. Do not carry valuables in your pockets or backpacks with front pockets; if you must, carry the backpack on your chest rather than your back. If you walk through crowded areas or go on public transportation, keep a hand on your purse or wallet. If you are sightseeing, carrying cameras and valuables, *do not* use these services; take a taxi instead. Smartphones are a particularly common target; you should not take out your smartphone in the street or leave it on restaurant tables.

The historic center is surprisingly dodgy

at night, and it is not recommended to walk around at night except for the pedestrian street of La Ronda. Be aware that the popular nightlife district, La Mariscal, seems safer than it is at night. Though there is lots of pedestrian traffic along clean, well-lit streets, it is the other hot spot for pickpockets, many of whom flock here to opportunistically prey on drunk partiers from the district's many bars. Be aware of your surroundings at night, and if you plan on drinking a lot, take a taxi back to your hotel. Lastly, do not walk the road between downtown and El Panecillo even during the day; there have been several incidents of **robberies** on that road.

Another problem in Quito is *secuestros exprés,* or express kidnappings. This occurs when unsuspecting victims take a taxi and the taxi driver takes them to an ATM and forces them (usually at gunpoint) to withdraw money. Quito now requires all officially registered taxis to have a video camera (which tapes the inside of the taxi) and a red emergency button that alerts the authorities with the location of the taxi. It is preferable to ask your hotel to call you a taxi from a reputable company. If you hail a cab in the street, inspect the video camera when you get in. It should have a piece of tape over it, which indicates it has not been tampered with. If anything happens, push the red emergency button.

The last and scariest problem in major cities in Ecuador (including Quito and Guayaquil) is **scopolamine drugging.** Scopolamine is a hypnotic drug also known as the zombie's breath because victims are coherent but without free will of their own, and they wake up with no memory of the last night. Scopolamine is administered through food, drinks, aerosols, or, in some cases, even touch. Victims have been sexually assaulted and robbed during scopolamine incidents. Avoid strangers offering food, drink, and cigarettes, and, of course, watch your drinks at the bar.

Quito

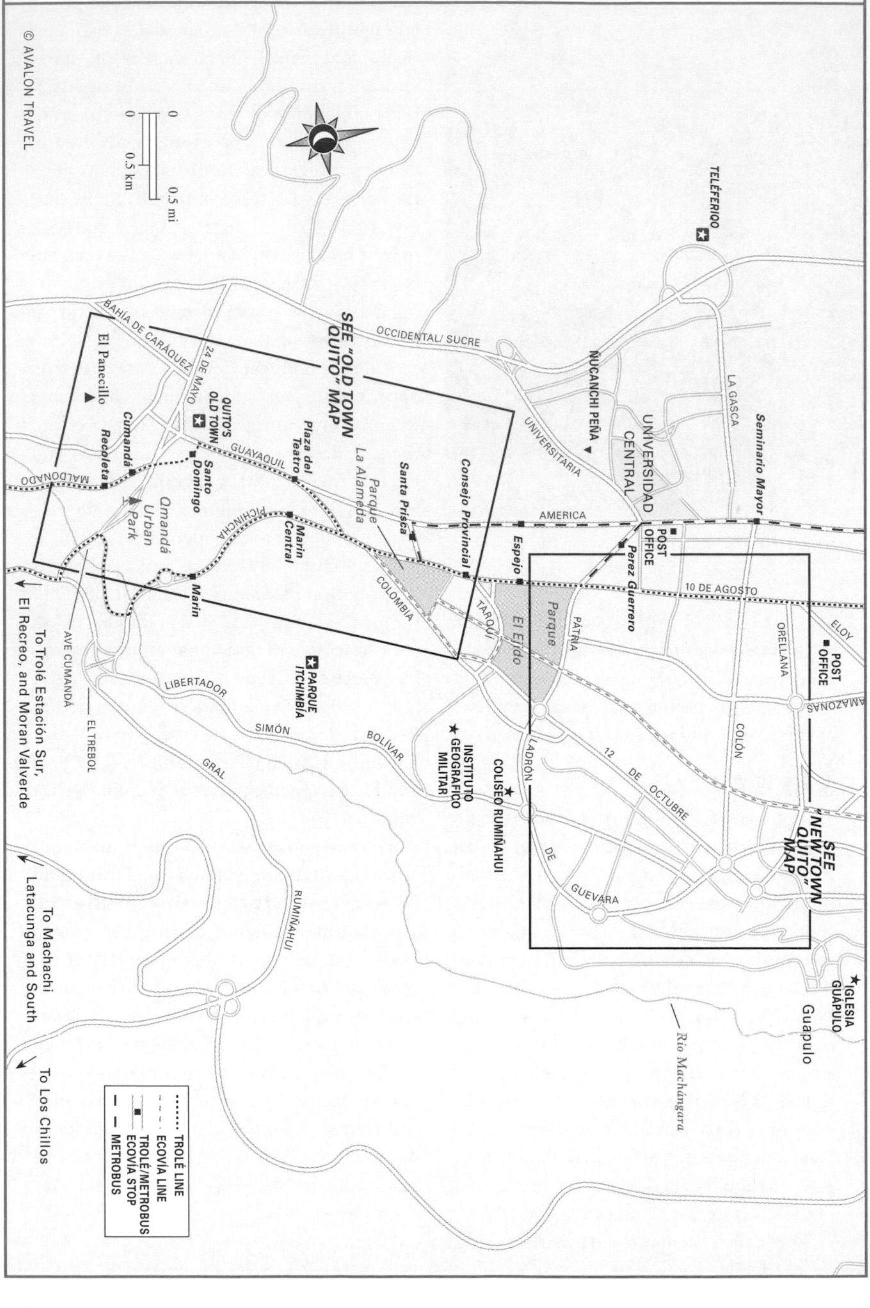

© AVALON TRAVEL

0
0   0.5 mi
0.5 km

TELEFÉRICO

SEE "OLD TOWN QUITO" MAP

OCCIDENTAL/ SUCRE

BAHIA DE CARAQUEZ

El Panecillo ▲

24 DE MAYO

QUITO'S OLD TOWN

Cumandá
Recoleta

GUAYAQUIL

Santo Domingo

Plaza del Teatro

Parque La Alameda

Santa Prisca

Consejo Provincial

NUCANCHI PEÑA ▼

UNIVERSITARIA

LA GASCA

Seminario Mayor

UNIVERSIDAD CENTRAL

MALDONADO

Omandá Urban Park

PICHINCHA

Marín Central

COLOMBIA

Espejo

AMERICA

POST OFFICE

Perez Guerrero

10 DE AGOSTO

POST OFFICE

Marín

AVE CUMANDA

EL TREBOL

LIBERTADOR

SIMÓN

GRAL

TARQUI

EL EJIDO

Parque

PATRIA

ORELLANA

ELOY

AMAZONAS

COLÓN

12   DE   OCTUBRE

PARQUE ITCHIMBIA

BOLIVAR

INSTITUTO GEOGRAFICO MILITAR

COLISEO RUMIÑAHUI

LADRÓN

DE

GUEVARA

SEE "NEW TOWN QUITO" MAP

RUMIÑAHUI

To Trolé Estación Sur, El Recreo, and Moran Valverde

To Machachi Latacunga and South

To Los Chillos

IGLESIA GUAPULO

Guapulo

Río Machángara

TROLÉ LINE
ECOVIA LINE
TROLÉ/METROBUS
ECOVIA STOP
METROBUS

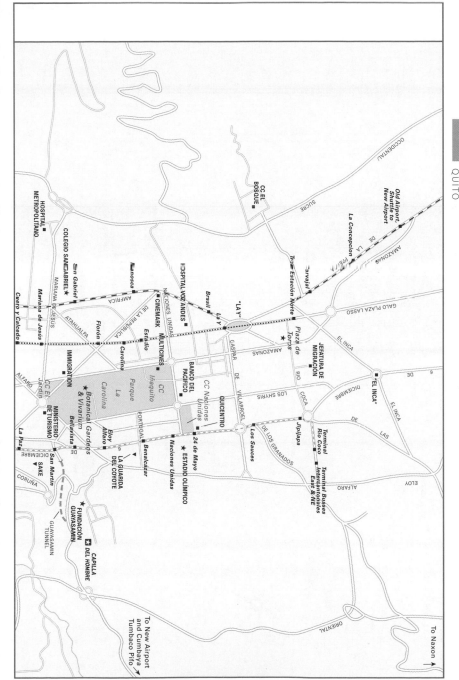

Old Town Quito

© AVALON TRAVEL

···· Trolé Line
----- Ecovía Line
■ Trolé/
  Ecovía Stop
— Metrobus

MARISCAL SUCRE

CHIMBORAZO

ROCAFUERTE

LOJA

LÓPEZ

BOLÍVAR

BAHÍA DE CARÁQUEZ

AMBATO

IMBABURA

MIDEROS

CHILE

El Panecillo

MONASTERIO EL CARMEN ALTO

BOUTIQUE PORTAL DE CANTUÑA

IGLESIA SAN FRANCISCO

CASA GANGOTENA

▼ TIANGUEZ
Plaza San Francisco

CENTRO CULTURAL METROPOLITANO

PALACIO DE PRESIDENCIAL ★
HOTEL PLAZA GRANDE
ARCHBISHOP'S PALACE ★

Plaza Grande

IGLESIA SAN AGUSTÍN ★

▼ VISTA HERMOSA

MUSEO DE LA CIUDAD ★

MUSEO NUMISMÁTICO ★

CASA MARÍA AUGUSTA URRUTIA ★

SUCRE

LA COMPAÑÍA ★

CATHEDRAL ★

IGLESIA EL SAGRARIO ★

QUITO VISITORS' BUREAU

LA

RONDA

MASAYA HOSTEL

Santa Domingo

GUAYAQUIL ST

QUITO'S OLD TOWN ✚

POST OFFICE

ESPEJO

GALLETTI

SANTA CATALINA ★

LA PURÍSIMA ▼

PIZZERIA S.A

TEATRO BOLÍVAR ★

Plaza Grande

24 DE

RONDA

LEÑA QUITEÑA ▼

CASONA DE LA RONDA

LA CASA DEL POZO

MAMACUCHARA

IGLESIA SANTO DOMINGO ✚

Plaza Santo Domingo

5 DE

MALDONADO

La Recoleta

Cumandá

LOJA

24 DE MAYO

OMANDA PARQUE URBANO

TEXEIRA

JUNÍN

PICHINCHA

CHILE

María Terminal

↙ To Trolé Estación Sur

0   250 yds
0   250 m

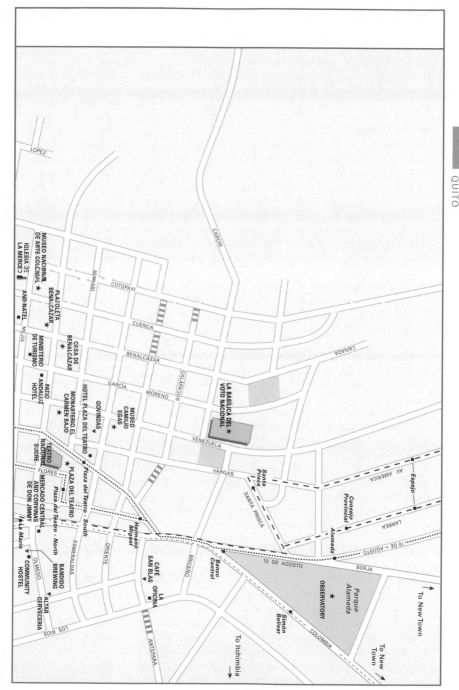

SIGHTS AND TOURS

If the altitude doesn't make your head spin, the amount to see in Quito probably will. Visitors could easily spend weeks here seeing the sights. If you only have a couple of days, spend one day in Old Town and one in New Town.

★ Old Town

Quito's Old Town is a joy to wander around following a multimillion-dollar regeneration. Though you do see some recently built structures, many of the buildings date from the Spanish colonial era; the oldest is the Iglesia San Francisco, which dates from 1536. Sunday is the best day for sightseeing because cars are completely prohibited in central Old Town between 9am and 4pm. Pedestrians, bicycles, and street performers take over the streets. The city plans to make several streets in Old Town pedestrian-only around the clock.

A good starting point is **Plaza Grande,** once the focal point of colonial-era Quito and now a popular gathering place. On the plaza's southwest side, the **Catedral Metropolitana de Quito** (mass 6am-9am daily) is actually the third to stand on this site. Next door, formerly the main chapel of the cathedral, the **Iglesia El Sagrario** (tel. 2/228-4398, 9am-5pm Mon.-Fri., 7am-8pm Sat., free) houses impressive paintings and stained-glass windows. On the northwest side lies the **Palacio Presidencial** (tel. 2/382-7118, tours 9am-4pm Tues.-Sun., free), where you can take a tour when the government is not in session (bring your passport). On the northeast side of the plaza lies the **Palacio Arzobispal** (Archbishop's Palace), a colonial house with wooden balconies, thick whitewashed walls, and an indoor courtyard housing small shops and eateries.

Around the corner from the Plaza Grande is the opulent **La Compañía church** (tel. 2/258-1895, 9:30am-4:30pm Mon.-Thurs., 9:30am-5:30pm Fri.-Sat., 12:30pm-4pm Sun, $5), one of the most beautiful churches in the Americas and certainly the most extravagant. Seven tonnes of gold supposedly ended up on the ceiling, walls, and altars of "Quito's Sistine Chapel," which was built by the wealthy Jesuit order between 1605 and 1765.

Turn right up the hill past La Compañía to **Plaza San Francisco,** one of Quito's most beautiful squares. The plaza is dominated by the wide facade of the **Iglesia San Francisco** (tel. 2/228-1124, 5pm-6pm Fri.-Sun., free), the largest religious complex in South America. Notice how many of the design motifs come from indigenous cultures, including the faces of sun gods and harvest symbols of flowers and fruit. To the right of the main entrance, the **Museo San Francisco** (tel. 2/295-2911, 9am-5:30pm Mon.-Sat., 9am-1:30pm Sun., $2) houses one of the finest collections of colonial art in Quito, dating from the 16th-19th centuries. On the other side, the **Capilla de Catuña** (tel. 2/228-1124, 8am-5pm Tues.-Thurs., free) also has colonial art on display. According to legend, this chapel was constructed by an indigenous man named Catuña who sold his soul to the devil in order to complete it on time.

Down the hill southeast of Plaza San Francisco is the elegant **Plaza Santo Domingo.** In the middle of the square is a statue of Antonio José de Sucre, a Venezuelan independence leader, pointing to the site of his victory on the slopes of Pichincha. Bordering the plaza is **Iglesia Santo Domingo** (no phone, 9am-5pm Mon.-Fri., 9am-2pm Sat., free) and the attached **Museo Fray Pedro Bedón** (tel. 2/228-2695, 9am-4:30pm Mon.-Fri., 9am-2pm Sat.-Sun., $2), which has obligatory tour guides to take you through the chapels.

Nearby is one of the best-preserved colonial streets in Old Town. **La Ronda** was nicknamed for the evening serenades (*rondas*) that once floated through its winding path. The narrow lane is lined with painted balconies, shops, traditional art workshops, tiny art galleries, and cafés. It's reached most easily via Guayaquil, sloping down from the Plaza Santo Domingo. This is one of the most popular evening haunts for *Quiteños* and visitors to soak up the atmosphere with a drink and

However, its two imposing, 115-meter towers make this the tallest church in Ecuador. Notice that the "gargoyles" are actually a menagerie of local animals, including armadillos. You can ride the elevator and then climb the northern steeple or east tower for the fantastic views.

Above Old Town
EL PANECILLO

Old Town's skyline is dominated by **El Panecillo,** a 30-meter statue of the Virgin of Quito on the hill at the southern end. You can climb up inside the base (9am-6pm Mon.-Thurs., 9am-9pm Fri.-Sun., $1) to an observation platform for a spectacular view of the city. Note that the neighborhood on the way up is dangerous, so take a taxi and ask the driver to wait. The area at the top of the hill has security until 7pm. A taxi ride costs about $3-4 one-way, $8 round-trip including a short wait.

★ PARQUE ITCHIMBÍA

Parque Itchimbía is Quito's most spectacular park—complete with the ultramod **Itchimbía Cultural Center** (tel. 2/295-0272, ext. 137, 9am-5pm daily, $1) and 34 hectares of gardens where the locals picnic, go running, and enjoy the stunning panoramic views of Old Town. Just below on Samaniego is the restaurant **Mosaico,** along with several happening spots for drinks and elite elbow-rubbing that justify their prices every evening at sunset. A taxi from Old Town costs $3.

New Town

Casa de la Cultura (6 de Diciembre and Patria) is one of the best collections of museums in Ecuador. The centerpiece of the complex is **Museo del Banco Central** (tel. 2/222-3528, 9am-5pm Tues.-Fri., 10am-4pm Sat.-Sun., free), a world unto itself and easily Ecuador's most impressive museum. The collection includes more than 1,500 pieces of pre-Inca pottery, gold artifacts, and colonial and contemporary art.

To learn about the indigenous cultures of the Ecuadorian rainforest, head to **Museo**

the spectacular views from Parque Itchimbía

some traditional music. It is well guarded and a completely pedestrian-only zone.

Just up from La Ronda is **Museo de la Ciudad** (García Moreno and Rocafuerte, tel. 2/228-3882, www.museociudadquito.gob. ec, 9:30am-5:30pm Tues.-Sun., $3). One of Old Town's best museums, it traces the history of the city from precolonial times to the beginning of the 20th century, with displays of replica households so you can understand the changing ways of life. Tours in English, French, Italian, and German can be arranged for an extra charge.

Across Mejía is the **Museo Nacional de Arte Colonial** (Cuenca and Mejía, tel. 2/228-2297, 9am-4:30pm Tues.-Fri., 10am-2pm Sat., $2), home to Quito's finest collection of colonial art.

Walk uphill eight blocks northeast from Plaza Grande on Venezuela for the best view of Old Town from within its boundaries. Even though construction began in 1892, **La Basílica del Voto Nacional** (no phone, 9am-5pm daily, $2) is still officially unfinished.

New Town Quito

QUITO TERRACE HOTEL

POST OFFICE

MERCADILLO

MARICHENA

SANTA CLARA MARKET

DAVALOS

ULLOA

SANTA MARIA SUPERMARKET

VERSAILLES

SAN GREGORIO

CARRION

DARQUEA

CORDERO

LARREA

Pérez Guerrero

Mariscal

PEREZ GUERRERO

Elido

10 DE AGOSTO

Santa Clara Park

CARRION

ROCA

VENTIMILLA

Colón

COLON

AZCASUBI

0 150 yds

0 150 m

Parque El Ejido

To Old Town/ La Marín

Casa de la Cultura

AV. PATRIA

18 DE SEPTIEMBRE

9

JORGE WASHINGTON

ROBLES

PAEZ

OCTUBRE

AMAZONAS

SANTA MARIA

ORELLANA

TEATRO PROMETEO

CASA DE LA CULTURA

LA MARISCAL

CULTURA MANOR

REINA

VICTORIA

ROCA

EL ARABE

DULCE ALBAHACA

BAQUEDANO

SEE DETAIL

TAME (GALAPAGOS TICKETS)

UNIVERSIDAD CATOLICA

PLAZA

TAMAYO

CARRION

VENTIMILLA

BAALBEK

TOURIST POLICE

Galo Plaza

WILSON

Plaza del Quindé

Manuela Canizares

DIEGO

FOCH

CALAMA

JUAN LEÓN MERA

LA RABIDA

SAFARI TOURS

POST OFFICE

JW MARRIOTT HOTEL QUITO

CREPES AND WAFFLES

LA PINTA

MINDALAE

HOTEL VIEJA CUBA

Orellana

POLITECNICA

T2 DE OCTUBRE

CAFELIBRO

ISABELLA CATOLICA

RODRIGUEZ

6 DE DICIEMBRE

DE

ALMAGRO

PINZÓN

LA NINA

SUPERMAXI

MADRID

LIZARDO GARCIA

MORENO

PLAZA

BAQUERIZO

CORDERO

COLON

Baca Ortiz

SAN

IGNACIO

CORUÑA

ORELLANA

SWISSOTEL

GALAVIS

BAEZ

SALAZAR

MUROS

GONZALEZ SUAREZ

To Ananké, Parque Guápulo, and Guápulo

WILSON

REINA

DIEGO DE ALMAGRO

LEÓN MERA

FOCH

Plaza del Quindé

NUHOUSE

MAGIC BEAN

MCCOOL'S

FINN

VICTORIA

CORDERO

LA CANOA MANABITA

LA PETIT MARISCAL

DOLCE DE LOBO

ACHIOTE

CALMA

EL CAFECITO

CAYMAN HOTEL

QUITU

Manuela Canizares

····· Trolé Line
—■— Trolé/ Ecovia Stop
— Ecovia Line
— Metrobus

© AVALON TRAVEL

Amazónico (12 de Octubre 1436, tel. 2/256-2663, 8:30am-12:30pm and 2pm-5pm Mon.-Fri., $2). Guided tours are available in Spanish to take you past stuffed rainforest animals, stunning Cofán feather headdresses, and real Shuar *tsantsas* (shrunken heads).

Another option is the five-story, modern **Mindalae Ethnic Museum** (Reina Victoria and La Niña, tel. 2/223-0609, www.mindalae.com, 9am-6pm Mon.-Fri., 10am-5:30pm Sat., $3), which showcases all of Ecuador's indigenous cultures through clothing, artifacts, and ceramics.

North of New Town
★ CAPILLA DEL HOMBRE

To learn about Ecuador's most famous artist, Oswaldo Guayasamín, visit the **Capilla del Hombre** (Calvachi and Chavez, tel. 2/254 8492, www.capilladelhombre.com, 10am-5pm Tues.-Sun., $6). You can see the artist's former house as well as his masterpiece, a chapel dedicated to the struggles endured by the indigenous peoples of the Americas before and after the arrival of the Spanish. Huge paintings fill the open, two-story building, which is centered on a circular space beneath a dome mural portraying the millions of workers who died in the silver mines of Potosí,

Bolivia. Guided tours are offered in English and Spanish. To get there, take a bus bound for Bellavista from Parque Carolina (marked "Batan-Colmena") or hail a taxi ($3).

PARQUE CAROLINA

For a refreshing walk after sightseeing, head to **Parque Carolina,** a huge urban park. You can relax in the green spaces or check out the **Jardín Botánico** (between Ciencias Naturales and Shyris, tel. 2/333-2516, 9am-1pm Mon., 9am-4:30pm Tues.-Sun., $3), botanical gardens that showcase Ecuador's vast array of flora, including some 500 species of orchids in the greenhouses.

Outside Quito
★ TELEFÉRIQO

Outside Quito you may have time to take the **TelefériQo** cable car ride (tel. 2/225-0825, 8am-8pm daily, $8.50), which climbs the slopes of **Volcán Pichincha** to 4,000 meters in 18 minutes. A beautiful lookout point and a fast-food café await at the top. If you get an early start and are well acclimatized to the altitude, you can hike to the peak of Volcán Pichincha (elevation approximately 4,784 meters) from the top of the cable car. The hike is moderately difficult and takes about three

the trail to Volcán Pichincha at the top of the TelefériQo

QUITO **GATEWAY CITIES**

hours each way; there are steep, rocky scrambles toward the end. Try to get to the cable car before opening, or else budget extra time to wait in line to board, which can take up to an hour. The easiest way to get there is to take a taxi from downtown ($5-6). The adventurous can try taking some of the municipal buses ($0.25), which run by the bottom of the hill, and then taking the free mini-shuttle from the bottom to the top of the hill. Shared ride vans usually leave from the TelefériQo and drop people off in the Mariscal or Old Town for $1-2 per person.

MITAD DEL MUNDO

Mitad del Mundo (Middle of the World, Manuel Córdova Galaraza km 13.5, tel. 2/239-5637, 9am-6pm Mon.-Fri., 9am-8pm Sat.-Sun., www.mitaddelmundo.com, $3) is a tourism complex 14 kilometers north of the city at zero degrees latitude. Tourists flock here to take a picture standing on the bright yellow line that delineates the northern and southern hemispheres. A 10-meter-high monument housing an ethnographic museum, exhibits on science, souvenir shops, and restaurants complete the complex. Down the road, **Museo de Sitio Intiñan** (Manuel Córdova Galarza km 13.5, tel. 2/239-5122, www.en.museointinan.com. ec, 9:30am-5pm daily, $4) showcases scientific experiments about the significance of the equatorial line. To get there, take the Metrobus on Avenida América to the Ofelia terminal and catch the connecting "Mitad del Mundo" bus. Alternatively, walk to the El Tejar station on the west side of downtown and catch the "Mitad del Mundo" bus directly (approximately one hour).

Tours
CITY TOURS

The municipality of Quito has put together excellent **guided maps** to historic walks through Old Town, available at tourist offices. Even better are the **multilingual walking tours** given by municipal officials from the tourist office (walk into the municipal tourist information office in Plaza Grande to make a reservation in advance; $15 pp).

Private tour agencies are scattered throughout Old Town and can arrange **tours of the Old Town** ranging $6-15 per person, and a tour of Mitad del Mundo and the TelefériQo is typically $40. Typically these are bus tours that include transportation between Old Town and Mitad del Mundo or the TelefériQo, plus a walking tour of each spot.

If your Spanish isn't too shabby, you can see Old Town by means of a theatrical tour of the nonprofit group **Quito Eterno** (tel. 2/228-9506, www.quitoeterno.org, 3pm or 4:30pm Sat., $8). The costumed tour guides mix historical reenactment into the tour. Advance reservations are required.

The hop-on/hop-off **Quito Tour Bus** (tel. 2/243-5458, www.quitotourbus.com, 9am-6pm daily, $12) visits all of Quito's most popular attractions, with recorded narration in Spanish and English.

MINDO

To get out of town, travel agencies can arrange trips to neighboring **Mindo** (about three hours away), a small town on the edge of the tropical rainforest where you can find toucans, frogs galore, and waterfalls in front of a lush green backdrop. Alternatively, take the public bus (3.5 hours each way).

OTAVALO

Otavalo is one of South America's largest indigenous handicrafts markets, where you can buy anything from hand-woven tapestries to dolls. Hundreds of stalls cover the main square and several streets. If you are able to make it early Saturday morning, you can even buy your own goat at the livestock market. It is about four hours from Quito by bus, but tour agencies in town organize day trips for about $50, cutting the transportation time down to about three hours each way.

COTOPAXI

Another popular option for a day trip from Quito is visiting **Cotopaxi volcano,** about two hours from Quito, and hiking around the refuge and Limpiopungo lagoon. Some tours include a downhill bike ride down the slope. Note that summiting Cotopaxi is a different, more specialized tour usually done while based out of Latacunga rather than Quito.

ENTERTAINMENT

Nightlife

OLD TOWN

The classic way to experience nightlife in Quito is in **La Ronda,** a pedestrian-only cobblestone street lined with bars and restaurants, many playing live music.

Some of the best live music is at **La Casa del Pozo** (Calle Morales OE 384 at Venezuela, tel. 99/910-0386, live music every day at 9:30pm, $2 cover)—you can listen to acoustic music and munch on local snacks in a candlelit, intimate maze of small adjoining rooms. Specialties include huge *empanadas de viento* (sugary, deep-fried pastries) and *canelazo de naranjilla* (a spiced hot liquor mixed with tropical fruits).

A less traditional alternative is to make an artisanal beer crawl through the many breweries in **La Tola,** a neighborhood on the outskirts of Old Town. While La Tola has widely been viewed as a dangerous place, the opening of budget hostels in the area, and then local businesses, has revitalized the neighborhood.

In La Tola, the **Bandido Brewery Company** (Pedro Fermin Cevallos and Olmedo, tel. 2/228-6504, www.bandidobrewing.com, 4pm-11pm Mon.-Sat., beers $4) is a cozy brewery and pizzeria owned by expats from Portland. They also make their own hard cider and kombucha with local fruits such as mango, passion fruit, and pear.

Up the hill, the hip **Altar Cervecería** (Vicente León at Olmedo, tel. 99/772-1197, http://altarceveceria.com, 5pm-midnight Mon.-Sat., beers $4, entrées $6-10), run by a Queensland expat, serves up five in-house beers that are brewed near La Ronda, as well as a rotating selection of craft brews from smaller local producers. The brews are flavored with guayusa from the Amazon, and

local cacao and coffee. You can also find craft Ecuadorian wine, which, because of the lack of locally grown grapes, is made from *mora* (blackberries).

La Oficina (Antepara E4-55 at Los Rios, tel. 0967145478, 6pm-midnight Mon.-Sat. 6pm-10pm Sun., beers $4) is a dim, artsy space run by expats from New York. It doubles as an event space and microbrewery, where batches of 100 liters are made every other day. You can find movie nights, salsa dancing, and live music depending on the night.

NEW TOWN

Nightlife in the Mariscal is centered around **Plaza Foch,** where several international theme bars serve a crowd of young locals and tourists in outdoor patio seating. The scene outside the main plaza, particularly along **Lizardo García** street, is far trashier, with hole-in-the-wall *discotecas,* karaoke, and shot bars. Watch out for broken glass on the sidewalk, drug dealers, and pickpockets. One of the most popular is **Finn McCools** (Diego de Almagro N24-64 at Pinto, tel. 2/252-1780, 5pm-2am daily), a crowded, loud Irish bar with disco lights, huge kegs of beer to share, billiards, and foosball.

If club dancing isn't your thing, try salsa or Argentine tango nights at the bohemian restaurant-cultural center **CafeLibro** (Calle Leonidas Plaza N 23-56, between Wilson and Veintimilla, tel. 2/250-3214, www.cafelibro. com, cover $5-7 plus minimum consumption), or take a taxi north of the Mariscal to **Salsoteca Lavoe** (Iñaquito and Naciones Unidas, tel. 2/243-5429, www.salsocalavoe. com, 9pm-3am Wed.-Sat., $5-10), Quito's biggest *salsoteca*, with a large wooden dance floor and a live DJ or band.

Theater

One of Quito's finest theaters is **Teatro Nacional Sucre** (Manabí N8-131, between Guayaquil and Juan José Flores, tel. 2/295-1661, www.teatrosucre.org), located in a gorgeous historic building and showing plays and concerts, including opera, jazz, ballet, and international traveling groups.

The opulent **Teatro Bolívar** (Pasaje Espejo 847 at Guayaquil, tel. 2/258-3788, www.teatrobolivar.org) is a 2,200-seat theater built in 1933 by a pair of American theater architects, and it incorporates elements of art deco and Moorish styles. It hosts world-class performance, dance, and concert events.

Both theaters have only occasional events, so plan in advance.

FOOD

For restaurants, you are spoiled for choice for international options in the **New Town.** The places close to Plaza Foch are mostly bar-restaurant combinations. **Old Town** has plenty of places for cheap set meals, but quality varies widely. Old Town increasingly has more upscale traditional Ecuadorian restaurants but is somewhat lacking in international food.

Old Town

La Ronda pedestrian street has several mid-range to pricey Ecuadorian restaurants. One casual choice is the relaxed outdoor patio of **Leña Quitena** (Morales 911 at Guayaquil/La Ronda, noon-midnight Tues.-Thurs., 2pm-2am Fri.-Sat., noon-10pm Sun., entrées $10-20). You won't leave hungry: The specialties are big plates of grilled meats—tenderloin, chicken, *cuy* (guinea pig), or their special grilled variety platter (*cariucho*).

For a wide variety of cheap, authentic eats, head to **Mercado Central** (Pichincha and Esmeraldas, 9am-6pm), a two-story farmers market with food stalls and produce. You can find a simple *almuerzo* for $2-3, a bowl of *encebollado* (soup with tuna, onions, and yucca) for $2, and snacks like *humitas* for $1. If you're feeling adventurous, you can try the *yaguarlocro* (blood and tripe soup)

The most famous stall in Mercado Central is ★ **Corvinas de Don Jimmy** (Mercado Central, 2nd floor, no phone, 7:30am-4:30pm Mon.-Sat., 7:30am-3pm Sun., $6-8.50), originally opened by Don Jimmy in 1953 and now run by Don Jimmy's son. The signature dish is *corvina* (a white sea bass), deep-fried and served over boiled potatoes with a side of ceviche, popcorn, and spicy *ají* sauce.

If you're out sightseeing, there's a small food court on Chile street in **Plaza Grande,** with outdoor seating and several hole-in-the-wall eateries offering inexpensive local snacks and entrées.

Another convenient, fun option is **Café Tianguez** (Plaza San Francisco, tel. 2/295-4326, www.tianguez.org, 10am-6pm Mon.-Tues., 10am-11pm Wed.-Sun., entrées $3-5). Choose from traditional snacks such as tamales and well-presented entrées such as *fritada* (fried pork) and *llapingacho* (cheesy potato pancake). Don't miss wandering the maze-like gift shop with fair-trade goods.

Inside the historic Teatro Bolívar building, **Purísima** (Guayaquil at Espejo, tel. 2/295-6527, noon-10pm daily, entrées $10-18) is a popular place with a café atmosphere and fun splashes of color. The food is traditional, well-presented Ecuadorian dishes. Try the hearty roasted pork or the lamb medallions.

Next door, **Galletti** (Espejo Oe2-43 and Guayaquil, tel. 2/258-9703, www.cafegalletti.com, 9am-7pm daily, drinks $3, snacks $2-6) is a "third-wave" coffee shop where fanatics can get their fix of the good stuff. There are standard espressos and lattes, and snacks like *humitas* and cookies, but the real specialty is the pour-over coffees that are made to order using single-source beans from various regions of Ecuador. See if you can taste the terroir in the *Expresso de los Volcanes* (volcanoes), *Bosque Nublado* (cloud forest) or *Amazonas* beans.

Across the street, **Pizza SA** (Espejo and Guayaquil, tel. 99/831-1478, 10am-9pm Mon.-Fri., 11am-11pm Sat., 10am-8pm Sun., $6-12), a centrally located pizzeria in Old Town, has all your standard toppings, plus local novelties—the fig, mozzarella, and basil pizza is savory-sweet, and you can shock your friends by ordering the *cuy* (guinea pig) pizza. Outdoor patio seating and rustic wood benches make a relaxed atmosphere.

Govindas (Esmeraldas 853, tel.

2/296-6844, 8am-4pm Mon.-Sat., entrées $3) is one of the few completely vegetarian restaurants in Old Town. Lunch items include veggie burgers and spinach-egg tortillas, though the most popular is the fixed-price *almuerzo*. The cheerful courtyard is filled with locals and backpackers alike. The *almuerzo* ends at 3pm; afterward there is just coffee, desserts, and reheatable but unappealing deep-fried items from the deli.

The penthouse-floor ★ **Vista Hermosa** (Mejía 453 at García Moreno, tel. 2/295-1401, 1pm-midnight Mon.-Sat., entrées $12-27) offers spectacular 270-degree views of Old Town Quito at night from a fifth-floor terrace. There are ample heat lamps to stay warm. The food is well-done local specialties, with everything from the typical potato soup *locro de papas* and *seco de chivo* (goat stew) to fine dining *langostinos al ajillo* (king prawns). There's live music Thursday-Saturday at 9:30pm.

Just outside Old Town, **Café San Blas** (José Antepara E4-09 at Vicente León, tel. 2/228-6762, 6pm-10pm Mon.-Sat., $3-6) in La Tola neighborhood is popular with locals and tourists alike for its reasonable prices, cozy atmosphere, and cheap pizzas. They also serve salads, sandwiches, and heaping piles of pasta. The pizza marinara is topped with local seafood.

New Town

There are tons of international and Ecuadorian options in New Town. **Plaza Foch** is mostly bar-restaurants with forgettable bar food. **Lizardo García** street is full of cheap shawarma and hamburger joints. The following recommended restaurants are scattered around the **Mariscal.**

La Canoa Manabita (Calama E-736 at Reina Victoria, tel. 2/256-3349, 10am-8pm Tues.-Sun., $7/plate), a hole-in-the-wall, authentic Ecuadorian seafood eatery run by a couple from the small coastal town of Vicente in Manabí province. On offer are ceviche, rice dishes, soups, and fried fish. If you're hungry, try the *bandera* (a huge mixed platter) or the *viche mixto* (a soup with shrimp, tuna, yam,

and corn in a broth made out of plantains and peanuts).

A more upscale seafood option is **La Petite Mariscal** (Diego de Almagro N24-304 at Juan Rodríguez, tel. 2/604-3303, lapetitemariscal. com, noon-3pm, 6pm-9:30pm Mon.-Fri., entrées $10-20, *almuerzo* $7), an inviting, dimly lit café serving Ecuadorian and French seafood. You can find everything from ceviche, fish in coconut sauce, and grilled seafood platters to bouillabaisse and coq au vin. There's also a moderately priced *almuerzo*.

★ **Achiote** (Juan Rodríguez 282 at Reina Victoria, tel. 2/250-1743, noon-10pm daily, entrées $15-20) is one of the best upscale places to try Ecuadorian food. The candlelit, sleek interior and impeccable service bring in the locals and tourists alike. If you are daring, try the *seco de chivo*, a local specialty that is surprisingly flavorful and tender, or the *cuy*. There are good chicken and beef dishes as well, in case you had either of the previously mentioned animals as pets.

Crepes & Waffles (Rábida N26-249 at Orellana, tel. 2/250-0658, www. crepesywaffles.com.ec, noon-10pm Mon.-Sat., 9:30am-9pm Sun., $7-12) in New Town is a trendy South American chain. Aside from their namesake dishes, there's a huge menu including pita sandwiches, large salads, decadent bread bowls, and ice cream. The salad bar is notably awesome with local ingredients like toasted corn, hearts of palm, and quinoa. The outdoor heated patio is particularly nice.

★ **Dulce Albahaca** (Juan León Mera 23-66 and Baquedano, tel. 2/510-3881, 8am-8pm Mon.-Fri., 10am-6pm Sat.-Sun., entrées $7-10) is a California-style health food café. The gluten-free, spiralized zucchini "pasta" is excellent. The veggie burger comes with several choices for toppings and patties (quinoa and amaranth, black bean, chickpea). Wash it down with a local *guanábana* (soursop fruit) kombucha or something from the custom tea bar, where you pick dehydrated fruits, spices and herbs. There are also salads, sandwiches, and bread bowls.

The Magic Bean (Foch 681 at Juan León

Mera, tel. 2/256-6181, www.magicbeanquito. com, 7am-11pm Mon.-Sat., $10) is a casual, popular gringo-haunt with large portions. For breakfast, try the banana-nut pancakes and cappuccino, for lunch or dinner a Santa Fe chicken salad, homemade veggie burger, or big plate of nachos. The cheery outdoor patio is a nice place to have brunch with friends.

Baalbek Comida Lebanesa (6 de Diciembre N23-103 at Wilson, www.restaurantbaalbek.com, tel. 2/255-2766, noon-5pm Sun.-Tues., noon-10:30pm Wed.-Sat., $8-16) is a classy restaurant for authentic Lebanese food in New Town. Baalbek has all the usual Middle Eastern suspects (hummus, tabbouleh, falafel, dolma) plus the house specialties— *mansofh* is a pile of spiced rice with ground beef, chicken, nuts, and yogurt sauce. It is a popular dinner spot, particularly on Thursday nights when there is live belly dancing.

Foodies, rejoice: **Quitu** (Juan Rodríguez 159 at 6 de Diciembre, tel. 2/513/8887, 6pm-9pm, tasting menus $35-70), is Quito's most creative, expensive, and ambitious restaurant. The 6- and 12-course tasting menus ($35 and $70) are a culinary exploration of the different regions of Ecuador. The ingredients are sourced from all over the coast, the Andes, and Amazonia. Though the ambience in the restaurant is quite unassuming, the artistic presentation, creativity, and quality of the food inspire comparisons with Michelin-starred restaurants from its raving fans.

ACCOMMODATIONS

Most visitors stay in the **New Town** because there are so many amenities for visitors, including international restaurants and a plethora of bars. A wide selection of poorly maintained budget hostels attracts backpackers, though many have sagging beds and loud bar noise. There is a good choice of midrange and luxury hotels, including large chain hotels—**Marriott, Swissôtel,** and the **Hilton.** In contrast, staying in **Old Town** is an authentic, immersive experience. The downside is that it is not a safe place to wander at night with the exception of police-patrolled

La Ronda. Since the **airport** is far from downtown, a handful of hotels close to the airport are recommended for visitors just passing through Quito to the Galápagos. Breakfast is included unless otherwise noted.

Under $50
OLD TOWN

Unsurprisingly, the reason to choose **Community Hostel** (Pedro Fermin Cevallos N6-78 at Olmedo, tel. 2/228-5108, www.communityhostel.com, $10-12.50 dorm, $30 d, breakfast not included) is the community. Though it's not a "party" hostel, it has a great social atmosphere because a lot of guests tend to center their day around the hostel. Wake up with free morning yoga and a cheap breakfast, then go on tours organized through the in-house tourist agency, eat dinner at the hostel's big communal table, and finish with one of the organized nighttime activities (movie night, pub crawls, etc). It is also perhaps the best option for those who want to cook their own food in the shared kitchen, since the huge municipal market is next door. There is also a great free walking tour that leaves from the hostel most days.

★ **Masaya Hostel** (Rocafuerte OE3-85 and Venezuela, tel. 2/257-0189, www.masaya-experience.com, $10-$14 dorm, $40-50 d, breakfast and towels not included) is a stylish "luxury hostel" in a fantastic location a stone's throw from La Ronda. Dorms are built into solid wood cubes, each complete with immaculate linens, individual outlets, reading lamps, and roll-down privacy shades. You could easily fit a person inside the tall lockers, each equipped with shelves for keeping your stuff safe and organized. An interior garden space is complete with beanbags, a treehouse-inspired raised deck, and a bonfire pit. Indoors, you'll find spacious sitting areas, a movie room, and nightly free activities. The only downside is the lack of shared kitchen.

NEW TOWN

A great-value place to stay near New Town is **Quito Terrace Hostel** (Av. 10 de Agosto

N17-275 y Asunción, tel. 2/252-4502, quito-terrace@gmail.com, $9 dorms, $25 s, $30-35 d). The doubles and triples are brand-new. The interior-facing dorm rooms lack natural light, but they are spacious and have twin beds rather than bunks. The real selling point, however, is the gorgeous, sunny terrace filled with succulents and overlooking Parque El Ejido. It is less convenient walking to Plaza Foch and the restaurants in that vicinity (a little under a mile), but it is very close to the *mercado artisanal* and Casa de la Cultura. No breakfast is offered, but there is a communal kitchen for cooking. Avoid the second-floor street-facing rooms as there is a busy street below.

$50-100

OLD TOWN

Boutique Portal de Cantuña (Bolívar Oe6 at Cuenca, tel. 2/228-2276, www.portalde-cantunaquito.com, $79 d, $105 t) is a charming family-run hotel in an old colonial house centrally located near Plaza San Francisco in Old Town. Much of the original house remains—a 16th-century confessional, mosaic tile floors, and baroque furniture. The owners have added modern touches such as a Jacuzzi on the terrace and recycled-glass-metal art covering the courtyard glass ceiling. Rooms are comfortable and bright, most facing the inner courtyard. There's Wi-Fi in the common areas only.

NEW TOWN

A short walk from Plaza Foch, the **Cayman Hotel** (Juan Rodríguez 270 [E7-29] at Reina Victoria, tel. 2/256-7616, www.hotelcayman-quito.com, $35 s, $50 d, $64 t) is a breath of fresh air with light, airy rooms and a sunny garden area with a resident hummingbird. Rooms are fully equipped with hair dryers, fluffy white duvets, and large beds. The hotel attracts international tourists due to the friendly English-speaking service, central location, and modern amenities. Fun extras include a DVD collection, board games, and a large book exchange. You can help yourself to tea, coffee, and bananas all day.

Just down the street, the eight-room ★ **Dolce de Lobo Boutique Stay** (Juan Rodríguez E8-34 at Diego de Almagro, tel. 2/223-0798, www.lacasasol.com, $60 s, $65 d, $90 suite) feels artsy and more exclusive than its price tag warrants. Chandeliers, gilded mirrors, and white linens are punctuated by bright pops of art-deco color and well-curated artwork. Aside from the design, the personalized service, spacious rooms, and waterfall showerheads make it a solid choice. There's no sitting area or dining room, but who can object to breakfast delivered by room service?

For a thematic vacation-in-a-vacation, go to **Hotel Vieja Cuba** (La Nina N26-202 at Diego de Almagro, tel. 2/290-6729, www.hotelviejacuba.com, $61 s, $101 d, $119 q) in the northern end of the Mariscal. The hotel may not be owned by Cubans, but you just might forget that after seeing the beautiful mosaic spiral staircase, bodega adorned with fake fruit and kegs, and ivy-covered exterior. Rooms are white, bright, and modern in furnishings and technology, with cable TV and a separate Wi-Fi router for each room.

AIRPORT HOTELS

If you just have a brief overnight layover on the way to Galápagos, you may want to stay near the airport rather than downtown. At the airport, there is currently only one hotel, the **Wyndham Quito Airport Hotel;** a pre-security lounge **(Layover Stay Quito)** has recliners, showers, and snacks for $36 for 12 hours.

The rest of the options for a layover are in the sleepy neighboring towns of **Tababela** and **Puembo.** Staying in Tababela and Puembo has become less desirable lately, as a new bridge has shortened transit time to downtown Quito. Getting to downtown Quito via taxi now takes 40-60 minutes and $25 each way by taxi, compared to 10-15 minutes and $10 each way to Tababela and Puembo. The majority of accommodations in Tababela and Puembo are *hosterías*, countryside retreats with pools and large event spaces that were built before the airport moved nearby. These hotels are not very walkable, so book in advance.

Quito Airport Suites (971 Alfonso Tobar and Tulio Garzon, tel. 2/239-1430, www.airporthotelquito.com, $49 s, $49-55 d, $65 t, $75 q) is much smaller than its name implies, with nine clean though nondescript rooms, a living room, and an on-site soccer field. They have both private rooms and suites (two adjoining rooms with queen-size beds sharing one bathroom).

Casa Puembo Quito Airport (Calle José Gallardo S6-171 at J. Tobar García, Esquina, tel. 098/371-4706, casadeartepuembo@gmail.com, $55 s, $72 d, $92 t, $108 q) is a converted house with modern rooms tastefully decorated in whites and neutrals; there is cable TV. It is located within a beautiful green garden space complete with pool.

Over $100

OLD TOWN

If you want to stay right on Quito's most historic street, look no farther than **Casona de la Ronda Boutique** (Calle Morales/La Ronda OE1-160 at Guayaquil, tel. 2/228-7501, www.lacasonadelaronda.com, $160 d, $230 junior suite). Restaurants and bars are just outside along the safe, pedestrian-only Calle La Ronda. The hotel itself is built in a renovated 18th-century colonial house and boasts a cozy inner courtyard, vertical garden, and a sunny terrace with views of the city. Rooms are elegant, with carved wood furniture and white linens.

Get a sense of how Quito's elite lived by staying at **Patio Andaluz** (García Moreno and Olmedo, tel. 2/228-0830, www.hotelpatioandaluz.com, $200 d, $244 suite), a former home of nobles and now one of Old Town's most distinguished establishments. Here you can walk through hallways wider than most other hotel rooms, rest in a king-size bed, and have a drink in the medieval-themed bar. Rooms are spacious yet inviting, and suites

are two floors with an extra sitting area and balcony.

If money is no object, stay at the elegant five-star ★ **Casa Gangotena** (Bolívar Oe6-41 at Cuenca, tel. 2/400-8000, www.casagangotena.com, $461 d), winner of several awards in the hotel industry, located right in Plaza San Francisco. The hotel is in a restored historic mansion, and it mixes modern luxury—marble, crisp linens, and red velvet—with original historic touches, such as antique mirrors, high ceilings, and some of the house's original museum-quality murals. The top-floor terrace has fantastic views of El Panecillo and Plaza San Francisco.

NEW TOWN

Cultura Manor (Robles 513 at Reina Victoria, tel. 2/222-4271, www.cafecultura.com, $200-300 d), is a romantic boutique hotel with history. The colonial-style building was built in 1933 and formerly served as an elite social club. After careful renovation, it preserves its historic charm with old-world murals, antiques, and roses. Each room has a unique collection of alfresco paintings and artwork, as well as clawfoot tubs for soaking. Common areas include a comfortable sitting room with a fireplace and board games.

Nuhouse Quito (Foch E6-12 at Reina Victoria, tel. 2/255-7845, www.nuhousehotels.com, $159 s, $169 d, $189 t, $249 suite) is modern and trendy five-floor hotel in Plaza Foch. While it's not Quito's most unique accommodation, it checks all the boxes travelers expect from the large international luxury chains. It has a business center, in-house travel agency, on-site restaurant with room service, and bilingual staff. All rooms have double-paned noise-blocking windows, but for the quietest room, pick a room in Tower A on one of the upper floors. Premium suites have a separate dining room and in-room Jacuzzi.

INFORMATION AND SERVICES

The **Corporación Metropolitana de Turismo** (Quito Visitors Bureau) is the best visitor information bureau in Ecuador and an excellent source of information on Quito, with maps, brochures, leaflets, English-speaking staff, and a regularly updated website. The main office is at the Palacio Municipal (Plaza de la Independencia, Venezuela and Espejo, tel. 2/257-2445, www.quito.com.ec, 9am-6pm Mon.-Fri., 9am-5pm Sat.). There are also branches in Mariscal (Reina Victoria and Luis Cordero, tel. 2/255-1566), the airport (tel. 2/330-0164), the Museo Nacional del Banco Central (6 de Diciembre and Patria, tel. 2/222-1116), and at Quitumbe bus terminal.

ATMs for most international systems (Plus, Cirrus, Visa, and MasterCard) can be found at major banks along Amazonas and around the shopping centers. These tend to have limits on how much you can withdraw per day (usually $600), so if you need to pay cash for a Galápagos trip, you'll have to go to a bank branch. It's best to take a taxi straight to the travel agency if you're withdrawing a large amount of money, as robberies are a problem in Quito. **Banco del Pacífico** has its head office at Naciones Unidas and Los Shyris, and there is a branch on Amazonas and Washington. **Banco de Guayaquil** is at Reina Victoria and Colón and at Amazonas and Veintimilla; **Banco de Pichincha** is at Amazonas and Pereira as well as on 6 de Diciembre. **Banco Bolivariano** is at Naciones Unidas E6-99.

To reach the police, dial 101. There is also a special **tourist police office** (Roca and Reina Victoria, tel. 2/254-3983) that is geared to foreigners in New Town.

There are several hospitals in Quito. Frequently recommended modern hospitals are **Hospital Vozandes** (Villalengua and 10 de Agosto, tel. 2/226-2142, www.hospitalvozandes.org) and **Hospital Metropolitano** (Mariana de Jesús and Occidental, tel. 2/226-1520, www.hospitalmetropolitano.org).

GETTING THERE AND AROUND
Airport
The **Mariscal Sucre International Airport**

(airport code UIO, tel. 2/294-4900, www.aeropuertoquito.aero), 24 kilometers east of downtown Quito, was finished in 2013—a $500 million, multiyear project to replace the old airport in central Quito. The airport serves international and domestic routes. It is one of only two airports with routes to the Galápagos Islands (the other is Guayaquil). To get there, take the public bus, express shuttle bus, or taxi. Although the airport is not many miles away from downtown, be aware that the road is very windy and traffic can cause significant delays. By taxi the trip can be as quick as 45 minutes or take an hour and a half. The express shuttle takes longer than a taxi, and public transportation usually takes around two hours.

The **public bus** costs $2 and is the cheapest way to get to the airport, though it can take two hours from Old Town depending on traffic. Take the Ecovia ($0.25) to Río Coca stop (30-40 minutes), cross the street, and then catch the bus to the airport. The bus makes 11 intermediate stops and takes approximately one hour. The bus runs every 20 minutes Monday-Friday 4:45am-9:20pm and every 30 minutes Saturday-Sunday 5am-9pm. Note that the bus lacks good storage for luggage, can be standing-room only, and is frequently boarded by touts hawking everything from candy to erasers.

Express shuttle buses (tel. 2/604-3500, www.aeroservicios.com.ec) cost $8 and go directly between the former airport in central Quito and the new airport, leaving every 30 minutes, 24 hours a day, 365 days a week. The shuttles are more comfortable than the bus—you are guaranteed a seat, and there is onboard Wi-Fi. From the new airport, take a taxi to your hotel.

Taxis are the fastest way to get to and from the airport. The fees to different areas of the city are fixed by the city—$22 to La Mariscal or $26 to Old Town.

Services at the airport include visitor information, a post office, late-night money exchange, duty-free shops, the phone company Andinatel, the pre-security lounge **Layover**

Stay Quito, and a decent selection of restaurants and cafés.

Trolley

Quito's network of three electric trolley buses is the best of its kind in Ecuador: It is cheap, clean, fast, and well organized, although it's very crowded and may be elbow-to-elbow standing room only during rush hour. Beware of pickpocketing. Flat fare for all services is $0.25, payable at kiosks or machines on entry. Trolleys pass every 5-10 minutes and are run by the **Quito Public Transport System** (tel. 2/266-4023, www.trolebus.gob.ec).

El Trole (5:30am-11:30pm Mon.-Fri., 6am-10pm Sat.-Sun.) runs north-south from Estación Norte north of New Town near La Y, south past sts at Mariscal and Colón, through Old Town past Chimbacalle train station, to the new southern bus terminal at Quitumbe. It takes about an hour to get to Quitumbe from New Town. The main *trole* thoroughfare, 10 de Agosto, reserves a pair of center lanes for the service, detouring down Guayaquil and Maldonado in Old Town, then continuing on Maldonado south of El Panecillo.

The **Ecovia** (6am-10pm Mon.-Fri., 6am-9:30pm Sat.-Sun.) is similar, but without the overhead wires. It also runs north-south from its northern Río Coca terminal along 6 de Diciembre past La Casa de la Cultura to La Marín near Old Town. Most trolleys turn around at La Marín, where there are interchanges with many country bus routes to the south and the valley; an extension continues past the exit of the old Cumandá bus terminal to Avenida Napo.

The third line, called **Metrobus** (5:30am-10:30pm Mon.-Fri., 6am-10pm Sat.-Sun.) is, like Ecovia, a trolley without overhead wires. It runs from La Marín in Old Town up Santa Prisca and along Avenida América, La Prensa, and north to both the Ofelia and Carcelén terminals, where there are connections to the

northern highlands, cloud forest, and northern coast. It takes about 40 minutes to get to these terminals from New Town.

Bus

Blue city buses run all over Quito and are operated by the city. There are too many routes to list and no comprehensive route maps. Luckily these buses list the destinations on the windshield.

The most popular bus line used by tourists is the Mitad del Mundo bus, which runs rather infrequently once or twice an hour. One line runs between El Panecillo, passes through the El Tejar station west of Old Town, and continues to the Mitad del Mundo monument ($0.40). Another Mitad del Mundo line runs between the Ofelia bus station in north Quito and the Mitad del Mundo monument ($0.40).

Taxi

Taxis are good value in Quito and are recommended at night. Most taxis use a meter during the day and early evening, and fares should be no more than $2-3 from the Old Town to the New Town. Taxis charge fixed rates to the airport, at night, and to popular tourist destinations. Official taxis in Quito are yellow. If you hail a yellow cab, make sure that it has a registered taxi number on the side of the car and on the windshield, and that the driver has official ID. The safest option is to ask your hotel manager to recommend a company and prebook it for you.

If you have data service, **Uber** ridesharing services are also available in Quito and are less expensive than taxis, particularly at night when traditional taxis turn off the meter and negotiate rates, sometimes overcharging foreigners.

Metro

Quito's metro is under construction and is currently scheduled to open in mid-2019.

Wildlife Guide

I t seems incredible that a set of rocky islands, parched in the equatorial sun and covered with blackened lava, could be teeming with so much life.

However, it's precisely because of the inhospitable landscapes that creatures have been forced to adapt; in doing so, they provided the living proof for Darwin's theory of evolution.

The Galápagos archipelago has 5,000 species, and 1,900 are endemic: a third of the plants, almost half the birds, half the fish and insects, and 90 percent of the reptiles have all adapted so well to life in the archipelago that they barely resemble their original mainland ancestors. Famous endemic animals include many species of the iconic giant tortoise, marine iguanas, land iguanas, flightless cormorants, Galápagos penguins, Darwin's finches, many species of mockingbirds, the Galápagos hawk, and the waved albatross. Some even rarer species are "locally endemic" or found on only one island in the archipelago.

Some 1,000 kilometers west of the South American mainland is a very long way to swim or fly, never mind crawl, so how on earth did the wildlife of the Galápagos come to be here? Nobody knows for sure, but it seems likely that the strengths of the ocean currents brought mammals such as sea lions to the archipelago, and they flourished in islands surrounded by waters teeming with marine life. Birds may have been blown off course, but more likely migratory birds came and knew they were on to a good thing, with an endless supply of fish, and returned year after year. Insects and plant seeds could also have been carried from the South American continent by high winds, whereas other seeds were probably excreted by birds or arrived stuck to their feet.

Explaining how terrestrial reptiles and rodents arrived is trickier, the most common theory being that they drifted on rafts of vegetation that still wash down Ecuador's ocean-bound rivers. Any animals or plants that happened to be aboard, provided they could survive the journey, stood a slim chance of riding the currents all the way to the Galápagos. With their ability to slow their own metabolism, reptiles are particularly suited for such a long, difficult journey, while larger mammals would have died quickly, which explains the lack of mammals on the islands.

Previous: a land iguana on Plaza Sur; blue-footed booby. **Above:** Galápagos sea lion.

Did You Know...?

- **Giant tortoises** are not fully grown until they are 100 years old. Many live to the age of 160, although nobody knows their maximum age for sure.

- When a **land iguana** nods its head, watch out; this is a territorial threat to other males, also employed against humans who get too close.

- **Blue-footed boobies** encircle their nests with a ring of excrement (guano). If the chick ventures outside the ring, it will often be rejected by its parents.

- **Marine iguanas** work hard to keep warm after staying underwater for more than an hour. On cold nights, they often congregate together into huge piles.

- **Booby** is a rude name for a bird, but not in the way you'd expect; it derives from **bobo**, meaning "stupid," in Spanish. It was coined by sailors derisive of the birds' friendly nature. Boobies are no chumps, though, and are very talented at fishing.

- Not all **finches** are cute. The sharp-billed ground finch is nicknamed "vampire finch" because it pecks at the base of a booby's tail to drink blood. It also rolls other birds' eggs until they break and then eats the insides.

- **Nazca booby** chicks are fratricidal. Two eggs are hatched, and the first chick to hatch pushes the other egg out of the nest, killing it.

- **Sea lion colonies** are split into harems, where one dominant bull lives with up to 15 females, and bachelor colonies where other males congregate. Dominant bulls have to repel regular challenges and only last a few weeks or months before they are displaced by a stronger bull.

- **Penguins** and **waved albatross** are among the most romantic of Galápagos birds and usually mate for life. The **Galápagos hawk** has the most unusual mating system, known as cooperative polyandry, whereby up to four males mate with a single female and then help to incubate and raise the young.

- **Albatross** can fly at speeds of 80 kilometers per hour and often spend years in flight without touching land.

Reptiles

The Galápagos were named after the giant reptiles that inhabit them, and this is one of the only places on earth where reptiles rule the land with no natural predators. Thus the archipelago gives us a glimpse of what life might have been like millions of years ago when dinosaurs ruled the planet. More than 90 percent of the reptile species in the Galápagos are endemic.

GIANT TORTOISES

Of the 20 species of endemic reptiles, these slow giants are the most famous. They also gave the islands their name—**galápago** is an old Spanish word for a saddle similar in shape to the tortoise shell. The tortoises are found only on the Galápagos and, in smaller numbers, on a few islands in the Indian Ocean. They reach sexual maturity at about 25 years and are not fully grown until age 100, reaching 1.5 meters in length and weighing up to 250 kilograms. Many live to the age of 160, although nobody knows their maximum age for sure.

The shell of a giant tortoise reveals which island its owner originates from. Saddle-shaped shells evolved on low, arid islands where tortoises needed to lift their heads high to eat tall vegetation, while semicircular domed shells come from higher, lush islands where vegetation grows closer to the ground. The vice governor of the Galápagos boasted to Charles Darwin that he could distinguish the island of origin of a tortoise by the shape of its shell—just one piece of evidence that helped Darwin to form his theory of evolution.

The tortoises' famous slow, languid demeanor is what allows them to live so long, and perhaps we should all take a cue from them and slow down a little. They spend 16 hours a day sleeping and are most active in the early morning and late afternoon. With minimal movement, their metabolism slows significantly, and digestion takes 1-3 weeks, allowing them to survive with very little food and water during the dry season. When the rains come, the tortoises come alive, eating, drinking, mating, wallowing in pools of water,

and sleeping contentedly in large groups. They feed on a wide variety of plants, particularly opuntia cactus pads, fruits, water ferns, and bromeliads.

The only time tortoises make much noise is during mating season, when their unearthly groans echo for long distances. Males become surprisingly aggressive, pushing each other and rising up on their legs to stretch out their necks in a battle for dominance. The shorter male will usually retreat, while the larger male will ram a female's shell and nip her legs before mounting her from behind and bellowing. The process is long, arduous, and fraught with problems—males sometimes fall off and have great difficulty righting themselves.

When her eggs are ready to hatch, the female will journey for long distances to find dry sandy ground, usually on or near beaches, to dig a 30-centimeter-deep hole to bury the eggs, which hatch in the spring after about four months. The temperature of the nest has a marked effect on the gender of the hatchlings: Lower temperatures lead to more males and warmer temperatures to more females.

Of the original 14 subspecies, 10 remain, and 4 subspecies (Santa Fé, Floreana, Fernandina, and Pinta) have been hunted into extinction. Indeed, the giant

giant tortoise roaming the highlands at El Chato on Santa Cruz

Bringing Tortoises Back From Extinction

At a glance, the newest research in the Galápagos sounds disturbingly like the plot of *Jurassic Park*: Scientists are bringing back the extinct Pinta and Floreana giant tortoises.

This work was envisioned in 2012, when scientists discovered hybrid tortoises living on the remote northern tip of Isabela Island. These tortoises had genetic ancestry from Pinta Island and Floreana Island, two species assumed to be extinct. Research at Yale University is under way to analyze the genes of each of the tortoises and identify the breeding pairs that could produce the highest diversity and percentage of original genes of the extinct species.

Once the breeding pairs are identified, the selectively bred tortoises will repopulate Floreana and Pinta islands, effectively bringing these species back from extinction. Though some question the amount of human intervention, most agree that repopulating the islands will have a key impact on the ecosystem, as the tortoises play a key role in island ecosystems by dispersing native seeds.

You might ask what Pinta and Floreana Island tortoises were doing so far away from home. The current theory is that they owe their survival to pirates and whalers, who often took tortoises alive from the islands as a supply of fresh meat, but occasionally threw them overboard to make room for more valuable cargo. In many cases the tortoises would have drowned, but maybe some lucky individuals beat the odds, washing up on shore and surviving on a new island. And now these tortoises will become the future of their species.

tortoise population has plummeted from some 250,000 before humans arrived to just 20,000 now. Sailors used to be the tortoises' main enemy, taking them on long voyages as sources of fresh meat (the tortoises took up to a year to starve to death). Today, the main danger comes largely from introduced species: Pigs dig up nests, cats eat hatchlings, and goats and cattle eat the vegetation and cut off the tortoises' food supply. It's not all bad news, however, because there is a comprehensive rearing program to release tortoises back into the wild, most recently on Pinta Island.

It's hard to visit the Galápagos without hearing about "Lonesome George." The Pinta Island tortoise was widely regarded as extinct until the discovery of a single male on Pinta in 1971. All attempts at breeding were unsuccessful, leading to his moniker "Lonesome George." Over the years, as the last of his species, he became an icon for conservation. Fishers famously held Lonesome George for ransom in activism for fishing quotas in the Galápagos. After his death in 2012, his body was meticulously preserved and exhibited in international museums before it returned to the Charles Darwin Research Facility.

Five of the remaining subspecies are found on the five main volcanoes of Isabela, and the other species are found on Santiago, Santa Cruz, San Cristóbal, Pinzón, and Española.

Where to See Them

Charles Darwin Research Station on Santa Cruz is the most famous place to see these amazing creatures. There is a breeding center with 10 subspecies. Visitors used to be able to walk among the tortoises, but now you must observe from outside the walled enclosures. Lesser known but with a larger population is the **Centro de Crianza** breeding center on Isabela, which has more than 800 tortoises in eight separate enclosures, and there's a tortoise enclosure at **Asilo de la Paz** on Floreana.

To see tortoises in a semi-natural environment, check out **La Galapaguera,** a reserve and breeding center on San Cristóbal where tortoises reside in 12 hectares of dry forest. Alternatively, wander around **El Chato Tortoise Reserve,** which fills the entire southwest corner of Santa Cruz.

SEA TURTLES

There are four species of marine turtles in the archipelago. The eastern **Pacific green turtle,** known rather confusingly as **tortuga negra** (black turtle) in Spanish, is the most common species. Also present but rarely seen are the **Pacific leatherback,** the **Indo-Pacific hawksbill,** and the **olive ridley** turtles.

Green sea turtles are rarely seen in large numbers, preferring to swim alone, in couples, or next to their young. They usually weigh 100 kilograms but can weigh up to 150 kilograms. The females are bigger than the males and can grow to 1.2 meters long. They feed mainly on seaweeds and spend long periods of time submerged, even resting on the seabed and surviving without oxygen for several hours.

The mating season, November-January, is the best time to see them. Both genders are polygamous, and several males often mate with the same female. Mating is particularly tiring for the female, who has to do most of the swimming while the male holds on.

sea turtle near La Lobería on Floreana

Sea turtles must come ashore to lay eggs, and females often do this as many as eight times during the mating season, laying dozens of eggs each time. The female climbs the beach above the high water mark and digs a pit to lay the eggs before returning to the sea. If the eggs can evade the attention of predators, particularly pigs, rats, and even crabs and beetles, then the hatchlings emerge and make their way to the sea, where they may be gobbled up by sharks or even pelicans.

Despite the high mortality rate, green sea turtles thrive in the islands and spread far from the archipelago. Turtles marked in the Galápagos have been found as far away as Panama and Costa Rica as well as commonly off the coast of Ecuador.

Where to See Them

With a little luck, sea turtles can be seen swimming all over the archipelago, but the best-known sites are **Punta Vicente Roca** and **Los Túneles** on **Isabela, La Lobería** on **Floreana,** and **Gardner Bay** on **Española.**

MARINE IGUANAS

The only seafaring lizards in the world, **Galápagos marine iguanas** are living proof of evolution. Scientists estimate that this species adapted over 2-3 million years from their land iguana cousins in order to find food underwater in the form of nutritious coastal seaweed. A flattened snout allows them to press against the rocks to feed, a flattened tail propels them more effectively underwater, long claws grab the rocks firmly, and salt-eliminating glands in their nostrils cleanse the sea salt from their bodies. These iguanas can dive more than 12 meters below the surface. They feed for an hour a day, always at low tide, and can stay underwater for more than an hour by lowering their heart rate by half.

The seaweed they feed on is true to its name—it's a weed that grows incredibly quickly throughout the coastline of the islands and supports more than 200,000 marine iguanas on the Galápagos. Males measure about one meter in length and weigh up to 20 kilograms. They are mostly black, with red

Travels with Charlie

When in the water this lizard swims with perfect ease and quickness, by a serpentine movement of its body and flattened tail—the legs being motionless and closely collapsed on its sides. A seaman on board sank one, with a heavy weight attached to it, thinking thus to kill it directly; but when, an hour afterwards, he drew up the line, it was quite active.

Charles Darwin in *The Voyage of the Beagle,* on marine iguanas

and green tinges on their backs becoming particularly prominent during the mating season.

After feeding, regulating its body heat fills much of the rest of the marine iguana's day. After a long dive, they must warm up, but not too quickly and not to more than 45°C. To do so, iguanas face the sun, exposing as little surface area as possible, and raise their bodies off the ground to allow air to circulate underneath—they often look like they're striking a yoga pose. On cold days and at night, iguanas congregate into huge piles to conserve heat.

Marine iguanas congregate in colonies for most of the year. During the mating season, which usually corresponds with the rainy season, males become more brightly colored, and their black coloring is punctuated by red, orange, and green spots. Males become more territorial and aggressive, standing proudly and bobbing their heads up and down rapidly to warn off other males. This head-bobbing is also used to court females. After mating, females lay their eggs in sandy burrows on beaches, and hatchlings emerge after three or four months. Young ones and even slow, elderly iguanas have one predator to fear: the Galápagos hawk.

Like much of the wildlife on the archipelago, iguanas were affected by El Niño conditions in the 1980s and 1990s, when abnormally warm waters killed the shallow-growing seaweed. The marine iguanas were not strong enough to dive deeper, and thousands perished. Their numbers have slowly recovered, but who knows if they will evolve further over time to become better divers?

Marine iguanas on Española turn Christmas colors around mating season.

Clockwise from top left: The female lava lizard has a bright red head; A humpback whale breaches off the Galápagos; a land iguana basks in the sun.

Where to See Them

There are marine iguanas throughout the archipelago, even in the port towns, and almost all visitors will see them at some point or another. There are sizable populations of marine iguanas on **Seymour Norte, James Bay** on **Santiago, Gardner Bay** and **Punta Suárez** on **Española,** and various sites on **Isabela.** However, the biggest population by far is at **Punta Espinosa** on **Fernandina.**

LAND IGUANAS

The Galápagos have seven subspecies of land iguana. How they arrived on the island is the cause of much debate—they may have floated on vegetation from the South American coast—but they almost certainly came after their marine cousins, when there was enough vegetation on the Islands for them to survive on land. They live in dry areas and eat anything from berries, flowers, and fruits to cactus pads, ingesting most of their water from food. Like their marine cousins, newborns are one of the few terrestrial creatures that have to fear the Galápagos hawk. They are also prey for many introduced species until they are big enough to defend themselves. As a result, the land iguana species on Santiago and Baltra are extinct, while those on other islands are endangered. A captive-breeding program at the Charles Darwin Research Station is working to boost the population.

Males grow to over one meter in length, can weigh up to 13 kilograms, and live more than 50 years. The Galápagos species are distinctively more yellow than greener mainland iguanas, particularly the subspecies on Santa Fé. There are also hybrids born from mating with marine iguanas. While most of the land iguanas range from brown to yellow-orange, one species stands out: The rare pink land iguana has unusual pink and black markings and inhabits only northern Isabela Island.

Like their marine cousins, the males can be very territorial, exhibiting brighter colors in the mating season and engaging in head-bashing battles with other males. They are famous for their head nodding, a threat that can also be employed against humans if they get too close. Note that male iguanas can also whip their tails up if startled, so be careful approaching them. They are also surprisingly fast and can run across the rocks at high speeds. Females need to be fast, too, as males are extremely persistent in attempting to mate, employing the same head-nodding movement and chasing them for long periods of time. The female is considerably smaller and so often unable to resist advances, during which the male holds her neck and hooks a leg over her to bring his tail in contact with hers. After mating, the female lays eggs in burrows, and hatchlings emerge after three or four months. Hatchlings need to avoid the attention of herons, egrets, hawks, and owls, but once they grow, they have no natural predators.

Where to See Them

While marine iguanas are all over the Galápagos, land iguanas are a little harder to see. You have to get away from the port towns. The best places to see land iguanas are **Cerro Dragón** on **Santa Cruz, Seymour Norte, Plaza Sur,** and **Santa Fé.** They can also be seen at **Urbina Bay** on **Isabela.**

LAVA LIZARDS

Although hardly as impressive as their larger relatives, the seven species of lava lizard are certainly faster—and they have to be to avoid being gobbled up by birds or snakes. You'll see them scurrying over sand and rocks all over the islands. They have various other evasive techniques—changing color to camouflage themselves, and leaving a breakaway tail in predators' mouths while they make a getaway and grow a new one. They feed on insects, plants, and occasionally each other. The males can often be seen doing a type of push-up as a show of strength, and their Spanish name **(lagartija)** has become a common slang term for this type of exercise.

Where to See Them

Lava lizards are common throughout the

Galápagos and can be found on all the major islands. Look for them on the shore and in dry zones.

OTHER REPTILES

On land, there are three species of **snakes** on the islands; all are brown and feed on rats, geckos, lava lizards, and marine iguana hatchlings. They are venomous but rarely seen by humans, and there have been no reports of bites. Underwater, the yellow-bellied sea snake is also venomous. **Geckos** come out to feed on insects at night and spend their days resting under rocks. Like lava lizards, they can lose their tails and regenerate them easily.

Where to See Them

Geckos are small and hard to spot because they are nocturnal, but you may not have to go far to spot one; they are known to crawl up the walls of hotels and restaurants at night. Snakes are also difficult to spot; your best bets are **Santa Fé** and **Seymour Norte.**

Mammals

In contrast to the abundance of plants, insects, fish, and lizards, the archipelago has only six types of mammals. These include sea lions, fur seals, whales, and dolphins, all of which must have swum to the Galápagos. There are also bats, which flew over, and, most impressive of all, rice rats, which most likely arrived by floating on rafts of vegetation.

GALÁPAGOS SEA LIONS

A close encounter with sea lions is for many people the highlight of a Galápagos trip. While other creatures show a mild disdain for humans, sea lions are very communicative and the pups are particularly playful in the water, which makes for an incredible snorkeling experience. They seem to delight in playing impromptu games of peek-a-boo and demonstrating their acrobatic skills underwater. After a hard day's fishing and playing, the sea lions sprawl over beaches and rocks, snoozing to replenish their oxygen supplies. Walking among a colony is another highlight of any trip. Outside their colonies, sea lions are often found dozing on boats and docks.

However, they are not called lions for nothing (or "wolves" in Spanish—**lobos marinos**). The mature males can reach 2.5 meters in length, considerably bigger than the females, and they are more than a little scary. Males mate with about 10-15 females and can be very territorial, so be advised that although most of this posturing is harmless, sea lions occasionally attack—it's the principal cause of animal injury to visitors in the Galápagos. Steer well clear of patrolling males, especially when snorkeling. Their behavior is understandable, though—with such an uneven ratio of cows to bulls, many bulls are left fending for themselves and plotting their next move, and territorial battles are common. There are several bachelor colonies in the archipelago, where surplus males congregate. Dominant bulls are soon tired out, and territory tenure ranges from a few days to a few months before a new bull comes along and makes a successful challenge.

Mating usually takes place in shallow water or on land. Females give birth to a single pup, which is suckled for 1-3 years. The pups often congregate in "nurseries" while the adults are out fishing. Pups rarely swim without adults until they begin to fish for themselves, at about five months. The adults continue to accompany them, mindful that they do not swim too far out and attract predators in the form of sharks and killer whales.

Unfortunately, the sea lion population has declined considerably in recent years due to a lack of fish after the 1998 El Niño, but there are still more than 25,000 in the archipelago. Females live to age 20, males slightly less.

Males are territorial, so steer well clear of patrolling males, especially when snorkeling. Males can be identified by their larger size and a characteristic bump on their foreheads. Take special care not to accidentally touch the pups while on land. You can transfer scents that can cause the mother to abandon the pup.

Where to See Them

Sea lions are very easy to spot in the Galápagos, inhabiting shores all over the archipelago. You can even find them right in all the ports, most notably in Baquerizo Moreno on San Cristóbal, where they sunbathe on all the town benches. The best places to walk among a colony are at **Gardner Bay** on **Española** and **La Lobería** on **San Cristóbal.**

The best places to snorkel with sea lions are at **Enderby** on **Floreana's north shore; Isla Lobos** on **San Cristóbal; James Bay** on **Santiago; Gardner Bay** on **Española; Bartolomé;** and **Rábida.**

GALÁPAGOS FUR SEALS

Smaller than sea lions and with a thick, furry coat, the Galápagos fur seals are also harder to see because they prefer shaded areas and cooler waters. We are lucky that these endearing animals with their bearlike snouts and small external ears exist at all after they were hunted to the brink of extinction in the 19th century. The warm, two-layered pelt was in high demand in Europe and the United States, leading to slaughter on a mass scale.

The seal population recovered slowly through the 20th century but has suffered at the hands of nature as well as people. The warm currents of the El Niño phenomenon were particularly devastating, killing their supply of fish. Although they are endemic to the islands, many seals have now emigrated to the coast of Peru. There are still estimated to be over 20,000 fur seals inhabiting the northern and western islands of Pinta, Marchena, Santiago, Isabela, and Fernandina. The social behavior and breeding of fur seals is very similar to that of sea lions, although bulls establish their territory on land in contrast to sea lions, which tend to defend it from the sea.

Fur seals' preference for cooler water also puts them at greater risk from sharks that inhabit these waters, and attacks are frequent.

Where to See Them

Fur seals are much harder to see than sea lions, and if you stay in hotels you are not likely to see them at all. The best opportunities

Galápagos fur seal yawning at Puerto Egas

are the fur seal grottoes at **Puerto Egas** on **Santiago, Punta Vicente Roca** on **Isabela, Fernandina,** and **Genovesa.**

WHALES AND DOLPHINS

The mammals that pop in and out of the water are far easier to see than the several cetaceans (completely aquatic mammals) that live in the waters around the archipelago. There are many species of whales, but it's rare to see them. The massive blue whale is an occasional visitor, but you're more likely to spot humpback whales breaching. The killer whales or orcas are the most feared, preying on sea lions and fur seals. They often swim in small groups and are known to use sonar to locate their prey. Far more commonly seen are schools of bottlenose dolphins surfing the bow waves of cruise boats and leaping in unison.

Where to See Them

The best spot to see humpback whales is **west of Isabela and Fernandina** from July to September. Whale sharks can only be seen on **live-aboard dive cruises** going to the northern islands of **Wolf** and **Darwin.** Dolphins can be spotted throughout the archipelago, usually in open seas from boats.

BATS

Two endemic species of bats made the long crossing from the South American mainland—probably by accident—to settle in the Galápagos. They roost in trees and mangroves, feeding on insects.

Where to See Them

Bats are hard to spot because they are

Bottlenose dolphins can be found playing in the wake of cruise ships and speedboats.

nocturnal. They can occasionally be found flying around at night in the port towns.

RATS

Two species of rice rats are left from the original seven that must have arrived floating on vegetation. The rest have been driven to extinction by the larger Norway rat, which was introduced by visiting ships and remains a major threat to native species. They feed mainly on seeds and vegetation.

Where to See Them

The two species are found on **Fernandina** and **Santa Fé.**

Seabirds

Surrounded as the islands are by water rich in fish, it's no surprise that the Galápagos teem with birdlife. Only a relatively small minority of species—5 out of 19—are endemic: the Galápagos penguin, flightless cormorant, waved albatross, lava gull, and swallow-tailed gull. The other species, including the boobies and frigates that receive a lot of attention from visitors, are found elsewhere in Ecuador and along the South American coast.

BOOBIES

The Spanish sailors who first discovered the Galápagos were very unimpressed by a bird that would simply peer at them curiously instead of fleeing, so they called these birds *bobos* (stupid), and the name stuck. *Amigos* would have been nicer and more appropriate for these amenable birds, who are completely unfazed by humans walking within a meter or two of them on island trails. The insult to their intelligence is particularly unfair because boobies are no chumps—they are astonishingly adept at catching fish, dive-bombing the waters from as high as 25 meters

before popping up to the surface and gulping down the luckless prey. The shock of the impact with the sea is diffused by air sacs in the boobies' skulls.

The **blue-footed boobies** are the most commonly seen because they nest on the ground. There are actually far more **red-footed boobies** in the archipelago, but these smaller birds tend to feed farther out to sea and are mainly found on the more remote islands. In contrast to the other species, they nest in trees and shrubs. The **Nazca boobies** are the largest booby, with a wingspan of 1.5 meters. They are easily differentiated from the other boobies by their distinctive black eye mask, which contrasts with their bright white plumage. They nest on cliff edges, finding it difficult to take off from level ground. They were formerly thought to be a subspecies of masked boobies, but were later recognized as a separate species.

If you're lucky enough to see the blue-footed booby's mating ritual, it's hilarious: The male marches around, kicking his feet up high, then raises his beak skyward, whistles,

Blue-footed boobies dance at Punta Pitt.

Clockwise from top left: Male frigate birds inflate their red chest pouches to attract mates; Red-footed boobies are the only booby species that nest in trees; flamingos in Laguna Salinas on Isabela.

and opens his wings as if to say, "How can you resist my bright-blue feet?" The bluer the better, in the view of the female, who responds with a honk if she likes what she sees. After mating, the couple often begins to build a nest together, 1-3 eggs are laid, and the couple takes turns incubating them for about 40 days.

After the chicks hatch, the nest area is surrounded by a ring of excrement called guano. If the chick ventures outside the ring, it will often be rejected and could end up as lunch for a hawk or frigate. The male does most of the fishing, and females also help out, but only when the chicks are large enough to defend themselves.

Where to See Them

The **blue-footed boobies** are best seen on **Seymour Norte**, at **Punta Pitt** on **San Cristóbal**, and on **Española**, though you may find a couple individuals scattered throughout the archipelago. The largest colony of **red-footed boobies** in the world is on **Genovesa**, but there is a much smaller colony at **Punta Pitt on San Cristóbal**. The **Nazca boobies** can be seen on **Genovesa**, **Española**, and **Punta Pitt**, the last being the only place where all three booby species can be seen together.

If you're a frigate bird, size clearly matters. These scavengers are most famous for the bright red chest pouches that males inflate to the size of a basketball to attract females in the mating season. Once inflated, the male spends the entire day that way, calling and flapping his wings at passing females, hoping to attract one to the nest he has built for her. It's particularly romantic because once the female chooses the best-chested male, they mate for life. The sight of the inflated pouches is one of the highlights of bird-watching on the archipelago.

After mating, a single egg is laid, and both parents share the incubation duties for 7-8 weeks. After hatching, the young have to wait five months before they are able to fly and learn from their parents how to scavenge. Frigates don't reach maturity until age five.

Mating aside, though, frigates are actually the bad guys of the archipelago; they are scavengers that live mainly by stealing food from other birds. There are two species of frigates on the islands: the great and the magnificent. They are very similar in appearance, and both have the famous red sacs. They have a wide wingspan that can reach over two meters, but they cannot swim. Instead, frigates harass

SEABIRDS · **WILDLIFE GUIDE**

Nazca boobies nesting on Española

other birds, particularly boobies, into coughing up their hard-earned meal in an unpleasant show of avian bullying; sometimes they even steal fish right out of a chick's mouth. However, they are very resourceful and sometimes catch flying fish from just above the surface. Frigates have also learned that humans are a good source of food and are often seen following fishing boats in the hope of scavenging scraps.

Where to See Them

You will likely see frigate birds flying in the air throughout the islands. There are large colonies on **Seymour Norte, San Cristóbal,** and **Genovesa.** To see them close up and doing the famous mating display is trickier. The best place is undoubtedly Seymour Norte, where the mating display occurs year-round. You can also see the mating display from March to April on Genovesa and San Cristóbal.

WAVED ALBATROSS

If you don't go to Española, you probably won't see the largest seabird in the archipelago—it's as simple as that. Nearly the entire world population of waved albatross nests on this island April-November before migrating to Peru. They have a wingspan of 2.5 meters,

so it is quite a sight to see them taking off and landing. Española gets so busy in mating season that landing areas, most famously Punta Suárez, are nicknamed "albatross airports." Once they're out of the skies, these graceful fliers become surprisingly awkward; they often fall over after landing and then waddle around clumsily. It's not a surprise when you consider that many birds have not walked on land for months or even years. They travel without actually "landing," only leaving the skies to float on water far out in the ocean.

True to the Galápagos tradition, albatross have an entertaining mating ritual. The couples perform an elaborate courtship display, clacking their bills together, sky calling, and dancing around in a synchronized, circular walk. They sometimes do this for several hours, and the island turns into a kind of open-air avian disco. However, albatross are not the faithful birds we once thought they were, and research has shown that some have several partners while others are monogamous.

The first birds arrive on Española at the end of March, and courtship reaches its peak in April. The egg is incubated by both parents for two months. The birds quite often move the egg around rather than staying in

waved albatross nesting on Española

The Galápagos penguin is the only tropical penguin in the world.

while other species like iguanas and sea lions warm up on the rocks, the penguins struggle to cool down by swimming, standing with their wings out at 45-degree angles, and even panting rapidly. They rise early and spend most of the day swimming and fishing before returning to their colonies in the afternoon. You're most likely to see them standing around on the rocks, but in the water they are quite a sight—streaking after fish at speeds up to 40 kilometers per hour.

Galápagos penguins molt once a year, usually just before breeding, and during this period they do not enter the water. The penguins usually mate for life and lay eggs in crevices, caves, or holes to keep them out of the sun. The parents guard the eggs for five weeks until they hatch. Penguins do have to fear aquatic predators, but the main threat in recent years has been starvation. The 1998 El Niño had a severe effect on penguin numbers, and the latest estimates put the population at less than 2,000.

Where to See Them

The largest colonies are on **Fernandina** and **Isabela,** with far smaller colonies on **Floreana** and **Bartolomé.**

FLIGHTLESS CORMORANTS

Flightless cormorants are proof that evolution is not all about gaining skills but also about losing them. These birds spend so much time in water and have no predators to fear on land, so they have lost their ability to fly, the only species of cormorant to have done so. They have neither the chest muscles nor the wingspan to take to the air but instead have long necks, strong kicking legs, and webbed feet that make them experts at catching fish, eels, and even octopuses underwater.

They have an unusual courtship ritual, although you're unlikely to see it as it takes place underwater. The pair performs an aquatic "dance," swimming back and forth past each other before the male leads the female to the surface to mate. They build nests of seaweed

one nest. The first chicks arrive in June-July, and the adults feed them regurgitated fish oils until they are old enough to fly, usually by the end of the year, when they migrate.

Albatross can live up to age 50, and when not breeding, they spend their time at sea, sitting on the surface of the ocean to feed on squid and fish.

Where to See Them

You can only see these birds on a cruise April-November on **Punta Suárez** on **Española.**

GALÁPAGOS PENGUINS

The last thing you'd expect to see on the equator is a penguin, and these endearing little birds are special in two ways—they are the only penguin found in the northern hemisphere (the equator cuts across the north of Isabela), and at just 35 centimeters tall they are one of the smallest penguins in the world. They evolved from the Humboldt penguins that inhabit the coast of Chile but have retained much of their original insulation. So on rocks and beaches very close to the water-line—so close that some are washed away by high tides. Two or three eggs are laid, and incubation takes about 35 days.

Where to See Them
You can only see these birds on **Fernandina** and **western Isabela** while on a cruise.

ENDEMIC GULLS
There are over 35,000 **swallow-tailed gulls** nesting throughout the archipelago. These attractive birds sport a black head, a distinctive red eye ring, a white-and-gray body, and red feet. Unlike most gulls, swallowtails feed nocturnally, leave at dusk, and help to point boat captains toward land at dawn. The **lava gull** is thought to be the rarest gull in the world, with only 400 mating pairs nesting exclusively in the Galápagos. Their dark-gray plumage makes them difficult to pick out from the lava rocks they inhabit.

A flightless cormorant stretches its vestigial wings.

Where to See Them
Swallow-tailed gulls are usually flying over the ocean or nesting on rocky shores and cliffs throughout the archipelago, but the largest colonies are on **Española** and **Genovesa**. The lava gull is much rarer, but your best bets are **Santiago, Fernandina,** and **Genovesa.**

OTHER SEABIRDS
Elsewhere in the world, a pelican swooping into the sea to catch fish is considered an impressive sight. Here on the Galápagos, **brown pelicans** don't get as much attention as the more colorful and rarer birdlife. They are amazing creatures, though, filling their enormous 14-liter beak pouches on impact with the ocean, filtering out the fish, and gulping them down.

Red-billed tropic birds feed far out to sea and return to their nests on windy cliff-sides. They have a gray-and-white body and long, flowing white pintail feathers capped by a distinctive red bill and a black mask.

Where to See Them
Brown pelicans are common all over the Galápagos, including right in the port towns, where they can be found trying to steal scraps from the fishers. Red-billed tropic birds can be seen soaring along cliffs on **Genovesa, Española, Seymour Norte,** and **Plaza Sur.**

Coastal Birds

While they don't get nearly as much attention as their seafaring cousins, the islands' coastal and land birds are still fascinating, not least to Charles Darwin. One of the many mysteries of the Galápagos is how land birds that cannot fly over the sea could have arrived here; the most plausible conclusion is that they were blown all the way from the mainland by storms.

GREATER FLAMINGOS

Their distinctive pink makes these birds an attractive sight in the lagoons around the archipelago. They feed on shrimp by filtering through the salty lagoon water, and it is this shellfish diet that turns them pink from their original white. The population is relatively small, about 400-500 birds.

Where to See Them

The best places to see flamingos are the lagoons at **Punta Cormorant** on **Floreana, Red Beach** on **Rábida, Puerto Villamil** on **Isabela,** and **Bachas Beach** on **Santa Cruz.**

HERONS AND EGRETS

There are five species of herons, all prolific hunters of small lizards, rodents, insects, and fish. They stand motionless as statues and spear their prey with their long beaks. The largest is the **great blue heron,** 1.5 meters tall; the smaller **yellow-crowned night heron** feeds by night. The only endemic species is the small gray **lava heron** that hunts in rock pools.

Where to See Them

Herons and egrets are found in coastal areas and near lagoons, particularly on **Santa Cruz, San Cristóbal, Santiago,** and **Isabela.**

MIGRANT SPECIES

Six species of birds come down to the archipelago during winter in the northern hemisphere. They are the **semipalmated plover,** the **ruddy turnstone,** the **wandering tattler,** the **sanderling,** the **whimbrel,** and the **northern phalarope.**

Where to See Them

Look for migrant birds on rocky shores and coastlines in the winter.

Land Birds

DARWIN'S FINCHES

From a scientific viewpoint, these tiny birds are arguably the most important species in the Galápagos. The 13 species of finches with varied beak shapes were the most important inspiration for Charles Darwin's evolution theory. The key to the finches' survival, as Darwin noted, is the beak. Short, thick beaks enable **ground finches** to crack hard seeds, while longer, slimmer bills allow other species to probe crevices for insects and eat cacti or flowers. The finches obviously came from a common ancestor, but they are subtly different according to which island and even which part of the island they inhabit.

Finches are remarkably resourceful birds and are one of the few species to use tools to find prey. **Woodpecker** and **mangrove finches** use a cactus spine or small twig to get at grubs burrowed deep in tree branches.

The **sharp-billed ground finch** is the most unusual species, and a little sinister. It is nicknamed the "vampire finch" for its habit of pecking at the base of a booby's tail until it can drink a trickle of blood. The boobies offer little resistance, perhaps because the pecking also helps to remove parasites. This species also rolls other birds' eggs until they break and then eats the insides.

One aspect that unites the many species of finches is that they all have to fear the Galápagos hawk.

Where to See Them

The different species are found throughout the archipelago, but the best places to see them are in the **highlands of San Cristóbal, Santa Cruz, and Floreana,** as well as **James Bay** on **Santiago, Punta Suárez** on **Española,** and **Darwin Bay Beach** on **Genovesa.**

MOCKINGBIRDS

There are four species of mockingbirds endemic to the Galápagos, feeding mainly on insects and small reptiles. Sadly, though, mockingbirds are increasingly endangered due to introduced species, such as rats and cats, which hunt the chicks. Adults also need their wits about them to avoid the Galápagos hawk. They are slowly being reintroduced to Floreana following a large-scale extermination of invasive species.

a finch in the trees by Los Gemelos on Santa Cruz

Where to See Them

The four species of mockingbirds are endemic to different areas of the Galápagos. **San Cristóbal, Floreana,** and **Española** each have their own unique species endemic only to one particular island. The Galápagos mockingbird species is found on several islands, including **Santa Cruz, Santa Fé, Genovesa, Fernandina,** and **Isabela.**

GALÁPAGOS HAWKS

Out of the water, this fearless bird is the largest natural predator on the islands. It eats everything from baby iguanas and lizards to small birds, rodents, and insects, as well as scavenging on dead animals. It also has a highly unusual mating system known as cooperative polyandry: Up to four males mate with a single female, then help to incubate and raise the young.

Where to See Them

The hawks are found throughout the archipelago, but good spots include the **Santa Cruz highlands, Santa Fé, James Bay** on **Santiago, Bartolomé, Rábida,** and **Punta Suárez** on **Española.**

OTHER LAND BIRDS

The male **vermilion flycatcher** deserves special mention for its fiery red plumage, as does the **yellow warbler,** whose sunshine plumage is as beautiful as its songs.

Where to See Them

The vermilion flycatcher is rare but can be spotted in the **Santa Cruz highlands** and on **Isabela** near the Sierra Negra volcano. The yellow warbler is easier to spot flitting around trees in many areas of the archipelago.

Travels with Charlie

I have seen one of the thick-billed finches picking at one end of a piece of cactus whilst a lizard was eating at the other end; and afterwards the little bird with the utmost indifference hopped on the back of the reptile.

Charles Darwin in *The Voyage of the Beagle*, on the fearlessness of finches

Marine Life

The temperatures of the waters around the Galápagos are the foundation on which most life is built. These temperatures are as diverse as the wildlife, varying from a bone-chilling 15°C to the near-thermal-bath comfort of 30°C. With such a wide range of temperatures and depths, some 300 fish species inhabit the waters, which makes the Galápagos a wonderful snorkeling and diving destination. Snorkelers and divers can often gaze into a school of fish that seems to go on forever.

SHARKS

While there are few natural predators on land in the Galápagos, underwater is a different story. The cold waters are ideal for sharks, so sea lions have to be careful when swimming too far out. Luckily for humans, these sharks are mainly harmless. The most common are the docile **white-tipped reef sharks** and **black-tipped reef sharks,** which eat plankton and small fish. They tend to rest under rocks and in caves but are also commonly seen swimming close to shore.

The more adventurous can watch for scary-looking **hammerhead sharks.** Large schools of 30-40 of these incredible creatures are commonly encountered when diving, although they can occasionally be seen while snorkeling at Kicker Rock (León Dormido) or off the north shore of Floreana.

The largest shark in the archipelago is the huge **whale shark,** up to 20 meters long, found only at the outlying islands of Darwin

and Wolf, which are visited mainly by dedicated dive boats.

Where to See Them

Reef sharks are found all over the archipelago, but you are most likely to encounter them while snorkeling in the waters around **Española, Floreana, Seymour Norte, Bartolomé, Las Tintoreras** on **Isabela,** and **Kicker Rock (León Dormido)** on **San Cristóbal.** The larger Galápagos shark is another species that can be seen in these areas.

Divers can see hammerhead sharks at **Gordon Rocks, Kicker Rock,** and off **Floreana,** and whale sharks on **Darwin** and **Wolf.**

RAYS

Encountering a school of rays gliding along flapping their wings like underwater birds is unforgettable, and the Galápagos waters are filled with these beautiful creatures. When they swim past you, it's a highlight of any snorkeling or diving excursion, and on occasion they can also be viewed from boats. The most common are the **stingrays,** whose wings can span up to 1.8 meters, but be careful of the sting, which can whip up if you startle them. They are also found resting on sandy beaches, so watch where you step. More spectacular are the brightly colored **golden rays;** the massive **manta rays,** an incredible six meters across; and the rarer **spotted eagle rays,** found mainly in deeper waters.

Where to See Them

Rays are seen all over the archipelago and are easiest to see when snorkeling or diving, although they are also visible from boats. Good **snorkel sites** include **Kicker Rock (León Dormido), Gardner Bay,** and **Bartolomé.** Manta rays are harder to spot for snorkelers because they feed in deeper water, and thus are much more often spotted while diving. Good **dive sites** include **Gordon Rocks, Santa Fé, Mosquera, Daphne Minor, Cousins Rock,** and of course **Darwin** and **Wolf.**

FISH

Choosing highlights from the vast array of fish in the waters around the archipelago is tricky. **Surgeonfish** with bright yellow tails and gray bodies are commonly spotted in large schools. **King angelfish** are another common fish with blue-black coloring and yellow tails and fins. Silvery **salemas** can sometimes be found by the thousands in incredibly densely packed schools. If you look along the rocks, you might find the **hieroglyphic hawkfish,** named for the beautiful markings on its body. Among the most colorful are the iridescent blue-green **parrot fish** and the elegant **moorish idol,** with its long dorsal fin.

Where to See Them

You should be able to see many of these fish on snorkeling excursions throughout the archipelago.

INVERTEBRATES

Nobody expects crabs to be a highlight of a Galápagos trip, but you'll be surprised at how eye-catching some of the invertebrates are. Of the 100 crab species in the islands, the most colorful is the bright-red **Sally Lightfoot crab,** named for its fast movement across water over short distances. They are easily startled and can give a nasty pinch. They need to be fast to avoid the attentions of herons and moray eels. Other invertebrate species of note include **pencil-spined sea urchins,** many neon-colored species of **starfish (sea stars),** and the increasingly rare **sea cucumbers,** which have been harvested for their medicinal benefits and are now an endangered species.

Where to See Them

Crabs can be seen on rocky shores and beaches throughout the archipelago. Prime locations for the Sally Lightfoot crabs include **Bachas Beach, Seymour Norte, James Bay,** and **Gardner Bay.**

Sally Lightfoot crabs are scattered throughout the islands.

Background

The Landscape

The Galápagos's landscapes are as diverse and otherworldly as the wildlife that inhabits them: lush highland forests, pristine white-sand beaches, steaming volcanic peaks, and blackened lava trails strewn with cacti. The 13 volcanic islands and 16 tiny islets scattered over 60,000 square kilometers in the eastern Pacific Ocean have 8,000 square kilometers of land, including 1,350 kilometers of coast-line. The islands are actually the tips of un-derwater volcanoes, which become younger and higher to the west. Isabela, the largest island of the group at 4,275 square kilome-ters, has six volcanic peaks, and one of these, Cerro Azul, is the highest point on the islands at 1,689 meters.

Some 97 percent of the landmass is in the national park and uninhabited, and only the remaining 3 percent is inhabited. The latest estimated population of the archipelago is 30,000, of whom 7,000 are temporary resi-dents. The biggest population area is Puerto Ayora on Santa Cruz, followed by the capital, Puerto Baquerizo Moreno, on San Cristóbal, then Puerto Villamil on Isabela, and tiny Puerto Velasco Ibarra on Floreana.

GEOGRAPHY
Volcanic Origins

The Galápagos archipelago sits directly over a hot spot in the Pacific tectonic plate, where underlying magma bulges closer to the sur-face than usual. Millions of years ago, molten rock began to rise through the crust, cool-ing in the sea and forming mountains that eventually rose above the surface. New volca-noes quickly formed to take the place of older ones and were slowly eroded by the sea and weather, resulting in a rough chain of islands trailing off southeast toward the mainland.

Many volcanoes came and went over millions of years; Española, the oldest island in the ar-chipelago, is nearly 3.5 million years old. By comparison, Fernandina is less than one mil-lion years old, a mere infant in geologic terms. Geologists have found an island forming west of Fernandina, although it will be many thou-sands of years or so before it forms, so don't expect it to be included on your itinerary just yet.

Evidence of volcanic heritage is everywhere on the islands. Many lava flows have hardened into rocky trails, the most accessible being in Sullivan Bay on Santiago. In the highlands on Santa Cruz you can find collapsed calde-ras and lava tunnels, while Isabela offers the best close-up view of an active volcano, with trails leading past the second-largest crater in the world at Sierra Negra and into its pungent sulfur mines. Wolf volcano in the north of Isabela erupted in May 2015. Fernandina also has trails through lava fields, and it experi-enced the most recent eruption at La Cumbre in September 2017.

The Sea

The islands' unique ecosystem has been cre-ated by the interaction of several ocean cur-rents. The most famous and most powerful is the Humboldt Current, which brings cold water from the south along the coast of Chile and Peru. The warmer Panama Current flows down from Central America, and every few years it brings devastating warm El Niño con-ditions, most recently in 1998. A third cur-rent is the Equatorial Counter Current (also called the Cromwell Current), which flows deep below the surface and is deflected up-ward when it encounters the islands, bringing cool water, which is vital to the archipelago's

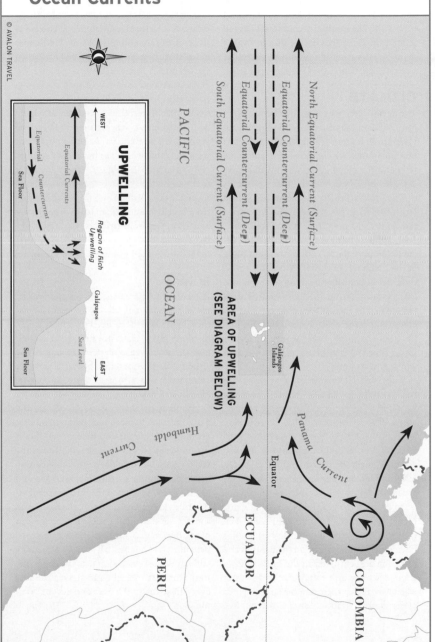

Ocean Currents

North Equatorial Current (Surface)

Equatorial Countercurrent (Deep)

Equatorial Countercurrent (Deep)

South Equatorial Current (Surface)

PACIFIC

OCEAN

**AREA OF UPWELLING
(SEE DIAGRAM BELOW)**

Galápagos
Islands

Humboldt Current

Panama Current

Equator

PERU

ECUADOR

COLOMBIA

UPWELLING

WEST

Equatorial Currents

Equatorial Countercurrent

Sea Floor

Region of Rich
Upwelling

Galápagos

Sea Level

Sea Floor

EAST

ecosystem. Algae thrive on the nutrients; fish and marine invertebrates feed off the algae; and whales, dolphins, sea lions, and birds eat these fish. The unusually cool waters found around the Galápagos ensure the survival of many species usually found only in colder waters, in particular the Galápagos penguin.

CLIMATE

The ocean currents determine the archipelago's subtropical climate. While there is no variation in hours of sunlight due to the fact that the islands are right on the equator, the temperature, cloud cover, and rainfall vary considerably throughout the year.

The hot or **rainy season** begins in December when the Panama Current warms the nearby waters to 26°C; it runs until May. Daily showers bring 6-10 centimeters of precipitation per month, with more rain falling in the highlands of the larger islands. As on the coast of Ecuador, the rainy season is also the warmest period, with hot, sunny days punctuated by intermittent showers. The average temperature climbs into the 30s, and the seas are comfortably warm for swimming; February and March are the warmest and sunniest months.

The June-November **dry season** arrives with the colder (20°C) waters from the Humboldt Current, and the average temperatures drop to less than 27°C. There is very little rain, but you often find **garúa,** a type of misty drizzle, in the highlands in August. Days are generally overcast, the seas colder and rougher, and the landscapes lose their greenery August-November, to be replenished again in the next rainy season. It's surprising how different the climate seems when climbing 500 meters into the highlands—it's often quite hot and sunny on the beaches and drizzling and chilly up in the hills, so it's a good idea to bring a rain jacket and sweater when heading up there. On the larger islands of Fernandina, Isabela, Santa Cruz, and San

Cristóbal, there is a distinctive type of cloud forest with mosses, lichens, and grasslands.

The biggest climatic problem in the archipelago is a lack of freshwater. The comparative lack of rain and the volcanic landscapes mean that there are few sources of water in the islands. Annual rainfall in the lower elevations is a mere 6-10 centimeters. This is the reason lizards, which require comparatively little water, thrive, and mammals do not. For humans, this has presented serious problems. The first islands to be populated were Floreana, which has freshwater springs, and San Cristóbal, which has freshwater lakes in the highlands. On Isabela most water is extracted from wells, and on Santa Cruz it comes from brackish water (a mixture of rainwater and seawater) from **grietas,** fissures in the lava rocks. However, large quantities of drinking water have to be brought to the islands.

El Niño

It seems ironic that such a destructive climatic phenomenon should be named after the Christ child. The "devil's current" might be more appropriate, but its arrival around Christmastime gave birth to the name "the child." The phenomenon brings a surge of warm water down from the north, forcing the Humboldt Current south for up to 18 months. Ocean temperatures rise, clouds gather, and 6-10 centimeters more rain falls per month. For humans, the main problems are flooding and crop loss, but for the wildlife of the Galápagos it is even more devastating. Strong El Niño conditions struck in 1982-1983 and again in 1997-1998, and the warmer sea temperatures killed algae and fish, the main food sources for much of the wildlife. Populations of marine iguanas, sea lions, waved albatross, penguins, and boobies fell sharply, and many still have not recovered. If past history is any indicator, a strong El Niño strikes roughly every 15 years, so the next one may be coming soon.

Plants

With such a bewildering array of wildlife and rugged volcanic landscapes to keep visitors busy, the plants of the Galápagos don't get much attention, and you're more likely to notice the absence of vegetation than its presence in often barren terrain. To put this in perspective, mainland Ecuador has 25,000 species of plants, while the Galápagos archipelago has just 550 species, only a third of which are endemic. However, the rainy season leads to an explosion of greenery on the larger islands, and there is much to admire in the hills.

The habitat of Galápagos plants is spread across three diverse areas: the coastal or littoral area, where fresh highland water meets saltwater; the semideserts of the dry areas; and the lush, humid, misty highland area.

MANGROVES

The coastal areas' flora is dominated by tangled mangroves, consisting of trees and plants that can only grow in brackish water. They weave themselves into the sand and send up small breathing roots called pneumatophores. The archipelago has four types: the **red mangrove** (the most common), found along sheltered shores and on the edges of lagoons, with larger, pointier, shinier leaves; the paler **white mangrove;** the darker **black mangrove,** found on sandy beaches; and the less common **button mangrove.**

PALO SANTO TREES

In the dry areas, the lifeless-looking palo santo tree blankets the landscapes. The trees may not look like much, but the smell of the wood is famously aromatic, used throughout Ecuador both as incense in church and to repel mosquitoes. The trees were given their name, which translates as "holy wood," for their habit of flowering near Christmas.

CACTI

Even more prevalent in dry areas are various species of cacti. The **opuntia** prickly pear cactus has evolved into 14 separate species throughout the archipelago. True to the Galápagos tradition, the species evolved according to which predator they have to repel. On islands with large populations of land iguanas and tortoises, the cacti are taller and thicker, growing up to 12 meters high, with stronger spines. On islands with no large predators, opuntia cacti grow low to the ground, and their spines are soft enough for birds to nest in and pollinate the cactus in return. Other Galápagos cacti include the endemic **lava cactus,** often the first thing to grow in new lava flows, and the more impressive **candelabra cactus,** which has branches that stretch up to seven meters across.

OTHER FLORA

The highlands of Santiago, Santa Cruz, San Cristóbal, and Floreana contain the richest variety of plantlife. Here you'll find dense forests of **lechoso trees,** a world away from the barren lowlands below. There are 90 species of **ferns,** some of which grow up to three meters high, and an equal number of mosses. **Orchids,** an endemic species of **mistletoe,** the purple and pink **cacotillo,** and purple-and-white **passion flowers** bring splashes of color to the highlands. Charles Darwin, of course, had a flower named after him— **Darwin's aster,** which has tiny white blossoms that can be seen in highland grass.

A rare edible endemic plant is the **Galápagos tomato,** which produces small green, yellow, and red fruits. There are 300 species of **lichens** on the islands, a symbiosis of algae and fungi. These lichens produce dyes ranging from purple, red, and orange to green and gray. Production of purple **dyer's moss** was a focus of some penal colonies on the islands in the early 20th century, but it was very labor intensive and not particularly lucrative. Make sure to stay clear of the **manzanillo,** also called the poison apple tree, as the fruit is highly poisonous, and even contact with the leaves can cause skin irritation. The trees can be found in highland areas and are commonly food for giant tortoises.

Conservation Issues

The Galápagos region is as delicate as it is unique. In an ecological Eden with few natural predators, the arrival of one particular predator—humans—has upset the balance considerably. Only time will tell if the balance can be restored. The following is a profile of the most serious problems and what is being done to solve them.

GROWTH OF TOURISM AND LOCAL POPULATION

The growth of tourism and the local population that supports tourism is one of the key drivers of other issues such as water pollution, the use of fossil fuels, and the introduction of invasive species. The number of tourists arriving yearly to the archipelago has grown enormously over the last 50 years. Tourism in the 1960s consisted of around 2,000 visitors a year sailing to the Galápagos on a handful of boats and hotels. Tourism grew to 40,000 visitors per year in 1990, 161,000 in 2007, and 224,000 visitors in 2015. These numbers continue growing around 4 percent per year.

The number of visitors who take cruises has remained flat for several years at around 70,000 people, due to the constant number of berths available on ships permitted to sail the Galápagos. All of the growth in the last decade has been due to land-based tourism, where visitors stay in hotels on the islands rather than on ships. As a result, the number of hotels has tripled between 2007 and 2015, from 73 to 291 registered hotels, and there are even more operating as unofficial guesthouses without permits. The local population has followed the growth pattern of land-based tourism and currently stands at about 30,000 people.

The islands are dependent on cargo ships for food and supplies.

FOSSIL FUELS AND TRAFFIC

As tourism grows, the islands require more electricity. Historically this has come from diesel, with its associated problem of causing air pollution. Diesel has also been the primary fuel for boats in the Galápagos. With increasing numbers of vessels in the archipelago, diesel has become particularly harmful to the coral. To cut costs, many boats use the cheapest fuel available, but the government is bringing in regulations to increase the use of less damaging biofuels. Transportation of diesel is also dangerous, as evidenced by the disastrous oil spill from the tanker *Jessica* off the shore of San Cristóbal in 2001.

Traffic is another pressing issue. Ecuadorians love their cars, and Puerto Ayora, the archipelago's main port, is overflowing with traffic. The government has brought in measures to try to restrict car use and is proposing a new public transportation system. But there are still more than 2,000 vehicles, including 200 taxis, plying the roads of the three populated islands, bringing danger and contamination with them. All too common are road kills, not just of birds but of iguanas and other lizards, and there are even road signs warning drivers to watch for giant tortoises crossing. It makes a good photo op, but it's sad that it is necessary.

There are ambitious plans to convert the islands to 100 percent renewable energy, and visitors can now see some of the progress. Baltra Airport is LEED Gold Certified and operates with 100 percent solar and wind energy. San Cristóbal now receives 30 percent of its energy from wind turbines.

WATER POLLUTION

With rising population come rising levels of waste, and the most pressing issue in Puerto Ayora at present is the sewage system. Freshwater has always been a problem in the archipelago, and most of Santa Cruz's municipal freshwater comes from **grietas,** fissures in the lava rocks. The island has no adequate water treatment system, and most residences and hotels rely on poorly maintained septic tanks. Municipal tankers clean the septic tanks by flushing the sludge into the ground inland. As a result, much of the island's water poses a health risk, and large areas around Puerto Ayora are polluted. Academy Bay in Santa Cruz is particularly polluted, as are some of the beaches surrounding Baquerizo Moreno on San Cristóbal. The municipal tap water is brackish and contaminated, and the population relies on private companies to provide desalinated bottled water for drinking. Nevertheless, incidents of gastritis and food poisoning, caused by dirty water, are common.

There are plans for a water treatment plant, but work is hampered by the enormous cost of drilling into the volcanic rock to construct a network of pipes. At present, the Finch Bay Eco Hotel is the only hotel that has its own water supply and sewage treatment plant on Santa Cruz.

ILLEGAL FISHING

Small-scale fishing within the Galápagos marine reserve is permitted under tight quotas. The growth of tourism has provided a relatively easy solution to the problem of illegal fishing—people working in fishing have been persuaded that they can make more money from tourism. Many have been given assistance to transition into the tourism industry as operators of artisanal fishing tours (which operate much like other day tours) or specialized sportfishing tours. However, environmentalists claim that even sportfishing is damaging.

Illegal fishing remains a serious problem, however; fishing for lucrative sea cucumbers only stopped because the species was fished to near extinction. Shark fishing continues to be a challenge, and there have been numerous incidents. Satellite technology has been introduced by the Ecuadorian navy, and more illegal vessels are being caught, but resources are limited. Many fishing boats use longlines that catch anything and everything, including sharks, dolphins, turtles, and seabirds. In July

2017, the Chinese fishing vessel *Fu Yuan Yu Leng 999* was caught in the Galápagos marine reserve near San Cristóbal Island. The vessel held 300 tonnes of catch, including 6,600 sharks of mostly protected species. The crew were sentenced to one- to four-year prison terms and a fine of $5.7 million.

INTRODUCED SPECIES

While humans have long posed a threat to the fragile ecosystem of the Galápagos, the animals and plants that they have brought with them have caused the most serious problems. There are believed to be nearly 1,000 introduced species in the archipelago. The vast majority are plants and insects, and fruit flies and fire ants have proven to be very difficult to remove. Larger creatures that have been introduced include 12 species of mammals, 6 species of birds, and 4 species of reptiles. Today, because agriculture has been largely abandoned in favor of tourism, the islands are highly reliant on supply cargo ships from the mainland for food, making it difficult to avoid introducing new insect species.

Introduced Animals

Most of the introduced mammals were brought over as domestic animals—as livestock, beasts of burden, or pets—before escaping into the wild. They all cause damage in their own way. **Donkeys** eat through cactustree trunks to get at the juicy pulp, killing the plant in the process. Scattered **horses** and **cattle** roam the highlands, trampling tortoise eggs, and the feral **pigs** are the worst enemy of giant tortoises, gobbling up as many turtle eggs as they can find and sometimes killing hatchlings.

Wild **dogs** are even more bloodthirsty. While pigs kill only for food, wild dogs have been responsible for senseless attacks on iguanas, sea lions, seals, and birds, particularly on Santa Cruz. **Cats** adapt very easily to the wild and are the biggest threat to small birds and chicks on many islands.

While these large animals have wreaked havoc, they are at least relatively easy to spot.

Rats, on the other hand, have been on the Galápagos even longer, arriving on whaling ships. As any city sanitation worker will tell you, they are extremely difficult to control. Black rats and Norway rats are the most common species. They spread disease to other species and are as much a danger as pigs to giant tortoises, eating hatchlings. The national park has been trying poison pellets to eliminate rats from smaller islands, such as Rábida, Bartolomé, and Plaza. It has been an effective program so far, but the problem is that the pellets are dangerous to Galápagos hawks, so the birds must be removed from the islands during the extermination process. Applying this method to the larger islands is fraught with difficulties.

Of all the introduced animals, the most damage has arguably been done by **goats.** They eat their way through pretty much anything, demolishing island vegetation and causing both erosion and food shortages for endemic species. They also reproduce at an astonishing rate—three goats left on Pinta in the late 1950s had produced more than 40,000 descendants by 1970. Luckily, goats are also very easy to eliminate, and some 250,000 have been culled in a large-scale extermination program on Isabela, Floreana, and Santiago. At present, only San Cristóbal, Santa Cruz, and the populated southern part of Isabela have remnant goat populations, but most goats are in enclosed areas.

Insects have caused major problems, too, the worst offenders being fire ants. These highly aggressive ants invade birds' nests as well as iguana and tortoise eggs. However, progress is being made to combat them. On the remote island of Marchena, trials with insecticide have successfully eliminated them, and the program will be extended to other islands, but it's a very slow process and will take many years. It also remains to be seen if the insecticide can be used over larger areas without degrading the ecosystem.

Introduced Plants

The growing human population has brought

enormous numbers of plants to the archipelago—more than 500 species is the latest estimate, and most of these have arrived in the past few decades. As any gardener can confirm, unwanted plants can strangle the life out of the endemic species, stealing sun, water, and nutrients. The main offenders are fruits—vines such as passion fruit (**maracuyá**) and blackberry (**mora**) grow quickly into impenetrable thickets, and trees such as the guava and red quinine take over entire hillsides. Weeds and flowers have spread from gardens to formerly arid zones on the major islands. Of all the plants, guava trees are perhaps the worst threat, and recent estimates show that they cover 50,000 hectares in the Galápagos. At present, the national park is investigating methods to control these plants, but they remain the biggest challenge of all invasive species.

Solutions

In the past decade, efforts to eliminate invasive species have been stepped up, but it's no easy task. To prevent the situation from getting worse, the Galápagos Inspection and Quarantine System (SICGAL) organization checks all luggage and packages, both entering the islands and moving between islands,

for organic materials of any kind. It may seem unnecessary to do this with foreign visitors, but even a piece of fruit could bring fruit flies onto the islands. However, the inspection system does not seem to prevent new insect species from arriving on the islands through tourist bags and cargo ships. The more rigorous checks and penalties for violations have discouraged the locals from importations and have led to confiscation of animals, plants, and seeds. Frustratingly, pets are still allowed, but they must be registered and neutered.

In terms of eliminating the species that are already on the islands, the best solution for larger animals is hunting, although with animal populations in the hundreds of thousands, it is costly and time-consuming. The alternatives are traps, which can ensnare other species, or poisoning, which is risky to the ecosystem. Hunting has reaped rewards, though; in 2002, a four-year campaign succeeded in ridding Santiago Island of 25,000 feral pigs. Even more impressive has been the elimination of goats from Santiago, northern Isabela, and Floreana—over 250,000 bit the dust by 2006, and the campaign is ongoing to remove them from San Cristóbal and Santa Cruz. How the hunters achieved this monumental task was highly impressive. Goats

Hundreds of thousands of goats used to roam Isabela.

were caught and fitted with radio-tracking collars, and their horns were painted bright colors. When they were released and rejoined the herds, hunters shot them from helicopters, and the carcasses were left to rot. There have been many other smaller-scale victories, but certain species, particularly rats, fire ants, and fruit trees, are proving far more difficult to control.

Regarding endangered species, progress is being made. Giant tortoise populations are being boosted by breeding centers on Santa Cruz, Floreana, San Cristóbal, and Isabela. In 2010, tortoises were reintroduced successfully to the remote island of Pinta, Lonesome George's original home. On Floreana, the population of dark-rumped petrels, which had been hunted to near extinction by dogs, cats, rats, and pigs, has recovered after a concerted effort to eliminate their predators. The endemic Floreana mockingbird is also being reintroduced to the island after its population had been confined to Champion Island.

Although the conservationists are winning battles, redressing the balance of the archipelago's ecosystem is a long, hard war, and it will take many years to undo the damage invasive species have caused.

If you're interested in helping the Galápagos solve environmental problems, tax-deductible **donations** for research, conservation, and environmental education can be sent

The Española tortoises are numbered due to breeding center programs.

to the **Charles Darwin Foundation** (407 N. Washington St., Suite 105, Falls Church, VA 22046, U.S. tel. 703/538-6833, www. darwinfoundation.org) or the **Galápagos Conservation Trust** (5 Derby St., London W1Y 7AD, U.K. tel. 20/7629-5049, www.gct. org).

History

The Galápagos Islands' isolation and inhospitable volcanic terrain have been their greatest assets for much of their history, saving them from colonization and degradation until relatively recently. With the South American coast 1,000 kilometers to the east and nothing but blue Pacific Ocean all the way to French Polynesia, over 5,000 kilometers to the west, the archipelago really was a hidden jewel for centuries.

EARLY VISITORS

It's not clear who the first visitors to the islands were, but it's probable that they were sailors blown off course or people on hapless fishing boats blown out to sea. Most of them were likely unimpressed by the lack of freshwater on the islands. Whether the Incas ever made it here is disputed; in 1572, Spanish chronicler Miguel Sarmiento de Gamboa claimed that the Inca Túpac Yupanqui had visited the archipelago, but there is little evidence for this, and many experts consider it a far-fetched legend, especially since the Incas weren't seafaring people.

The discovery of the islands by Europeans was officially made in 1535, when the ship of Tomás de Berlanga, Bishop of Panama, was pushed off course by the Panama Current on its way to Peru. The crew didn't stay long, but the bishop wrote to King Charles V of Spain enthusing about the giant tortoises with shells shaped like riding saddles (called **galápagos** in Spanish), and the name stuck. The islands appeared on a 1574 world map with the label "Insulae de los Galopegos." The islands were given their nickname, Las Islas Encantadas (The Enchanted Islands), by Spanish conquistador Diego de Rivadeneira, who believed the islands to be enchanted, moving with the ocean's currents. It made a better story than his navigation being a little off.

PIRATES AND WHALERS

During the 17th century, the Galápagos were used as a base for Dutch, French, and English pirates, most famously Sir Francis Drake, to mount raids on coastal ports and treasure-filled Spanish galleons. The pirate William Ambrose Cowley made the first working map of the Galápagos, naming islands after British royalty and aristocracy. Floreana and Santiago islands were originally called Charles and James, respectively, after British monarchs, and Isabela was once called Albemarle after a duke of the same title.

Given pirates' propensity to plunder, it's no surprise that they were the first humans to cause damage to the islands' ecosystem. The pirates realized the value of taking a giant tortoise on long voyages to provide fresh meat. Thousands were taken and stowed in ships' holds, enduring a slow death over the course of a year without food or water. This was the beginning of the drastic reduction in the giant tortoise population that had been over 250,000 before human arrival. Fur seals were another target, sold for their pelts, and by the early 19th century it became clear that the Galápagos were far more valuable than had previously been thought. On February 12, 1832, the newly independent Ecuador fought off halfhearted claims by the United States and Britain and annexed the islands officially.

CHARLES DARWIN AND THE GALÁPAGOS

In 1835, just three years after Ecuador annexed the archipelago, a young British scientist named Charles Darwin, then just age 26,

Whalers used to hand-deliver mail from a post office barrel on Floreana, a tradition that tourists carry on today.

Travels with Charlie

The staple article of animal food is supplied by the tortoises. Their numbers have of course been greatly reduced on this island, but the people yet count on two days' hunting giving them food for the rest of the week. It is said that the formerly single vessels have taken away as many as seven hundred, and that the ship's company of a frigate some years since brought down in one day two hundred tortoises to the beach.

Charles Darwin in *The Voyage of the Beagle*, on the marked effect of human colonization of Floreana on the giant tortoise population

visited aboard the HMS *Beagle*. Darwin collected crucial evidence, particularly from the many species of finches, that helped formulate his theory of evolution, published in *The Origin of Species* in 1859. This monumental work forever changed human beings' view of life on earth.

Charles Robert Darwin was born in Shropshire, England, in 1809 to an upper-middle-class British family. His father was a doctor and determined that his son would follow him into the profession, but Charles had other ideas, collecting specimens and studying botany in his spare time. He neglected his medical studies in Edinburgh in favor of his fascination with nature, and when his father transferred him to Cambridge to study theology, Darwin developed an interest in philosophical works on creation and adaptation.

Soon after graduating, Darwin was thrilled to be given the post of unpaid naturalist aboard the HMS *Beagle,* a small sailing vessel that left Plymouth, England, on December 27, 1831. The *Beagle* landed twice off the coast of Africa before crossing the Atlantic and beginning a two-year exploration of South America's eastern coast. Darwin explored the forests of Brazil and the high plains of Uruguay before the *Beagle* rounded Cape Horn in 1834 and headed up the western coast of Chile and Peru.

Darwin arrived in the Galápagos in September 1835 and spent five weeks here, visiting San Cristóbal, Floreana, Santiago, and Isabela. The evidence of evolution was everywhere—the different shapes of finches'

beaks, iguanas that had learned to swim, and cormorants that no longer needed to fly. The governor of the archipelago remarked to Darwin that he could identify which island a giant tortoise was from by the shape of its shell, and Darwin was particularly struck by the variation in mockingbirds caught on different islands. But far from having a eureka moment, Darwin took samples of species from as many islands as he could and took copious quantities of notes, which he analyzed for years afterward.

Even though he was a naturalist, he didn't take to all of the species he encountered, being particularly scathing about the marine iguanas, calling them "most disgusting clumsy lizards." Darwin was similar in his behavior to other sailors and wrote of his experience enjoying giant tortoise meat ("The breast plate roasted with the meat on it is very good") and the less enjoyable taste of iguana meat ("These lizards, when cooked, yield a white meat, which is liked by those whose stomachs soar above all prejudices").

DARWIN'S THEORY OF EVOLUTION

Darwin returned to England in October 1836. His visit to the Galápagos had changed him fundamentally. He had embarked on the *Beagle* voyage a firm believer in the biblical story of creation and the idea that God created perfect, immutable creatures. But the evidence of so many variations of subspecies on the islands was undeniable—why else did one finch have a slightly longer beak on an island where

Darwin's Voyage on the Beagle

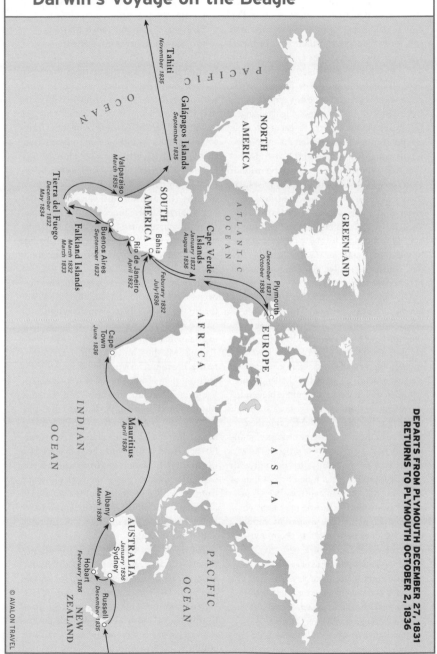

**DEPARTS FROM PLYMOUTH DECEMBER 27, 1831
RETURNS TO PLYMOUTH OCTOBER 2, 1836**

NORTH AMERICA

GREENLAND

SOUTH AMERICA

AFRICA

EUROPE

ASIA

AUSTRALIA

NEW ZEALAND

ATLANTIC OCEAN

PACIFIC OCEAN

INDIAN OCEAN

Tahiti
November 1835

Galápagos Islands
September 1835

Valparaiso
March 1835

Tierra del Fuego
December 1832
May 1834

Buenos Aires
September 1832

Falkland Islands
March 1832
March 1833

Río de Janeiro
April 1832
July 1836

Bahía
February 1832

Cape Verde Islands
January 1832
August 1836

Plymouth
December 1831
October 1836

Cape Town
June 1836

Mauritius
April 1836

Albany
March 1836

Hobart
February 1836

Sydney
January 1836

Russell
December 1835

© AVALON TRAVEL

its primary food source was insects living in crevices, while another finch had a shorter, stronger beak better for cracking nuts? The only logical explanation was that the finch species had adapted to their environment. Darwin was a meticulous and devout man, and it took him more than 20 years to finally publish his findings. A key reason for the delay was his concern over the impact of his theory on Victorian England's highly evangelical society. In the end, the threat of someone else publishing the theory first finally spurred him to act: A fellow naturalist, Alfred Russel Wallace—younger and less conventional than Darwin—was about to publish a similar theory in 1858. When Darwin's friends discovered this, they arranged for Darwin and Wallace to read a joint paper to the Linnean Society of London, formally presenting evolution to the public for the first time. To this day, Wallace is credited as the codiscoverer of natural selection.

On November 24, 1859, Darwin published *On the Origin of Species by Means of Natural Selection*, and the world would never be quite the same. The book's central idea, while being revolutionary to Victorian England, was extremely simple—that organisms change over time in order to adapt to the challenges presented in their habitats. One of the biggest inspirations for the idea was the beak shapes of Galápagos finches. This idea became the cornerstone of the concept of the process of natural selection. To explain the process, Darwin proposed a mechanism called descent with modification. He based it on observations of animals and plants in captivity, which produced many more offspring than their environmental "niche" could possibly support. Only the ones best-suited to their environment survived to reproduce.

> As many more individuals of each species are born than can possibly survive; and as, consequently, there is a frequently recurring struggle for existence, it follows that any being, if it vary however slightly in any manner profitable to itself, under the complex and sometimes varying conditions of life, will have a better chance of surviving, and thus be naturally selected. From the strong principle of inheritance, any selected variety will tend to propagate its new and modified form.

The process could even work in "reverse," leading to the loss of adaptations that were suddenly no longer beneficial. On an island with no predators, and hence no need for birds to fly to safety, wings might eventually just get in the way. Birds that could somehow forgo growing them would be able to swim after fish more efficiently and have more energy left over for other things—such as reproduction—than their fellows; thus the cormorant became flightless. The theory applied not just to physical attributes but also to behavior. Birds surrounded by predators would be naturally timid, while birds on the Galápagos, with no natural predators, were uncommonly docile.

Darwin was the first to admit that his theory was still full of holes, and that he was not the first to suggest this concept, having drawn on the work of a long list of scientists, including Jean-Baptiste Lamarck, Charles Lyell, Thomas Malthus, and Darwin's own grandfather, Erasmus Darwin. But his modesty did nothing to quell the uproar that it caused in Victorian England, just as he had feared it would. The church was particularly unhappy at Darwin's implication that God's work was not perfect but had to be changed over time. Darwin, who had recently been bereaved by the death of his infant son from scarlet fever, was suffering from illness that kept him away from public events and out of the storm. He remained a committed Christian and fervently disagreed that his theory was at odds with belief in God.

However, with the support of friends and scientific colleagues, toward the end of his life Darwin's theory gradually became accepted, and nowadays it is accepted as scientific fact. Darwin continued his work into old age, publishing several more books, and lived out the remainder of his days with his wife and 10 children in Downe House in Kent. He died on April 19, 1882, at age 73. He was given a state funeral, a rare honor outside the royal family, and buried in Westminster Abbey next to Sir Isaac Newton.

THE LATE 19TH AND EARLY 20TH CENTURIES

These so-called "enchanted islands" became anything but through the latter part of the 19th century, when most of the residents were convicts. Similar to the British policy of sending convicts to Australia, Ecuador commuted the death penalty to a life sentence of toil on the islands, where the convicts endured cruel treatment and scratched out a meager existence, such as by making dye from lichen. There were colonies on Floreana, San Cristóbal, and Isabela, the latter functioning until 1959.

As the world plunged into World War I, the Galápagos were used by the U.S. Navy to protect the entrance to the new Panama Canal, completed in 1914. After the war, the first permanent settlers (apart from the convicts) began to arrive.

The world had woken up to the wonders of the Galápagos, and it was only a matter of time before Europeans were attracted to escape to a place depicted in books and newspapers as a Pacific paradise. An eccentric German doctor named Friedrich Ritter was so taken with the Galápagos that in 1929 he set off for Floreana with his lover (and former patient), Dore Strauch. They were followed by the Wittmer family, and finally, a troublesome woman who claimed to be a baroness arrived with two lovers. The residents of Floreana drew international media attention, and the story of death and disappearance that ensued has been recounted in several books and a 2013 documentary.

During World War II, the U.S. Army Air Forces set up an airport on Baltra to monitor Japanese activity in the South Pacific, and then donated the airport to Ecuador after the war.

THE LATE 20TH AND EARLY 21ST CENTURIES

Conservation efforts increased in the mid-20th century, and after some islands had been established as wildlife sanctuaries in the 1930s, the whole archipelago became a national park in 1959. Three percent of the land was earmarked for use by the local population for housing, agriculture, and land-based tourism in the port cities. The Charles Darwin Research Station opened in Puerto Ayora in 1964, followed four years later by the Galápagos National Park Service. This was the start of an effort to study and conserve the islands' unique natural heritage, but it also coincided with an increase in tourism. Scheduled flights to the Galápagos began in the early 1970s, and tourism grew rapidly.

As word spread of fortunes to be made from fishing and tourism, immigration to the islands from the mainland gathered pace and led to increasing friction between conservationists, who wanted a minimal human population, and immigrants, who wanted to make a decent living. In 1978 the archipelago was among the first 12 regions in the world to receive UNESCO protection.

Paradise in Revolt

In 1986 the Galápagos Marine Resources Reserve was created to protect the waters around the islands. However, illegal fishing continued, and officials found encampments of *pepineros* (sea cucumber fishers) collecting tens of thousands of sea cucumbers per day on the coast of Isabela. Conflicts over the banning of fishing, the exposure of the **pepinero** camps, and other reforms sparked angry protests that shocked the international community. On one day, the carcasses of 80 giant tortoises were found slaughtered on the shores of Isabela. A militant group threatened to hold tourists hostage and burn the national park. A group of machete-wielding fishers seized the Charles Darwin Research Station and threatened to kill the national park's darling last-of-species tortoise Lonesome George. A park ranger's house was burned down.

In the meantime, the stakes increased for the conflicts as tourism continued to boom with 9 percent growth per year. There were no restrictions on immigration, and the local population grew as people from the mainland were lured to the island by higher wages and better opportunities.

The Special Law

The political turmoil put increasing pressure on the Ecuadorian government, and they finally responded with the Special Law of Galápagos in 1998. The law aimed to stabilize the resident population and encourage sustainable development. Critically, new immigration from mainland Ecuador was restricted for the first time; residency was restricted to people already living on the islands and their children. An eradication and quarantine program was set up, restrictions on illegal fishing expanded, and Galápagos residents were given preferential treatment for permits for new projects. The intent was to limit the growth of the local population and provide a better living standard for those who stayed.

Deportations of people without residency were common, but overall enforcement of the Special Law of Galápagos was inconsistent. As a result, the resident population continued to grow through illegal immigration as well as a high birthrate. Environmentalists also expressed criticism that the law crucially failed to limit the number of tourists permitted to visit the islands. Even with tighter regulations, the environmental situation deteriorated after 2001: The visitor numbers tripled in 15 years to reach 160,000 annually in 2007. Lucrative illegal fishing of shark fins and sea cucumbers continued, as the size of the Galápagos Marine Resources Reserve made it difficult to patrol.

Galápagos in Danger?

In 2007 the islands were placed on the UNESCO List of World Heritage in Danger. This widely publicized move seemed to focus minds locally, and Ecuadorian president Rafael Correa's government introduced a series of measures to improve the environmental situation through better controls on migration and checks for invasive species. The primary changes were the "Zero people on irregular status in Galápagos" policy, enforcement through deportation, and the implementation of a Transit Control Card (TCT) system to track visitors.

After this action, the Ecuadorian government successfully lobbied to have the islands removed from UNESCO's danger list in July 2010, a decision welcomed by the travel industry but heavily criticized by scientists and conservationists, who claimed it was premature to judge that the islands are out of danger. Galápagos continues to struggle with illegal fishing, water pollution, fossil fuels, invasive species, and growth in tourism and local population.

Government and Economy

GOVERNMENT

Democracy in Ecuador has been in place since the end of military rule in 1979. However, the military is never far from the political arena, and military-backed coups have removed several presidents, including Jamil Mahuad in 2000 and Lucio Gutiérrez in 2005.

From 2007-2017, leftist president Rafael Correa reduced political instability by forming a new political party, Alianza PAIS, which now dominates the National Assembly. Correa's administration presided over important legislation in the Galápagos, including tighter regulations on fishing and immigration as well as efforts to eliminate invasive species. Environmentalists applauded Correa's Yasuni-ITT plan, whereby he proposed that rich countries pay Ecuador not to drill for oil in the Yasuni region of the Amazon rainforest. The acclaim for this creative initiative quickly turned to criticism when Correa abandoned the plan in 2013, stating that not enough funds had been raised and authorized drilling in the Yasuni.

In 2017 former vice president Lenin Moreno was elected to succeed Correa. Moreno was shot and confined to a wheelchair in 1998, and he has been widely recognized for his advocacy for people with disabilities.

The Galápagos are among the 24 *provincias* (provinces), each ruled by a governor. The capital is Baquerizo Moreno on San Cristóbal, even though Puerto Ayora on Santa Cruz is considerably larger. The local government's focus on economic expansion has frequently come into conflict with the Galápagos National Park and Charles Darwin Research Station.

ECONOMY

Ecuador's economy balances between relatively small agricultural enterprises, businesses in the mountainous sierra, and huge export projects along the coast. Oil supplies half the country's export earnings, and bananas, cut flowers, shrimp, coffee, and chocolate are the other main exports. Since the economic crisis of the 1990s, when the national currency, the sucre, was replaced by the U.S. dollar, the Ecuadorian economy has recovered well, posting annual growth of 5 percent during 2002-2006, peaking at 7 percent because of high oil prices in 2007. However, low oil prices in recent years have caused stagnation. In 2016 a disastrous earthquake struck the coast, causing hundreds of casualties and $3 billion in damage. The government is financing reconstruction of disaster areas and infrastructure projects through higher taxes, which has also dampened the economy somewhat.

On the Galápagos, the main industries are tourism and fishing. Tourism has boomed recently, with tourist arrivals tripling over the past 20 years, and the industry generates more than $400 million. However, most of this income has not stayed on the islands, with profits taken instead by tour operators based on the mainland or abroad. The government has recently introduced measures requiring more profits to remain on the islands, and most employees have to be local residents with contracts granted to nonresidents only if the employer can prove that they bring special expertise not available on the archipelago.

The fishing industry has been particularly damaging to the local ecosystem, notably through overfishing and illegal fishing of sharks and sea cucumbers. Many of those working in fishing have been persuaded to move into tourism, and sportfishing has developed as a less environmentally damaging pastime.

People and Culture

POPULATION

Ecuador's population currently stands at 15 million and is growing at a rate of about 1 percent per year. Large families are still considered the norm, not least because the predominant Roman Catholic religion frowns on birth control. Women still tend to marry young and have children quickly. The result of this is a very young population—35 percent are under 15, while only 4.5 percent are over 65.

The population of the Galápagos has boomed in recent years alongside the growth in tourism, rising from under 10,000 in 1990 to over 30,000 currently. It is estimated to be growing at 5 percent per year. Most residents originate from the coast and the sierra, with Quito, Guayaquil, and Loja particularly well represented. More than 5,000 of the residents were estimated to be in the archipelago illegally, and several thousand have been deported back to the mainland since 2007. Tougher new residency laws have slowed immigration, but another key problem is a baby boom on the archipelago. Babies born here have automatic residency status, and recent estimates put the youth population at nearly 50 percent, a population time bomb that surely cannot be sustainable.

RACIAL GROUPS

The largest racial group in Ecuador is mestizo—people of mixed Spanish and indigenous heritage—although you'll rarely hear anyone refer to themselves by this word. They make up 65 percent of the population. Indigenous people make up 25 percent, mainly living in the mountains of the mainland. White people of Hispanic descent dominate Ecuador's richer classes (5-7 percent). A small Afro-Ecuadorian population, concentrated mainly in Esmeraldas, Quito, and Guayaquil, makes up 3 percent.

On the Galápagos, the vast majority of the residents—more than 80 percent—are mestizo, with a relatively small number of indigenous Ecuadorian people (8 percent) compared with mainland Ecuador, probably because most indigenous groups inhabit mountainous or rainforest regions and are not attracted to the Galápagos.

EDUCATION

The level of education on the archipelago is slightly higher than in the rest of Ecuador, with more than 40 percent of the population high school graduates, and 15 percent have university education. The Universidad Central in Puerto Ayora and the Universidad San Francisco in Baquerizo Moreno are branches of schools based in Quito.

LANGUAGE

Spanish is the official language of Ecuador and is spoken by the great majority of the people that visitors encounter. The Ecuadorian Spanish accent is generally considered relatively easy to understand, though there are strong regional variations and enough differences that Spanish speakers who learned in the United States can easily be confused. To add to the linguistic mix, there are more than 20 different languages spoken by the indigenous groups in Ecuador, so if you veer off the beaten path in Quito, you may encounter Quechua-speaking Ecuadorians who speak no English and very little Spanish. You may also hear Quechua words incorporated into Ecuadorian Spanish.

Basic English is widely understood and spoken to tourists in the tourist-geared hotels and restaurants in major cities such as Guayaquil and Quito. It's fun—and it will be appreciated—to put in a little effort to talk to the locals in Spanish when possible, but it is also possible to get by knowing almost no Spanish. It's even easier in the Galápagos, where the level of English is significantly higher due to the islands' focus on tourism.

Essentials

Transportation

GETTING THERE

The Galápagos can only be reached by flying into either of Ecuador's two international airports, located in Quito and Guayaquil, and then taking another flight from Quito or Guayaquil to one of two airports in the Galápagos: Baltra (just north of Santa Cruz) or San Cristóbal. Tracking down the cheapest fare is more problematic than finding a flight in the first place.

Air

TO AND FROM THE UNITED STATES

American Airlines (U.S. tel. 800/433-7300, Quito tel. 2/226-0900, www.aa.com) has daily flights to Ecuador from most major U.S. cities via Miami or New York. **United** (tel. 800/222-333, www.united.com) shuttles its planes through Houston and New York, and some stop in Panama. **Delta** (tel. 800/101-060, www.delta.com) has daily flights from its Atlanta hub. All these airlines can bring you to either Quito or Guayaquil. Newer routes are offered by **Copa** (www.copaair.com) through Panama and by **Lacsa/TACA** (www.taca.com) through Costa Rica. **AeroGal** (www.aerogal.com.ec) and **LAN** (www.lan.com) are competing with flights from Miami. The trip takes about four hours from Miami and five hours from Houston and Atlanta. Airfares vary greatly, so shop around; generally you can expect to pay $500-800 for a round-trip ticket.

TO AND FROM CANADA

Most flights from Canada connect through gateway cities in the United States. Air Canada and American Airlines fly from Toronto and Montreal via New York and Miami to Quito. **Travel Cuts** (www.travelcuts.com) is Canada's discount student travel agency, with more than 60 offices throughout the country.

TO AND FROM EUROPE

Of the major European carriers, only **KLM** (www.klm.com) and **Iberia** (www.iberia.com) fly their own planes to Ecuador. KLM goes from Amsterdam and Iberia from Madrid. **Air Comet** and **Air Europa** are newer competition from Europe. Other carriers make connections in Caracas, Bogotá, Miami, or New York. Flights take 15-17 hours and airfares vary widely, from $1,000 upward.

A competitive discount travel market in the United Kingdom keeps prices reasonable. **Journey Latin America** (12-13 Healthfield Ter., Chiswick, London W4 4JE, U.K. tel. 20/8747-3108, U.K. fax 20/8742-1312, www.journeylatinamerica.co.uk) and **Trailfinders** (63 Conduit St., London W1S 2GB, www.trailfinders.com) are both recommended.

TO AND FROM AUSTRALIA AND NEW ZEALAND

There are no direct flights to Ecuador from Australia and New Zealand. The best routes are on **Qantas** via Los Angeles and Miami, **Qantas/LAN** via Santiago, or **Aerolíneas Argentinas** via Buenos Aires. Travel times are a minimum of 24 hours, and the cost is about A$2,000.

TO AND FROM LATIN AMERICA

Although major airlines connect Quito and Guayaquil with most other capitals in South America, it's usually cheapest to cross borders by bus because international flights are highly taxed. South American airlines include: **Aerolíneas Argentinas** (Argentina), **Lloyd Aéreo Boliviano** (Bolivia), **Gol** and **Varig**

Previous: Expect wet landings, where you climb out of a small boat onto shore; *canhalagua ceviche*.

(Brazil), **LAN** (Chile), **Avianca** and **TAME Calí** (Colombia), **LAN Perú** and **Nuevo Continente** (Peru), and **SBA** (Venezuela).

Airlines that offer flights within Central America and the Caribbean include **Lacsa/TACA** in Costa Rica, **Cubana** in Cuba, and **Copa** in Panama. The least expensive air route between Central and South America is via Colombia's tiny Caribbean island of San Andrés, connecting to Cartagena and beyond.

TO THE GALÁPAGOS

Flights to the Galápagos are usually paid separately, although agents can arrange them for you. **TAME** (Quito tel. 2/397-7100, Guayaquil tel. 4/231-0305), **AeroGal** (Quito tel. 2/294-2800, Guayaquil tel. 4/231-0346), and **LAN** (tel. 800/101-075, www.lan.com) all offer round-trip flights to San Cristóbal and Baltra. Prices for foreigners are usually $350-400 from Guayaquil and $400-450 from Quito, although there are occasionally promotional fares. *Censo* (foreign-resident ID) holders pay less, about $260-300, and for local Galápagos residents the fare is less than $150.

Check-in is at least 90 minutes before departure because there are special procedures when you fly to the Galápagos. You need to first line up to get a transit control card (TCT card), which costs $20. Next, you need to get in the inspection line where your luggage will be scanned and inspected to make sure you are not bringing in fruit or other prohibited items. The inspectors will tag your luggage. Once you have your luggage tagged, you can proceed to the check-in counter and pass through security as usual.

All flights originate in Quito and stop in Guayaquil for at least one hour, where passengers usually disembark while the plane is refueled. The flight takes about three hours from Quito (inclusive of the stop), and you're allowed to bring one main piece of luggage up to 20 kilograms. Tours should reconfirm flights for you both ways, but if you booked independently, do this yourself. Independent travelers must also make sure they fly to the correct island at the correct time to begin the tour, and arrange this *before* booking the tour.

Once you arrive in the Galápagos, you'll stand in line to pay the **national park entrance fee,** which costs $100 per person for foreigners and a measly $6 for locals. It's payable in cash only upon arrival at the Galápagos airport. The **migratory control card** costs $20 and is for both Ecuadorians and visitors. Be sure to keep both the receipt

Visitors line up for special luggage inspection before boarding a flight to the Galápagos.

for the fee and the control card—if you lose them, you may have to pay again.

If you're arriving in the Galápagos on an organized tour, you won't have to worry about transfers because you'll be met at the airport by guides who will take you to your hotel or yacht. For independent travelers, it depends which island you arrive on. San Cristóbal is very easy because the airport is very close to the main port, Baquerizo Moreno. You can walk it in 20 minutes, but most people take a taxi ($2). For Santa Cruz, it's more complicated. Flights arrive on the tiny island of Baltra, just north of Santa Cruz. Reaching the main port of Puerto Ayora is a three-stage process. First, take the free 10-minute bus shuttle, followed by a 10-minute ferry crossing ($1), and then either wait for a bus ($3) or take a taxi directly to the port (45 minutes, $25). The entire journey from the airport takes over an hour, although you'll likely be too excited to complain. To return to the airport from Puerto Ayora, take a taxi to the bus terminal north of town, but note that the last bus usually leaves at 9:30am, after which a taxi is the only option.

GETTING AROUND

Getting around the Galápagos is easier than it used to be. If you have booked a tour, you don't need to worry about this because all transfers, shuttles, and cruises are prearranged.

Boat

Traveling between islands is easier nowadays, with daily services on small speedboats connecting Santa Cruz with San Cristóbal, Isabela, and Floreana. All routes cost $30 per person one-way and take 2-2.5 hours, depending on the sea conditions. You can buy a round-trip ticket for $50, bringing the price down to $25 each way. The ferries leave Puerto Ayora for San Cristóbal and Isabela at 7am and 2pm. The reverse trip from Isabela to Puerto Ayora leaves at 6am or 3pm. The reverse trip from San Cristóbal to Puerto Ayora leaves at 7am and 2pm. Ferries depart Puerto Ayora for Floreana at 8am and start the return trip from Floreana to Santa Cruz at 2:30pm.

Usually, several boats run each day between Isabela, Santa Cruz, and San Cristóbal. Getting to and from Floreana is trickier; the ferries only run three to four times a week, and the schedule isn't fixed to any particular day of the week. It's best to ask at the nearest travel agency. Ferries can get booked up,

Public speedboat ferries travel between the four inhabited islands.

Interisland flights are a more comfortable way to travel between inhabited islands.

ask the crew if you can sit up top. The second-best seats are in the back of the boat. Since this part of the boat is lowest in the water, it tends to rock the least, though in rough waters passengers will frequently get wet. The worst seats as far as seasickness goes are the interior cabin, especially toward the front. Seats are first come, first served, so try to line up and board early to get a good one. Pro tip: Try to be seventh or eighth in line at the dock; everyone takes a water taxi to get onto the speedboat, then the water taxi will disembark in reverse order. The last person on the water taxi is the first person on the speedboat.

Bus

Bus services are limited on the islands. There are buses on Santa Cruz from Puerto Ayora to Bellavista and Santa Rosa that run several times a day and are useful for visiting the highlands. There is also an airport bus that only runs a couple times a day. Bus service on the other islands is much more limited and less useful, though there are a few exceptions, such as the *chiva* (an open-air bus) on Floreana and the once-weekly Sunday bus to Puerto Chino from Baquerizo Moreno on San Cristóbal.

Interisland Flights

If you're in a hurry and can spare the extra cost, take an interisland flight with **Emetebe,** which has an office on Santa Cruz (Los Colonos and Darwin, top floor, Puerto Ayora, tel. 5/252-6177) or **FlyGalapagos** (tel. 98/354-1125 , www.flygalapagos.net). Small eight-seat planes fly half-hour routes among San Cristóbal, Baltra, and Isabela several times per week. Airfares start at $160 one-way, $260 round-trip.

Camionetas and Taxis

In each of the three main ports, white *camionetas* (pickup trucks) are available for hire, and most destinations in town cost $1.50-2. Trips into the highlands by taxi cost from $40 for a half day or $10 per hour.

so reserve one day in advance. Unfortunately, there are no public direct services between San Cristóbal, Floreana, and Isabela; all the boats stop or connect in Santa Cruz.

You will have to get your luggage inspected prior to boarding the boat, so arrive 15 minutes early. You are not allowed to transport most fresh produce between the islands except for things like apples and pears that have already been imported (and inspected) from mainland Ecuador.

It can be a bumpy ride, particularly in the afternoon and from June to September when the seas are at their roughest. To minimize seasickness, don't eat a big meal beforehand, take seasickness pills in advance if necessary, try to get a good seat, and watch the horizon.

The best seats by far are the second-floor cockpit where the captain sits, where there is less engine noise, a strong breeze, and the 360-degree view of the horizon to minimize seasickness. Not all speedboats have a second-floor seating area, though, and you have to

Walking and Biking

It's better for the environment to vote with your feet and either walk or rent a bike ($15/ day or $3/hour, deposit usually required) rather than taking a taxi or *camioneta*. Some higher-end hotels offer free use of bicycles.

Visas and Officialdom

Most travelers entering Ecuador are given a stamped **tourist visa** (also called a T-3) upon entry. The duration of the visa is 90 days. If you overstay your visa without extending it, you'll have to pay a $200 fine.

To enter Ecuador, all travelers must have a **passport** valid for more than six months from the date of entry, a return ticket, and "proof of economic means to support yourself during your stay," which is loosely defined and may involve showing a photocopy of a bank statement. The last requirement is seldom invoked.

To enter the Galápagos, you must obtain the mandatory $20 **transit control card** (TCT card) from your departure airport (either Quito or Guayaquil). This helps to regulate the exact number of visitors. Hold onto the card; you need it to exit the Galápagos. On arrival in the archipelago, there is a mandatory $100 national park entrance fee, payable in cash. It's a hefty fee, but it helps preserve the islands' fragile ecosystem. If you have a student or cultural visa, you should pay $25, while Ecuadorians pay just $6. Unlike the rest of mainland Ecuador, the maximum stay on the Galápagos is 60 days, although most visitors stay 5-10 days.

You can extend your mainland Ecuador visa past the original 90 days to a maximum of 180 days at the immigration offices in Quito or Guayaquil before your visa expires. However, this isn't particularly useful for Galápagos visitors because your Galápagos stay of 60 days cannot be extended.

At the time of writing, officials were considering implementing additional entry requirements, so double-check before your trip.

LEAVING THE GALÁPAGOS

Leaving the Galápagos is much simpler than entering; after a luggage inspection to make sure that you are not taking prohibited items from the islands, you simply turn in the TCT card that you were given on entry.

Once you are in Quito or Guayaquil, to exit Ecuador, you simply go to immigration and get an exit stamp.

CUSTOMS

The Galápagos has stricter regulations than other destinations because of the fragile ecosystem. All visitors have their luggage inspected at Quito and Guayaquil airports and before boarding shuttle ferry services between islands. There is a long list of items that are prohibited, including plants, flowers, fungi, seeds, animals, soil, and timber. More relevant to visitors are the regulations on food: Coffee beans, dairy products, meat, and especially fruit and vegetables can all pose risks and are often confiscated by bag inspectors. You're safe with packaged drinks and packaged snacks, but otherwise it's best not to bring any food and drink. If you do bring food, help out by taking the trash off the archipelago in your luggage, or at least make sure you use the recycling containers dotted around the towns. If your bag is searched several times during your visit, understand that this is an essential part of environmental protection, as many visitors either unwittingly or, in some cases, deliberately flout regulations. Customs has caught travelers attempting to smuggle out dried sea cucumbers in suitcases, for example.

Food and Accommodations

FOOD AND DRINK

Ecuador isn't known for gourmet cookery, but perhaps the best food is found on the coast, and many of these specialties are available on the Galápagos.

The biggest downside is that the majority of food on the islands is shipped in from mainland Ecuador. Compared to Quito and Guayaquil, food tends to be more expensive and less fresh. Fresh fish is the exception; most fish is excellent because it is caught right in the archipelago. There are some midrange and pricey restaurants that serve local produce, but at most inexpensive places, don't be surprised if you get only small portions of fruits and vegetables, and they aren't very fresh. Vegetarian and vegan options are available, but without much variety. If gourmet food tourism is on your agenda, there are much better choices in Quito and Guayaquil on your way in or out.

If you are on a tight budget, the best solution is to cook at the *hostal* or seek out favorite local haunts. Basic two-course meals vary depending on the port: In Baquerizo Moreno and Puerto Ayora, expect to pay $5; in Puerto Villamil, a two-course meal will set you back $8. Puerto Velasco Ibarra is the most expensive, with meals costing $12 at lunch and $15 for dinner. If you're not on a strict budget, Puerto Ayora and Puerto Baquerizo Moreno also have a decent selection of international restaurants, including Italian, sushi, and a couple upscale gourmet places.

Basic breakfast (usually $5-6) is nothing special and usually includes bread, butter, jam, eggs, coffee, and juice. Local breakfast specialties include *bolón (*a fried ball of green plantains filled with cheese or bacon), and *encebollado* (onion-tuna hangover soup).

For lunch and dinner the best food on offer is, of course, seafood. Popular fish include the bright-orange *brujo* fish and tuna. Fish is usually offered *frito* (fried), *apanada* (breaded

and fried), *a la parilla* (grilled), *al ajillo* (in garlic sauce) or *encocado* (in coconut sauce). Other locally caught seafood that you can find are *pulpo* (octopus) and *canchalagua* (a local mollusk). You can also find freshly caught *langostino* (langosteen) and *langosta* (lobster or jumbo shrimp), depending on the season. *Camarones* (shrimp) are also popular, but they are all imported from mainland Ecuador.

Seafood is usually served with rice and *patacones* (pieces of plaintain mashed flat and fried), whereas meat and poultry are served with rice and *menestra* (lentils or beans). Meats include *lomo* (beef, also called *res* or simply *carne*, "meat") and *chancho* (pork), served *a la parilla* (roasted) or *asada* (grilled).

To wash your food down, there are *jugos* (juices) and *batidos* (milkshakes). While the juice that's included in a set meal is usually very watery and sugary, there are excellent juices at midrange and upscale places, despite usually being made with imported fruit. You can ask for no sugar (*sin azúcar*). Local beers include Pilsener (small or large bottles), weaker Pilsener Light (small bottles), and stronger Club Verde (small bottles and cans), but beer connoisseurs will be disappointed.

Keep in mind that the cleanliness of the water supply in the ports of the Galápagos is poor. Hygiene in very cheap restaurants can be a problem, and food poisoning does happen, although a mild case of diarrhea is more common. In the good hotels and restaurants, you're less likely to be sick. The biggest culprits are unpeeled raw fruit and vegetables, salads, pork, and shellfish. Needless to say, never drink water from the faucet. Bring a refillable water bottle because most hotels have large dispensers of drinking water; in a pinch, you can buy bottled water. If you do get sick, medicine can be obtained easily from a pharmacy in the port or from the staff on your cruise.

Local Specialties

- *Cazuela de mariscos*—A rich casserole with fish, shrimp, and shellfish in a creamy plantain-peanut sauce.

- *Bolón* – A fried ball of plantain and cheese, served for breakfast alongside savory stews.

- *Seco de chivo*—For the more adventurous, a surprisingly tasty local dish is goat stew. It is easier to find in Quito than the Galápagos.

- *Canchalagua*—A mollusk local to Ecuador; try it in garlic sauce, in ceviche, or even as a hamburger.

- *Ceviche*—Mixed seafood either raw or cooked in lime and served with toasted corn tostado.

- *Encebollado*—The local cure for a hangover; this breakfast soup has tuna, yucca, and onions, and is traditionally served lukewarm.

- *Langosta al encocado*—Locally caught lobster cooked in coconut sauce. If you're on a budget, you can find *pescado* (fish) *al encocado* for less money.

- *Jugos*—Don't miss the juices made with tropical fruits such as *tomate de árbol* (a sweet tree tomato), *mora* (local blackberry), papaya, or mango.

- *Bollo*—Savory green plantain mush, usually mixed with fish and steamed in a banana leaf.

- *Maduro con queso*—A sweet, ripe plantain grilled over hot coals and filled with fresh cheese, usually found as street food.

- *Corviche*—Artery-clogging but delicious deep-fried plantain-peanut balls filled with tuna fish.

- *Pan de yuca*—Gooey, savory-sweet small rolls made with yucca starch and cheese.

HOTELS

The range of accommodations in the Galápagos is not nearly as diverse as on the mainland, and you wouldn't expect it to be. However, the number of hotels on the islands has grown rapidly in recent years. Most hotels are in the midrange to high-end category, catering to foreign tour groups, but there are a surprising number of budget lodgings. Puerto Ayora on Santa Cruz has by far the largest range of accommodations, followed by Baquerizo Moreno on San Cristóbal and a limited range in Puerto Villamil on Isabela. Puerto Velasco Ibarra on Floreana has the fewest, with just a handful of hotels and informal, family-run guesthouses. Prices range from $30 for a basic double room in a budget hotel in Puerto Ayora to $400 for a room at a top-class luxury hotel such as Hotel Royal Palm Galápagos on Santa Cruz. Be aware that prices go up and availability goes down during peak seasons (Christmas-Easter, and to a lesser extent July-August).

Foreigners sometimes get a few surprises when staying in hotels in Ecuador and the Galápagos:

- You always need to throw your used toilet paper in trash bins rather than the toilet. The hotel staff should come empty the bin frequently. The sewage system was not designed to handle paper waste.

- Some budget accommodations have electric showerheads that heat water by passing an electric current through it, rather than burning propane. Water temperature is usually not piping hot, and to get the water hot, you often have to turn down the water pressure. It is important not to touch the showerhead in electric showers because this often results in a mildly shocking experience.

- Water quality is poor throughout the islands, so never drink from the faucet.

- Accommodation is surprisingly reasonable for solo travelers; many budget *hostales* charge per person, not for the room. Conversely, if you're traveling with someone, make sure you clarify whether the price is per person or per room to avoid a nasty surprise when you pay.

- Tall travelers, beware: A lot of "king"-size beds or "matrimonial" rooms in the Galápagos just have two twin mattresses pushed together, with the same short length.

- Few hotels (especially in the budget and midrange categories) accept credit cards. Bring cash.

- Most hotels only provide a single room key; don't share a room unless you plan to be on exactly the same schedule.

- Some hotels on Floreana do not have locks on the doors at all; while some have safe-deposit boxes to store valuables, some do not. It is a very small community and considered safe.

Accommodation Types

The boundaries between various accommodation types are very blurred, so look at the room type and amenities to make sure you know what you are getting. **Hostels** are budget accommodations with shared dorms, though some also have private rooms. *Hostales* are usually budget-midrange accommodations. Some are primarily private rooms and some are primarily dorms. **Hotels** usually have private rooms, but the range is all over the place. They can be upscale accommodations or they can be more down-market establishments (like a budget *hostal*). *Casas,* or houses, can be anything from inexpensive hostels to midrange rooms to pricey boutique hotels.

CRUISE TOUR ROOMS

There is a huge variation in the quality of rooms aboard cruises. Most cruise tour rooms are quite small if you make the somewhat unfair comparison to a hotel room of the same class. Bunk beds are the norm aboard tourist and tourist-superior class boats, but you can find spacious suites with private balconies and sitting areas aboard the luxury-class cruise ships.

Conduct and Customs

Ecuadorians are renowned for their laid-back attitude, which contrasts strongly with North American and European reliance on rules, regulations, and schedules. This relaxed demeanor shows itself in many aspects of life in Ecuador—on the plus side, the people are very friendly, hospitable, and extroverted, while on the downside, they are infamously unpunctual, and the culture as a whole is comparatively disorganized.

The culture on the Galápagos Islands, although still officially Ecuadorian, is more organized than on the mainland. Due to the tight travel schedules, punctuality does tend to be respected. Additionally, the presence of so many international tourists and a permanent scientific community means that many people you meet—but not all—are also more open-minded and educated than on the mainland.

One area where people in the Galápagos are less laid-back is religion. As on the mainland, people are deeply religious, the vast majority Catholic, and evangelical Christianity is rising fast. Note that belief in God is usually assumed, and atheism is considered abnormal, so it's best to avoid too much religious discussion. Ironically, like creationists in North

America, many locals believe the world is 6,000 years old and reject the theory of evolution that made the Galápagos famous.

GREETINGS AND GENERAL POLITENESS

Latin Americans are much more physical in day-to-day interactions than their northern neighbors. Men give a firm handshake to other men both when arriving and leaving; women give a peck on the cheek when being introduced to another woman, and usually to another man. These actions aren't usually expected of foreign clients, but a handshake is always appreciated as a greeting or expression of gratitude at the end of a tour. Verbal greetings are essential; *hola* (hello) is often followed by *¿Como está?* (How are you?), even if you don't know the person. It's normal to begin any conversation with *Buenos días/tardes/noches,* and even complete strangers will greet each other this way, unprompted. If you see someone eating, it's polite to say *Buen provecho* (Enjoy your meal), again even to strangers. This use of physical and verbal greetings is all part of the Latin American concern for appearances. It is frowned upon to be rude in public, and foreigners often acquire a reputation for being unfriendly, bordering on rude, if they don't use greetings properly. Politeness is also a quick way to make friends.

GENDER AND SEXUALITY

Latin American culture is very polarized. Men tend to be the traditional heads of the household, and women manage the home and raise the children. Recently, though, Latin American women have begun to assert themselves and claim new freedoms in work and daily life. A great enemy of feminism is, of course, machismo, manifested in ways ranging from subtle to blatant. Whistles and catcalls are seen as harmless, but men find themselves feeling they have to prove their manhood in their posturing, driving, and womanizing. Unfortunately, the Galápagos are no exception to this, and female travelers frequently complain about unwanted attention from crew members and even guides. Make it clear that you're not interested, and perhaps regular references to a fiancé (*novio*) and a ring on the appropriate finger would help. Don't be afraid to confront locals about sexism, but bear in mind that making an Ecuadorian look bad in public is not to be treated lightly and will likely lead to resentment.

Machismo extends to attitudes toward gays and lesbians, and even though same-sex civil unions are now permitted in Ecuador, homophobia is still pervasive. Gay travelers need to bear in mind that being open about their sexuality can lead to anything from embarrassment and religious rants to violence. There is a burgeoning gay community in Ecuador, however; Quito has the biggest gay scene, and there are a few gay bars in Guayaquil and Cuenca. Some cruise operators offer gay-friendly tours.

Travel Tips

OPPORTUNITIES FOR VOLUNTEERS

Volunteer placements on the Galápagos are highly competitive, and it helps to be a science student or university graduate to secure the best opportunities. Most positions available involve either labor-intensive physical work, teaching, or administration based in one of the main ports, so don't come expecting to track wildlife or analyze coral reefs. The **Charles Darwin Foundation** (6 de Diciembre N36-109 at California, Quito, tel. 2/224-4803, Santa Cruz tel. 5/252-6146, www. darwinfoundation.org) and the **Galápagos National Park** (www.galapagospark.org) offer the best placements in conservation and environmental science. Other organizations to contact include **Ecuador Volunteers** (Mariscal Foch E9-20 at 6 de Diciembre, Quito, tel. 2/223-4708, www.ecuadorvolunteers.org) and United Kingdom-based **i-to-i** (U.K. tel. 800/11-1156, www.i-to-i.com), or visit **www.goabroad.com,** a useful directory of volunteering and teaching posts worldwide, including the Galápagos.

ACCESS FOR TRAVELERS WITH DISABILITIES

Ecuador is not very well prepared to receive disabled travelers. Wheelchair ramps are rare on buildings and sidewalks, and accessible toilets are rare. International airports and top-class hotels are the few places where travelers with disabilities can expect reasonable facilities. On the Galápagos, it's even more problematic because many trails are too uneven for wheelchairs, and wet landings are inaccessible. For more information, contact **Mobility International USA** (45 W. Broadway, Ste. 202, Eugene, OR 97401, U.S. TTY tel. 514/343-1284, U.S. fax 514/343-6812, www.miusa.org) and the online **Global**

Access Disabled Traveler Network (www. globalaccessnews.com).

Travelers with disabilities have a range of options for travel-planning assistance, including the **Information Center for Individuals with Disabilities** (P.O. Box 750119, Arlington Heights, MA 02475, U.S. fax 781/860-0673, www.disability.net) and the **Access-Able Travel Source** (www.accessable.com). Health escorts can be arranged through **Travel Care Companions** (Box 21, Site 9, RR 1, Calahoo, Alberta T0G 0J0, Canada, tel. 780/458-2023 or 888/458-5801, www.travelcarecompanions.com).

WOMEN TRAVELING ALONE

On the mainland, macho whistles and catcalls can be a constant problem for female travelers. On the Galápagos, the situation is far better. However, young women traveling without a romantic partner should not be surprised to experience unwanted attention from crew members and even guides. Try to make clear politely but firmly that you're not interested. Wearing a ring on the appropriate finger and regular mention of a fiancé may also help.

TRAVELING WITH CHILDREN

It is not too common to see families traveling with children in the Galápagos; the large majority of travelers are adults. Nonetheless, the Galápagos can be a fantastic trip for families; seeing giant tortoises up close, swimming with sea lions, and seeing the blue-footed booby dance can be great fun and inspiring for curious young minds. On the other hand, it's important not to bring children who are too young.

At a minimum, families should wait until their children are old enough to follow the Galápagos National Park rules and tackle all the fun activities the islands have to offer.

Bringing infants and toddlers in particular to the Galápagos Islands is not recommended. You can't bring a stroller on the lava-rock hiking trails at visitor sites. If your children don't swim yet, then the ubiquitous snorkeling activities will present another challenge. The other crucial requirement is that children need to be well-behaved enough to stay on the trails, keep the required distance from wildlife, avoid touching the animals, and obey the other national park rules.

A more subtle question is whether the Galápagos are the best choice for your family vacation. If you just wish to expose your children to the wonders of nature in general, there are far easier and less expensive destinations for sun, sand, and snorkeling. You may want to ask yourself if your children will understand the unique and most famous aspects of the Galápagos—endemic species that are uniquely adapted to their own island; inspiration for the theory of evolution; the fragility of this ecosystem.

If you decide to take your whole family, look for dedicated family departures on cruise ships. Your children will be able to find other kids their age, and there will often be dedicated activities for kids on board. Many Galápagos tour operators offer discounts of around 25 percent for children under age 12, but teenagers tend to pay full price. Staying in hotels can be another good option as it will give you more flexibility to tailor your itinerary to your family's needs.

GAY AND LESBIAN TRAVELERS

By and large Ecuador still has a homophobic culture, and many gay people are either in the closet or keep their sexuality well guarded. Things have changed in recent years, however, and the 2008 constitution guarantees civil rights to gays and lesbians and allows same-sex civil unions. Quito has the most developed gay scene, with several bars in the New Town, while Cuenca and Guayaquil also have a few bars. Despite this, gay and lesbian travelers are advised to keep a low profile on

mainland Ecuador. The Galápagos are considerably more liberal, and there is no need to hide your relationship. **Ecuador Gay** (tel. 2/252-9993, www.galapagosgay.com) organizes dedicated trips to the islands for gay and lesbian travelers.

SENIOR TRAVELERS

The Galápagos are very popular with senior travelers, and most operators are accustomed to dealing with older visitors. However, make sure you can handle the physical demands of the tours—some Galápagos hikes are steep and strenuous, and you need to be a confident swimmer to go snorkeling. Many sites have wet landings where you will need to swing your legs over the side of a small dinghy and wade to shore on a beach. Don't be embarrassed to sit out a hike or swimming trip if you feel tired.

The large first-class and luxury-class cruise ships have more senior travelers than the economy-class and tourist-class yachts, and may have an onboard doctor in case anything goes wrong. Some cruise ships also offer less strenuous alternative activities, such as glass-bottom boat tours or an extra *panga* ride rather than snorkeling.

Bring along a printed medical history and enough prescription medications for the entire trip, plus extra medications.

AARP (U.S. tel. 888/687-2277, www.aarp.org) offers a Purchase Privilege Program for discounts on airfares, car rentals, and hotels. **Road Scholar** (U.S. tel. 800/454-5768, www.roadscholar.org) is the educational program of Elderhostel, a nonprofit founded in 1975, and offers educational adventures for adults who are usually over age 50.

WHAT TO PACK

A trip to the Galápagos requires plenty of preparation. Independent travelers who plan to island-hop should pack light, as you will be frequently changing hotels and carrying your luggage on ferries. The baggage allowance for flights to the Galápagos Islands (20 kilograms) may be smaller than your international flight.

Packing Checklist

- Lightweight, breathable clothing

- Wide-brimmed hat

- Sunglasses

- Sweater or jacket

- Rain jacket (optional)

- Daypack

- Flip-flops

- Good walking shoes or water shoes that you can hike in

- Swimsuit

- Rashguard shirt and leggings

- Camera, memory, and accessories

- Underwater camera

- Cash and ATM cards

- Seasickness pills

- Sunscreen

- Insect repellent

- Any prescription medications you need

- Chargers and electrical adapters if necessary

If you plan to fly between the islands in the Galápagos, note that the baggage allowance is even smaller; for Emetebe, it is 9 kilograms (20 pounds) for checked luggage and 2.3 kilograms (5 pounds) for your carry-on, after which excess baggage fees apply.

Clothes

Most tourists pack summer clothes—tank tops and shorts. However, keep in mind that the naturalist guides usually wear long sleeves and pants for good reason—protection from the sun and insects. While sunblock and insect repellent help, the best protection is a physical barrier—consider taking lightweight, breathable, long-sleeved shirts and pants in addition to your summer clothes. Don't forget a hat and sunglasses (preferably polarized).

During the warm, rainy season, the sun is extremely strong, and smart travelers copy the locals, wearing hats with large neck flaps or a lightweight neck gaiter that can be pulled up to cover the nose and cheeks.

Also bring a light jacket or sweater for chilly mornings and cool evenings, plus a rain jacket for visiting the damp highlands. There are self-service laundries in the three main ports where you can wash your clothes during longer stays. Some sites on the populated islands have an introduced species of wasp that is attracted by bright shades of yellow, so avoid wearing yellow in these areas.

If you pass through Guayaquil on your way to the Galápagos, the hot and humid weather will make the same clothes suitable, but if you spend time in Quito, make sure to bring warm clothes for the cold weather there.

Shoes

Good walking shoes should be packed along with flip-flops for relaxing. Most cruises recommend that you take good water shoes (Tevas or similar) for wet landings followed by walks along rocky terrain. These will also come in handy for wandering around tide pools, but are not strictly necessary if you don't mind taking off your shoes, then putting them back on once you've landed. If you plan to hike the long route on Sierra Negra on Isabela Island, you may want to bring proper hiking shoes or boots and walking sticks.

Swimming Gear

Don't forget your swimsuit. You can bring your own mask and snorkel if you prefer, although tours usually provide them. Snorkels with valves to prevent intake of water are particularly awesome, and are only available at some tour agencies and on cruises. If you are planning to snorkel at the public beaches on your own without a tour, bringing your own snorkel (or at least some goggles) will save money at the expense of packing space.

During the cold season, wetsuits are necessary, and most tours either provide them or rent them. During the warm season, wetsuits aren't needed, but bringing a swimming shirt and rashguard leggings is a good way to protect your skin from sunburn while snorkeling.

Nicer hotels and cruises provide separate beach towels. However, if you plan to go to the beach on your own and stay in budget *hostales*, you may want to bring your own.

Toiletries

Bring your regular toiletries, plus plenty of high SPF sunblock to protect you from the fierce equatorial sun, as well as aloe vera in case you get burned anyway.

There are a lot of mosquitoes in the Galápagos, particularly during rainy season, and strong insect repellent is a must.

Seasickness is a common problem in the Galápagos, both on cruises and particularly on the fast ferries between islands, so bring seasickness pills.

Most public and restaurant bathrooms in Ecuador or in the Galápagos don't have disposable toilet seat protectors. If you can't live without them, bring your own.

Camera and Underwater Camera

The Galápagos are hard to beat for photography, so if you were going to consider upgrading, do it before you visit. Those with a DSLR camera should consider investing in a telephoto lens.

The right accessories can make a big difference; bring UV and polarizing filters, and a decent bag to protect the equipment from water. A brush for dusting off sand will come in handy if you bring your camera to the beach and drop a lens cap. Tripods come in handy for video, but setting one up will often make you fall behind the group when on tour. Monopods are more useful to steady your zoomed-in shots.

Bring far more memory than you think you'll need, and expect to take several hundred photos. Some guides on cruises will also take great pictures and/or video of the group for an end-of-trip slideshow. You can usually copy these images if you have extra space on your memory stick.

Don't forget that you will also want to take photos and video underwater. Snorkeling is often one of the highlights of a Galápagos trip, so travelers who do not have an underwater camera often regret it. Compact waterproof cameras are often the easiest and most cost-effective option. Alternatively, you can purchase an underwater housing made of plastic and rubber gaskets to waterproof your smartphone ($100-200), an existing compact camera ($300-500), or DSLR camera (over $2,000). Though these housings are more expensive, they can be submerged to a greater depth, usually deep enough to take scuba diving as well. The GoPro is one popular option, particularly with the extension stick that allows you to get your camera closer to the fish.

If you plan to scuba dive but do not want to invest in an underwater camera, some dive agencies will photograph and video your dive and provide you with the images. Ask about this when booking your dive tour.

Cash and ATM Cards

The Galápagos economy is extremely cash-based (the currency is the U.S. dollar), and if you don't want to deal with ATM runs, you will need to bring a lot of cash. Upon arrival you will need $100 in cash for the national park entrance fee and $20 for the transit control card. Once you get into the port, be prepared to pay for your restaurants and hotels (except the most expensive ones) in cash. Most tour agencies and operators also only accept cash, no matter whether it is a $150 day trip, $180 snorkeling trip, or $1,800 last-minute cruise. Gratuities on board cruises are also large ($100 or more) and paid in cash. Puerto

Ayora and San Cristóbal have ATMs with a $600 daily withdrawal limit.

It is crucial to note that Floreana and Isabela currently have no international ATMs. You will need to bring enough cash for your entire stay on these islands.

Other Items

Don't forget a daypack for storing a dry change of clothes, water, and your camera.

The electricity outlets in the Galápagos are the same as in North America: 120V. If you are visiting from Europe or elsewhere, you may need an adapter to plug in your electronic devices.

Bringing a refillable water bottle is strongly recommended because it reduces the islands' problem with plastic.

You can bring your favorite packaged snacks if you like, but do not bring fresh food to the Galápagos as it will likely be confiscated to protect the islands from invasive species.

Health and Safety

BEFORE YOU LEAVE

Travelers to tropical (i.e., northern) South America must take a number of specific health concerns into consideration. Major hospitals and those attached to universities in your home country usually have **traveler's clinics** or **occupational medicine clinics** that can recommend and administer pre-travel vaccinations. Also check with your local Department of Public Health for an **immunization clinic.** If you're sufficiently informed, you might just be able to walk in with a list of the shots and pills you want.

Note that regulations on dishing out medication are very loose in Ecuador. You can walk into a pharmacy and get hold of a range of medicines without a prescription; on the other hand, supplies are often low and you have to be wary of unqualified pharmacists trying to sell you expensive, inappropriate medication.

Make sure you know exactly what you're taking before it goes in your mouth (a quick Internet search can help).

To stay healthy, the best you can do while traveling—besides taking any prescriptions you brought along—is to wash your hands often, pay attention to what you eat and drink, and be on the lookout for any unusual symptoms. Buying alcohol-based hand sanitizer is very useful, and a basic first-aid kit is a must. The last thing you'd expect in the Galápagos is to catch a cold or the flu, but these illnesses are very common in Ecuador, even in tropical areas. The nature of a group tour means that illnesses can be passed on quickly, so take precautions when possible.

Recommended Vaccinations

Vaccinations are recorded on a yellow **International Certificate of Vaccination,** which you should bring with you to Ecuador. You may be asked to show this document to prove your immunizations, especially in the case of a yellow fever outbreak. Take care of these vaccinations as soon as possible, since some involve a series of injections and take a few months to take effect. Your doctor should know which ones not to mix with others (especially immunoglobulins) so as not to decrease their effectiveness. See your doctor at least 4-6 weeks before you leave to allow time for immunizations to take effect. The following vaccinations are recommended for travelers to Ecuador. Even if you are only spending minimal time on the mainland before traveling to the Galápagos, you should still consider these vaccinations.

Hepatitis A: This viral infection of the liver is contracted mainly from contaminated food and water. The vaccination is strongly recommended, and a booster after 6 or 12 months guarantees protection for over 10 years. Get the first shot before you leave; it's possible to get a follow-up shot from a good private clinic in Ecuador.

Typhoid fever: This dangerous gut infection is also acquired from food and water. The vaccination is strongly recommended and can be administered as a live oral vaccine or through two injections taken at least four weeks apart.

Yellow fever: This vaccination is necessary when entering Ecuador from Peru or Colombia (both officially infected countries), but it's a good idea in any case because it's a dangerous disease.

Hepatitis B: This is a less-common travelers' disease because it's contracted through sexual contact or exposure to infected blood. The vaccination is recommended for longer-term travel (more than six months) and if you are likely to come into close contact with locals (for example, working in medicine). This disease is more insidious than others, and you can be a carrier for years without symptoms, but it can cause serious liver damage. The complication is that you need three vaccinations spaced a month apart.

Routine immunizations: Any trip is a good time to update the following: diphtheria-tetanus, influenza, measles, mumps, poliomyelitis, and pneumococcus.

Rabies vaccinations: It's also recommended that visitors get rabies vaccinations if venturing into rural areas.

SUNBURN

The Galápagos straddle the equator, and all those hikes and swims in the equatorial sun, not to the mention the reflection of the sun off the sea, will leave you burned to a crisp if you don't take precautions. Sunscreen (SPF 50 and above), lip balm, and a wide-brimmed hat will help protect you. A good pair of polarized sunglasses is also essential.

DISEASES FROM FOOD AND WATER

If you're going to get sick while traveling, it will probably be from contaminated water or food. As a tropical country, Ecuador is full of bacteria and parasites, and the Galápagos are no exception. Get in the habit of washing your hands at least 2-3 times a day, preferably before every meal and certainly after every restroom visit.

Hygiene is generally of a good standard on organized tours, and you're more likely to get sick eating and drinking at cheap places in the ports. Even then, it's less likely than on mainland Ecuador. Obviously, drink only bottled water and never from the faucet. Regarding food, the biggest illness culprit is shellfish. In most cases, you should be fine, but consider reducing your consumption of shrimp and other shellfish if you have a delicate stomach.

No one is safe from **traveler's diarrhea,** although most cases are mild. Ease a low-grade case of the runs with Imodium A-D (loperamide) or Pepto-Bismol, but bear in mind that these medicines are often short-term solutions. Drink plenty of water and noncaffeinated fluids like fruit juice and ginger ale. Oral rehydration solutions are very handy, and if you haven't brought any, they're easy to make: One teaspoon of salt and 2-3 tablespoons of sugar or honey in a liter of water will work. More serious cases may require a doctor's appointment and antibiotics. Your guide may be able to recommend a good antibiotic for bacterial infection to get from the pharmacy.

Dengue fever, transmitted by *Aedes* mosquitoes, is present on the Galápagos, although it is rare. There have been outbreaks occasionally on San Cristóbal, but these are confined to urban areas because the mosquitoes live mainly in dirty water. Flu-like symptoms, such as nausea, bad headaches, joint pain, and sudden high fever are often misdiagnosed as other tropical diseases. Severe cases leading to shock syndrome or hemorrhagic fever are rare, but if you have already had dengue fever, a second case can be more dangerous. The only treatments known so far are rest, fluids, and fever-reducing medications. Medical attention is strongly recommended, if only for diagnosis.

ANIMALS

Most of the creatures on the Galápagos are very tame and pose little threat to humans. However, the national park advises you to keep a minimum distance of two meters from any animal. By far the biggest risk comes from

sea lions, usually elderly bulls, and you should stay farther than two meters from them. Attacks are rare, but you must take care and avoid getting too close. The bull will usually bark at you as a warning, which is generally enough to scare anyone off. Note that female sea lions with pups can also be aggressive if they feel threatened.

INSECTS AND OTHER ARTHROPODS

There are 1,600 species of insects in the Galápagos Islands, but unlike in the Ecuadorian rainforest, they are far harder to see (most are nocturnal).

Mosquitoes are the most irritating pests in the islands, though luckily they do not carry malaria. Almost everyone who visits gets bitten at least a couple of times, particularly during warm/rainy season. Make sure to bring insect repellent and/or long sleeves to protect yourself, and if all else fails, anti-itch cream.

There is an introduced species of **wasps** particularly common around the inhabited areas of the islands. Visitors are advised to avoid wearing bright yellow, as it can attract the wasps.

There are also a few species of other

Visitors need to keep 2 meters of distance from wildlife.

critters, such as bees, fire ants, spiders, and, less commonly, scorpions, that can inflict painful bites and stings, but they are not normally considered dangerous.

MEDICAL CARE

If you are staying on the islands, Santa Cruz and San Cristóbal both have **hospitals with emergency rooms,** and Floreana and Isabela have **medical clinics** with doctors who speak some English. Though they are far from top-notch facilities, they are perfectly capable of basic medical care. Most common problems tourists will run into (scrapes from slipping on trails, food poisoning, colds and flu) can be treated here, although serious emergencies may require medical evacuation to Guayaquil in mainland Ecuador, where there are hospitals with a full range of specialties. There are also **pharmacies** available on Santa Cruz, San Cristóbal, and Isabela.

If you are planning to scuba dive in the islands, be aware of the possibility of **decompression sickness.** Decompression sickness (aka "the bends") happens when divers surface too quickly and the dissolved nitrogen in the blood forms bubbles. It can be lethal if not treated promptly. Santa Cruz and San Cristóbal have **hyperbaric chambers** in the case of decompression sickness. Isabela currently does not have one, so divers may need medical evacuation to Santa Cruz. Also, if you are on a live-aboard dive boat a day's navigation from town and you get the bends, you may need medical evacuation via helicopter to Santa Cruz.

If you are taking a **cruise,** the medical care options change dramatically. Large cruise ships and yachts often have their own onboard nurse or doctor, but the small yachts do not. Depending on your cruise itinerary, you may be within striking distance of a large cruise with an onboard doctor who can help. However, if you're not in luck, you will need emergency helicopter transportation either to Santa Cruz Island or mainland Ecuador depending on the emergency.

Medical evacuation, though rare, is extremely expensive. The Ecuadorian government subsidizes the cost for Galápagos residents, but tourists are not so lucky. In 2013 a young British couple was flown to a hospital in mainland Ecuador after their tour bus crashed into the side of a volcano. They made the news after receiving a £16,000 bill. If you don't want to risk a five-figure hospital bill, check your insurance policy for medical evacuation coverage.

Information and Services

MONEY
Currency

In 2000, Ecuador officially laid the beleaguered old sucre to rest and replaced it with the **U.S. dollar.** In the short term, the devaluation of the sucre and its subsequent replacement were a financial disaster for millions of Ecuadorians, who saw the value of their savings plummet while prices of basic foods rocketed. Once one of the cheapest Latin American countries for traveling, Ecuador is now in the middle of the price range—cheaper than Colombia and considerably cheaper than Brazil and Chile, but more expensive than Bolivia and Peru. The biggest plus for visitors is that there's no need to worry about exchanging money. The Galápagos, however, are more expensive than mainland Ecuador, with prices comparable to the United States.

Crime is low on the Galápagos, but no one likes to carry large amounts of cash. Unfortunately **cash** is necessary. **Credit cards** are accepted in many higher-end shops, hotels, restaurants, and travel agencies, but there is often a surcharge of up to 10 percent. It's generally best to pay with cash whenever possible and save your credit cards for emergencies or ATM use. MasterCard and Visa are the most widely accepted. American Express, Diner's Club, and Discover are much harder to use.

If you've already booked your tour from abroad, you should only need enough cash for drinks, tips, and occasional meals. If you are traveling independently, just withdraw a couple hundred dollars at a time to pay for hotels and tours. If you are trying to pick up a last-minute cruise, you will unfortunately need to withdraw a lot of cash or else pay the credit card surcharges.

Automated teller machines (ATMs) are very common in mainland Ecuador. Most ATMs have a daily withdrawal limit of $600 at most. On the islands, there are ATMs and banks in Puerto Ayora and Baquerizo Moreno, but not in Puerto Villamil or Puerto Velasco Ibarra.

Taxes

A 12 percent tax called **IVA** is charged on tours, hotel accommodations, and food. Foreigners can get these taxes refunded on exiting the country at the airport. Purchases over $50 are eligible, so save your receipts. To get the refund, look for the **SRI** (Servicio de Rentas Internas) kiosk immediately after security at the Quito or Guayaquil airport. Fill out the form, enclose the receipts in the envelope, and drop it in the box. The refund comes via your credit card information after a lengthy delay.

Tipping

It's customary to tip at the end of a cruise. Remember that, although your tour is expensive, in a country as unequal as Ecuador, the big bucks don't filter down to the lowest level; the crew as well as the guide will very much appreciate your tip. Obviously, use your own judgment on how much to give, and your tip should reflect the level of service. Between 5 and 10 percent of the price of the cruise is considered standard. Tip the guide separately and use the tip box for the rest of the crew.

COMMUNICATIONS AND MEDIA
Mail

At the post offices in the Galápagos, airmail postcards and letters under 20 grams cost $3 to North and South America.

Don't mail any objects of value, as things go missing quite often from Ecuador's postal system, especially incoming packages. The regular mail service is notoriously unreliable, and packages are routinely opened by customs (ostensibly checking for contraband). It's better to use a private courier company like DHL or FedEx from Quito or Guayaquil.

Telecommunications

Two cellular companies, Movistar and Claro, offer chips and microchips that you can use with unlocked cell phones to make national calls within Ecuador and the Galápagos. You buy the chip at the airport and then you can buy *recargas* (or prepaid minute "recharges") at convenience stores. There is cell phone reception in all the port towns except Puerto Velasco Ibarra on Floreana; the locals there rely on landlines only, or use WhatsApp along with the town's Wi-Fi network. Cellular data can also be purchased for the SIM cards but is quite slow and only 3G speed within the Galápagos.

National calls (within the Galápagos and mainland Ecuador) are no problem. If you don't get a local SIM card, you can ask your *hostal* reception to make a call from their line. Note, however, that landlines cannot call mobile numbers (though mobile phones can call landlines). Mobile numbers start with 09, whereas landlines start with 05 in the Galápagos, 02 in Quito, and 04 in Guayaquil. To make long-distance calls within Ecuador, dial a 0 followed by the regional area code and the seven-digit phone number. Drop the 0 for calls within the same region. For directory information, dial 104; for help with national long distance, dial 105; and for international long distance, dial 116 or 117. Numbers beginning with 800 are toll-free.

International calls are expensive and must

be done at Internet/phone cabins. Some offices will charge you for calls if the phone rings more than eight times, even if no one answers.

To call Ecuador from the United States, dial the international access code (011), the country code for Ecuador (593), the regional area code (2-7) or cell phone code (8 or 9), and the seven-digit local number—that's 15 digits in all. The area code for the Galápagos is 5.

Internet

Internet service on the Galápagos is often notoriously slow, and Skyping can be problematic due to the speed. The fastest time to use the Internet is usually early in the morning when everyone is asleep; it gets progressively worse throughout the day. Many cruises have no Internet available, so get ready to unplug for a week. Others offer onboard Wi-Fi through a satellite connection, though it is slow by international standards. Internet/phone cabins are becoming harder to find in the Galápagos, though most hotels and some restaurants offer Wi-Fi, albeit slow.

Newspapers and Magazines

Local publications include national Spanish-language newspapers, such as Quito-based *Hoy* and *El Comercio*, Guayaquil-based *El Universo*, and government-owned *El Telégrafo*. These are sporadically available in the main ports on the islands. It's often easier to keep up to date with local and international news online—or, even better, forget about the rest of the world for a few days!

MAPS AND TOURIST INFORMATION
Maps

You can pick up useful city, town, and regional maps at tourism offices across the country. Dedicated maps of the Galápagos and detailed street maps of the three main ports are available from tourism offices in Puerto Ayora, Baquerizo Moreno, and Puerto Villamil.

WEIGHTS AND MEASURES

Ecuador and the Galápagos use the international metric system; distances are in kilometers. Food is usually sold in kilograms, although some products are also sold in pounds, and gas is sold by the U.S. gallon. To avoid confusion, you can always ask for a fixed monetary quantity, for example $3 of ham, $20 of gas.

Resources

Glossary

aguardiente: sugarcane alcohol
almuerzo: lunch, usually an inexpensive fixed-price menu with limited or no options
batido: fruit shake
cabaña: rustic cabin
camioneta: a taxi; a truck for hire as a taxi
canelazo: hot, sweet alcoholic drink made with sugarcane
cangil: popcorn
centro comercial: mall
ceviche: cold seafood dish in lime juice. Unlike ceviche in other countries, Ecuadorian ceviche is not usually raw.
chifa: Chinese restaurant or food
chifles: chips made with crispy fried plantains
chiva: open-top bus; some are used for parties, others for public transportation
costeño: person from the coast
criollo: originally a person of Spanish descent born in the colonies but now applied to anything traditional, especially food
cuy: roasted guinea pig
encebollado: a soup usually eaten for breakfast with tuna, onions, and yucca
fanesca: a fish and bean stew dish served during Lent
finca: small farm

gringo: term for North American, but applied to most white foreigners; not particularly derogatory
hacienda: farm or country estate
hostal: budget or midrange accommodation; may offer private rooms, dorms, or both
hostería: inn
indígena: indigenous person; note that indio is considered insulting
malecón: riverside or seaside promenade
menestra: lentils or beans cooked in sauce as accompaniment to rice
menú del día: set menu of the day
merienda: inexpensive set-menu dinners
mestizo: person of mixed indigenous and European blood
monos: monkeys, a slightly derogatory term used for people from Guayaquil
patacones: a popular side dish with smashed and fried plantains
pasillo: Ecuador's national music
peña: bar with traditional live music
quinua: grain native to the Andes
salchipapas: french fries topped with chunks of hot dog
salsoteca: Latin dance club
serrano: person from the sierra or mountains

Spanish Phrasebook

Many foreigners come to the Galápagos without any knowledge of Spanish and get along fine because naturalist guides and staff at the midrange to luxury hotels are bilingual. However, if you are in Ecuador for an extended period, eat at typical "locals" places, or stay in inexpensive *hostales*, basic Spanish becomes very important. Regardless, your adventure will be far more fun if you use a little Spanish, and it will also empower you to be more in control of your travels.

Spanish commonly uses 30 letters—the familiar English 26, plus four additions: ch, ll, ñ, and rr.

PRONUNCIATION

Spanish pronunciation rules are straightforward and easy to learn because—in contrast to English—they don't change. Spanish vowels generally sound softer than in English. (*Note:* The capitalized syllables below receive stronger accents.)

Vowels

a like ah, as in "hah": *agua* AH-gooah (water), *pan* PAHN (bread), and *casa* CAH-sah (house)

e like ay, as in "may": *mesa* MAY-sah (table), *tela* TAY-lah (cloth), and *de* DAY (of, from)

i like ee, as in "need": *diez* dee-AYZ (ten), *comida* ko-MEE-dah (meal), and *fin* FEEN (end)

o like oh, as in "go": *peso* PAY-soh (weight), *ocho* OH-choh (eight), and *poco* POH-koh (a bit)

u like oo, as in "cool": *uno* OO-noh (one), *cuarto* KOOAHR-toh (room), and *usted* oos-TAYD (you); when it follows a "q" the **u** is silent; when it follows an "h" or has an umlaut, it's pronounced like "w"

Consonants

b, d, f, k, l, m, n, p, q, s, t, v, w, x, y, z, and

ch pronounced almost as in English; **h** occurs, but is silent (not pronounced at all)

c like k as in "keep": *cuarto* KOOAHR-toh (room), *corazón* kor-a-SOHN (heart); when it precedes "e" or "i," pronounce **c** like s, as in "sit": *cerveza* sayr-VAY-sah (beer), *encima* ayn-SEE-mah (atop)

g like g as in "gift" when it precedes "a," "o," "u," or a consonant: *gato* GAH-toh (cat), *hago* AH-goh (I do, make); otherwise, pronounce **g** like h as in "hat": *giro* HEE-roh (money order), *gente* HAYN-tay (people)

j like h, as in "has": *Jueves* HOOAY-vays (Thursday), *mejor* may-HOR (better)

ll like y, as in "yes": *toalla* toh-AH-yah (towel), *ellos* AY-yohs (they, them)

ñ like ny, as in "canyon": *año* AH-nyo (year), *señor* SAY-nyor (Mr., sir)

r is lightly trilled, with tongue at the roof of your mouth like a very light English d, as in "ready": *pero* PAY-doh (but), *tres* TDAYS (three), *cuatro* KOOAH-tdoh (four)

rr like a Spanish r, but with much more emphasis and trill. Let your tongue flap. Practice with *burro* (donkey), *carretera* (highway), and Carrillo (proper name), then really let go with *ferrocarril* (railroad)

Note: The single small but common exception to all of the above is the pronunciation of Spanish **y** when it's being used as the Spanish word for "and," as in *Ron y Kathy*. In such case, pronounce it like the English ee, as in "keep": Ron "ee" Kathy (Ron and Kathy).

Accent

The rule for accent, the relative stress given to syllables within a given word, is straightforward. If a word ends in a vowel, an n, or an s, accent the next-to-last syllable; if not, accent the last syllable.

Pronounce *gracias* GRAH-seeahs (thank you), *orden* OHR-dayn (order), and *carretera* kah-ray-TAY-rah (highway) with stress on the next-to-last syllable.

Otherwise, accent the last syllable: *venir* vay-NEER (to come), *ferrocarril* fay-roh-cah-REEL (railroad), and *edad* ay-DAHD (age).

Exceptions to the accent rule are always marked with an accent sign: (á, é, í, ó, or ú), such as *teléfono* tay-LAY-foh-noh (telephone), *jabón* hah-BON (soap), and *rápido* RAH-pee-doh (rapid).

BASIC AND COURTEOUS EXPRESSIONS

Most Spanish-speaking people consider formalities important. Whenever approaching anyone for information or some other reason, do not forget the appropriate salutation—good morning, good evening, etc. Standing alone, the greeting *hola* (hello) can sound brusque.

Hello. *Hola.*
Good morning. *Buenos días.*
Good afternoon. *Buenas tardes.*
Good evening. *Buenas noches.*
How are you? *¿Cómo está usted?*
Very well, thank you. *Muy bien, gracias.*
Okay; good. *Bien.*
Not okay; bad. *Mal* or *feo.*
So-so. *Más o menos.*
And you? *¿Y usted?*
Thank you. *Gracias.*
Thank you very much. *Muchas gracias.*
You're very kind. *Muy amable.*
You're welcome. *De nada.*
Goodbye. *Adiós.*
See you later. *Hasta luego.*
please *por favor*
yes *sí*
no *no*
I don't know. *No sé.*
Just a moment, please. *Momentito, por favor.*
Excuse me, please (when you're trying to get attention). *Disculpe* or *Con permiso.*
Excuse me (when you've made a mistake). *Lo siento.*
Pleased to meet you. *Mucho gusto.*
What is your name? *¿Cómo se llama usted?*

Do you speak English? *¿Habla usted inglés?*
Is English spoken here? (Does anyone here speak English?) *¿Se habla inglés?*
I don't speak Spanish well. *No hablo bien el español.*
I don't understand. *No entiendo.*
How do you say . . . in Spanish? *¿Cómo se dice . . . en español?*
My name is . . . *Me llamo . . .*
Would you like . . . *¿Quisiera usted . . .*
Let's go to . . . *Vamos a . . .*
Where is the bathroom? *¿Dónde está el baño?*
bathrooms *baños* or *servicios higiénicos*

TERMS OF ADDRESS

When in doubt, use the formal *usted* (you) as a form of address.

I *yo*
you (formal) *usted*
you (familiar) *tu*
he/him *él*
she/her *ella*
we/us *nosotros*
you (plural) *ustedes*
they/them *ellos* (all males or mixed gender); *ellas* (all females)
Mr., sir *señor*
Mrs., madam *señora*
miss, young lady *señorita*
wife *esposa*
husband *esposo*
friend *amigo* (male); *amiga* (female)
sweetheart *novio* (male); *novia* (female)
son; daughter *hijo; hija*
brother; sister *hermano; hermana*
father; mother *padre; madre*
grandfather; grandmother *abuelo; abuela*

TRANSPORTATION

Where is . . . ? *¿Dónde está . . . ?*
How far is it to . . . ? *¿A cuánto está . . . ?*
from . . . to . . . *de . . . a . . .*
How many blocks/kilometers? *¿Cuántas cuadras/Cuántos kilómetros?*

Where (Which) is the way to . . . ? *¿Dónde está el camino a . . . ?*
the bus station *la terminal terrestre*
the bus stop *la parada de autobuses*
Where is this bus going? *¿Adónde va este autobús?*
the taxi stand *la parada de taxis*
the yacht *el yate*
the boat *el barco*
the launch/speedboat *la lancha*
the dock *el muelle*
the airport *el aeropuerto*
I'd like a ticket to . . . *Quisiera un boleto a . . .*
first (second) class *primera (segunda) clase*
round-trip *ida y vuelta*
reservation *reservación*
baggage *equipaje*
Stop here, please. *Pare aquí, por favor.*
the entrance *la entrada*
the exit *la salida*
the ticket office *la oficina de boletos*
(very) near; far *(muy) cerca; lejos*
to; toward *a*
by; through *por*
from *de*
the right *la derecha*
the left *la izquierda*
straight ahead *derecho; directo*
in front *en frente*
beside *al lado*
behind *atrás*
the corner *la esquina*
the stoplight *la semáforo*
a turn *una vuelta*
right here *aquí*
somewhere around here *por acá*
right there *allí*
somewhere around there *por allá*
road *el camino*
street *la calle*
block *la cuadra*
highway *la carretera*
kilometer *kilómetro*
address *dirección*
north; south *norte; sur*
east; west *este; oeste*

ACCOMMODATIONS

hotel *hotel*
Do you have a room available? *¿Tiene una habitación disponible?*
May I (may we) see it? *¿Puedo (podemos) verla?*
What is the rate? *¿Cuál es el precio?*
Is that your best rate? *¿Es su mejor precio?*
Is there something cheaper? *¿Hay algo más económico?*
reservation *una reservación*
a single room *una habitación sencilla*
a double room (with 2 beds) *una habitación doble*
a double room (with a bed to share) *una habitación matrimonial*
with private bath *con baño privado*
with shared bath *con baño compartido*
hot water *agua caliente*
shower *ducha*
towels *toallas*
soap *jabón*
toilet paper *papel higiénico*
blanket *cobija; manta*
sheets *sábanas*
air-conditioned *aire acondicionado*
fan *ventilador*
breakfast included *desayuno incluido*
key *llave*
manager *gerente*
Wi-Fi password *contraseña de Wi-Fi*

FOOD

restaurant *restaurante*
menu *carta; menú*
order *orden*
glass *vaso*
fork *tenedor*
knife *cuchillo*
spoon *cuchara*
napkin *servilleta*
soft drink *refresco*
coffee *café*
tea *té*
drinking water *agua pura; agua potable*
bottled carbonated water *agua con gas*
bottled uncarbonated water *agua sin gas*

beer *cerveza*
wine *vino*
coffee *café*
milk *leche*
juice *jugo*
cream *crema*
sugar *azúcar*
cheese *queso*
ice cream *helado*
snacks *antojitos*
breakfast *desayuno*
lunch *almuerzo*
daily lunch special *almuerzo; menú del día*
dinner *merienda* (early dinner, often with an inexpensive fixed-price menu), *cena* (dinner, usually à la carte)
the check *la cuenta*
eggs *huevos*
bread *pan*
rice *arroz*
lentils or beans, which often accompany rice *menestra*
stew (often served with rice) *seco*
salad *ensalada*
sandwich *sánduche*
fruit *fruta*
watermelon *sandía*
banana *banano*
apple *manzana*
orange *naranja*
lime *limón*
chicken *pollo*
pork *cerdo; chancho; horneado*
beef; steak *carne, res, lomo; bistec, lomo fino*
bacon; ham *tocino; jamón*
goat *chivo*
fish *pescado*
shellfish *mariscos*
shrimp *camarones*
lobster *langosta*
fried (or deep-fried) *frito*
breaded and fried *apanado*
roasted *asado/a*
grilled *a la parrilla*
in coconut sauce *encocado*
vegetarian *vegetariano*
vegan *vegano*
gluten-free *sin gluten*

tip *propina*

SHOPPING

shop *tienda*
handicrafts *artesanías*
made by hand *hecho a mano*
How much does it cost? *¿Cuánto cuesta?*
What is your final price? *¿Cuál es su último precio?*
expensive *caro*
cheap *barato; económico*

HEALTH

Help me please. *Ayúdeme por favor.*
I am ill. *Estoy enfermo.*
I am nauseous/seasick *Estoy mareado.*
Call a doctor. *Llame un doctor.*
Take me to ... *Lléveme a ...*
hospital *hospital*
drugstore *farmacia*
hyperbaric chamber *cámara hiperbárica*
pain *dolor*
fever *fiebre*
headache *dolor de cabeza*
stomachache *dolor de estómago*
the bends (decompression sickness) *enfermedad del buzo*
burn *quemadura*
cramp *calambre*
nausea *náusea*
vomiting *vomitar*
medicine *medicina*
antibiotic *antibiótico*
pill; tablet *pastilla*
aspirin *aspirina*
ointment; cream *crema*
insect repellent *repelente*
sunblock *bloqueador*
Band-Aids *curitas*
sanitary napkins use brand name; e.g., Kotex
tampons *tampones*
birth control pills *pastillas anticonceptivas*
seasickness pills *pastillas para el mareo*
contraceptive foam *espuma anticonceptiva*
condoms *preservativos; condones*
toothbrush *cepillo dental*

dental floss *hilo dental*
toothpaste *crema dental*
dentist *dentista*
toothache *dolor de muelas*

BANK

bank *banco*
money *dinero*
ATM *cajero automático*
money-exchange bureau *casa de cambio*
I would like to exchange traveler's
  checks. *Quisiera cambiar cheques de*
  viajero.
What is the exchange rate? *¿Cuál es el*
  tipo de cambio?
How much is the commission? *¿Cuánto*
  cuesta la comisión?
credit card *tarjeta de crédito*
Do you accept credit cards? *¿Acepta*
  tarjetas de crédito?
money order *giro*

POST OFFICE AND OTHER SERVICES

Laundromat/laundry service *lavandería*
municipal market (which sells produce
  and staples in small stalls) *mercado*
  municipal
supermarket *supermercado*
post office *correo*
letter *carta*
postcard *postal*
stamp *estampilla*
air mail *correo aéreo*
package; box *paquete; caja*
Internet booth *cabina de Internet*
international call *llamada internacional*
I would like to call . . . *Quisiera llamar a . . .*
collect *por cobrar*
cell phone *celular*

AT THE BORDER

border *frontera*
customs *aduana*
immigration *inmigración*
tourist card *tarjeta de turista*
inspection *inspección; revisión*
passport *pasaporte*

profession *profesión*
marital status *estado civil*
single *soltero/a*
married; divorced *casado/a; divorciado/a*
widowed *viudo/a*
insurance *seguros*
title *título*
driver's license *licencia de manejar*

SIGHTSEEING

What time does . . . leave? *¿A qué hora*
  sale . . . ?
. . . the tour . . . *. . . el tour?*
. . . the speedboat . . . *. . . la lancha?*
. . . the bus . . . *. . . el bus?*
How many people? *¿Cuántas personas?*
scuba diving *buceo*
snorkeling *buceo de superficie*
wetsuit *traje de neopreno*
walking *caminata*
hiking *senderismo*
horseback riding *cabalgata*
(day-long) tour *tour diario*
cruise *crucero*
yacht *yate*
speedboat *lancha; fibra*
dinghy *panga*
volcano *volcán*
lagoon *laguna*
beach *playa*
sea lion *lobo del mar*
blue-footed/red-footed/Nazca
  booby *piquero de pata azul / de pata roja*
  / Nazca
frigate bird *fragata*
giant tortoise *galápagos; tortuga gigante*
sea turtle *tortuga marina*
fish *peces*
shark *tiburón*
marine iguana *iguana marina*
land iguana *iguana terrestre*

VERBS

Verbs are the key to getting along in Spanish. They employ mostly predictable forms and come in three classes, which end in *ar*, *er*, and *ir*, respectively:

to **buy** _comprar_
I buy, you (he, she, it) buy _compro, compra_
we buy, you (they) buy _compramos, compran_

to **eat** _comer_
I eat, you (he, she, it) eat _como, come_
we eat, you (they) eat _comemos, comen_

to **climb** _subir_
I climb, you (he, she, it) climb _subo, sube_
we climb, you (they) climb _subimos, suben_

Here are more (with irregularities indicated):

to **do or make** _hacer_ (regular except for _hago, I do or make_)
to **go** _ir_ (very irregular: _voy, va, vamos, van_)
to **go (walk)** _caminar_
to **love** _amar_
to **work** _trabajar_
to **want** _desear, querer_
to **need** _necesitar_
to **read** _leer_
to **write** _escribir_
to **repair** _reparar_
to **stop** _parar_
to **get off (the bus)** _bajar_
to **arrive** _llegar_
to **stay (remain)** _quedar_
to **stay (lodge)** _hospedar_
to **leave** _salir_ (regular except for _salgo, I leave_)
to **look at** _mirar_
to **look for** _buscar_
to **give** _dar_ (regular except for _doy, I give_)
to **carry** _llevar_
to **have** _tener_ (irregular but important: _tengo, tiene, tenemos, tienen_)
to **come** _venir_ (similarly irregular: _vengo, viene, venimos, vienen_)

Spanish has two forms of "to be":
to **be** _estar_ (regular except for _estoy, I am_)
to **be** _ser_ (very irregular: _soy, es, somos, son_)

Use _estar_ when speaking of location or a temporary state of being: "I am at home." _"Estoy en casa."_ "I'm sick." _"Estoy enfermo."_ Use _ser_ for a permanent state of being: "I am a doctor." _"Soy doctora."_

NUMBERS

zero _cero_
one _uno_
two _dos_
three _tres_
four _cuatro_
five _cinco_
six _seis_
seven _siete_
eight _ocho_
nine _nueve_
10 _diez_
11 _once_
12 _doce_
13 _trece_
14 _catorce_
15 _quince_
16 _dieciséis_
17 _diecisiete_
18 _dieciocho_
19 _diecinueve_
20 _veinte_
21 _veinte y uno_ or _veintiuno_
30 _treinta_
40 _cuarenta_
50 _cincuenta_
60 _sesenta_
70 _setenta_
80 _ochenta_
90 _noventa_
100 _ciento_
101 _ciento uno_
200 _doscientos_
500 _quinientos_
1,000 _mil_
10,000 _diez mil_
100,000 _cien mil_
1,000,000 _millón_
one-half _medio_
one-third _un tercio_
one-fourth _un cuarto_

TIME

What time is it? *¿Qué hora es?*
It's one o'clock. *Es la una.*
It's three in the afternoon. *Son las tres de la tarde.*
It's 4am. *Son las cuatro de la mañana.*
six-thirty *seis y media*
a quarter till eleven *un cuarto para las once*
a quarter past five *las cinco y cuarto*
an hour *una hora*

DAYS AND MONTHS

Monday *lunes*
Tuesday *martes*
Wednesday *miércoles*
Thursday *jueves*
Friday *viernes*
Saturday *sábado*
Sunday *domingo*

today *hoy*
tomorrow *mañana*
yesterday *ayer*
January *enero*
February *febrero*
March *marzo*
April *abril*
May *mayo*
June *junio*
July *julio*
August *agosto*
September *septiembre*
October *octubre*
November *noviembre*
December *diciembre*
a week *una semana*
a month *un mes*
after *después*
before *antes*

Suggested Reading

The titles here are all available on Amazon.com, either new or used in the case of many that are out of print. In Ecuador, the Libri Mundi bookstore in Quito and Guayaquil is your best bet, or try The English Bookshop (Calama and Diego de Almagro, Mariscal Sucre) in Quito.

HISTORY

Angermeyer, Johanna. *My Father's Island: A Galápagos Quest.* New York: Viking, 1990. Out of print. Life in the Galápagos through much of the 20th century.

Latorre, Octavio. *The Curse of the Giant Tortoise.* Quito: National Culture Fund, 1997. A collection of short stories about the exploitation, colonization attempts, and mysteries throughout the history of the Galápagos Islands, including pirates, whalers, and penal colonies.

Strauch, Dore. *Satan Came to Eden: A Survivor's Account of the "Galápagos Affair."* Troising Publishing, 2nd edition, 2014. A firsthand account of the mysterious events of the 1930s on Floreana Island, written from the perspective of one of the first settlers, Dore Strauch, who has a different opinion as to what really happened compared to the more popular rendition of the story by Margret Wittmer.

Wittmer, Margret. *Floreana: A Woman's Pilgrimage to the Galápagos.* Wakefield, RI: Moyer Bell, 1990. Firsthand account of early Floreana settlers, including Margret's account of the mysterious events of the 1930s.

ENVIRONMENT AND CONSERVATION

Bassett, Carol Ann. *Galapagos at the Crossroads: Pirates, Biologists, Tourists and Creationists Battle for Darwin's Cradle of Evolution.* Washington, DC: National

Geographic, 2009. Provocative analysis of the islands' environmental problems.

Nicholls, Henry. *Lonesome George: The Life and Loves of the World's Most Famous Tortoise.* New York: Pan Macmillan, 2007. The story of the last of the Pinta Island tortoises, who becomes a conservation icon worldwide.

DARWIN AND EVOLUTION

Darwin, Charles. *The Origin of Species by Means of Natural Selection.* New York: Signet Classics, 2003. The book that shook the world—and, as a bonus, it's one of the few groundbreaking scientific works that's truly readable.

Darwin, Charles. *The Voyage of the Beagle.* New York: Penguin USA, 1999. A classic of early travel literature written by a wide-eyed, brilliant young man setting out to see the whole world. You can almost witness his theories being born.

Darwin, Charles, and Mark Ridley, ed. *The Darwin Reader.* New York: W. W. Norton & Co., 1996. Selections from Darwin's works, including *The Voyage of the Beagle* and *The Origin of Species.*

Weiner, Jonathan. *The Beak of the Finch: A Story of Evolution in Our Own Time.* New York: Vintage Books, 1995. An award-winning account of the work of Rosemary and Peter Grant, who have meticulously studied 20 generations of finches on Daphne Major over two decades.

WILDLIFE AND PHOTOGRAPHY BOOKS

Castro, Isabel. *A Guide to the Birds of the Galápagos Islands.* Princeton, NJ: Princeton University Press, 1996. Presents every species to have been recorded within the archipelago, including accidentals and vagrants; 32 color plates.

Deloach, Ned, and Paul Humann. *Reef Fish Identification: Galápagos.* Jacksonville, FL: New World Publications, 2003. This is the go-to field guide for identifying fish and other marine species in the Galápagos. It is a favorite in dive agencies, but it is also accessible to casual snorkeling and scuba enthusiasts.

De Roy, Tui. *Spectacular Galapagos: Exploring an Extraordinary World.* Westport, CT: Hugh Lauter Levin, 1999. Text and breathtaking photographs by one of the islands' foremost advocates. De Roy lived in the Galápagos for 35 years and also wrote *Galápagos: Islands Born of Fire* (Lexington, KY: Warwick Publications, 2000).

Jackson, Michael. *Galápagos: A Natural History.* Calgary, Alberta: University of Calgary Press, 1994. This definitive guide to the islands' geology and wildlife is a must-read for every visitor.

McMullen, Conley. *Flowering Plants of the Galápagos.* Ithaca, NY: Cornell University Press, 1999. A field identification guide to the plants of the Galápagos. The plants are much less famous than the animals, but for enthusiasts there is a wealth of unique species, some endemic to the islands.

Suggested Films

A Galápagos Affair. Daniel Geller, Geller/ Goldfine Productions, 2014. The movie version of the famous murder-mystery history of Floreana Island, with voiceovers by Cate Blanchett as Dore Strauch.

Galápagos—Islands That Changed the World. Tilda Swanson, BBC, 2007. By far the most popular and famous Galápagos documentary, with high-budget filming, aerial shots, and animals galore; it will inspire you to take a trip.

Galáapagos 3D. David Attenborough, Colossus Productions, 2013. A 3-D documentary about the Galápagos Islands, by famous documentary director and Britain's national treasure, Sir David Attenborough.

Sharkwater. Rob Stewart, Sharkwater Productions, 2006. An award-winning documentary about shark hunting in the Galápagos and Costa Rica and the environmental consequences of the sharkfin industry.

Internet Resources

GALÁPAGOS WEBSITES
Charles Darwin Foundation
www.darwinfoundation.org
News about the foundation's research and volunteer opportunities.

Galápagos Conservancy
www.galapagos.org
U.S. organization focused exclusively on conservation in the Galápagos, with up-to-date news about scientific research and conservation initiatives.

Galápagos Conservation Trust
www.galapagosconservation.org.uk
U.K.-based charity that funds conservation projects on the archipelago.

Galápagos National Park
www.galapagospark.org
Comprehensive website with news and descriptions of visitor sites.

International Galápagos Tour Operators Association
www.igtoa.org

List of accredited tour operators and nonprofit organizations.

ECUADOR TRAVEL AND TOURISM
Ecuador's Ministry of Tourism website
http://ecuador.travel
Complete online guide.

Quito Official Travel Information
www.quito.com.ec
City tourism office's website, with comprehensive information.

GOVERNMENT
British Foreign Office Travel Advice
www.fco.gov.uk/en/travel-and-living-abroad/
Click on "Ecuador" in the country menu.

Ecuadorian Embassy in Washington DC
www.ecuador.org
Up-to-date information on visas and immigration issues, in English.

Ecuador's Ministry of External Relations

www.cancilleria.gob.ec
Up-to-date information on visas and immigration issues, in Spanish.

Presidency of Ecuador
www.presidencia.gob.ec
The latest news and views from Ecuador's government.

U.S. Department of State Ecuador Country Profile
http://travel.state.gov
Click on "Ecuador" in the country menu.

U.S. Embassy in Ecuador
www.ecuador.usembassy.gov
The official government office for assistance with lost passports, obtaining other records, notarizing forms, and other services.

WEATHER AND THE NATURAL WORLD
Politécnica Nacional
www.igepn.edu.ec
Local volcano watchers provide daily updates, seismograms within 15 minutes of events, and photos.

Weather.com
www.weather.com
Five- and ten-day forecasts throughout Ecuador.

NEWS AND MEDIA
El Comercio
www.elcomercio.com
Quito-based national daily newspaper, in Spanish.

El Universo
www.eluniverso.com
Guayaquil-based national daily newspaper, in Spanish.

LANGUAGE
Learn Spanish
www.studyspanish.com
Free, award-winning online tutorial.

Spanish Dictionary
http://SpanishDICT.com
Online Spanish dictionary.

Index

List of Maps

Photo Credits

Stunning Sights Around the World

Guides for Urban Adventure

MAP SYMBOLS

≡≡≡ Expressway	○ City/Town	✈ Airport	⚓ Golf Course
Primary Road	⊙ State Capital	✈ Airfield	P Parking Area
Secondary Road	⊛ National Capital	▲ Mountain	≜ Archaeological Site
Unpaved Road	★ Point of Interest	✛ Unique Natural Feature	Church
Feature Trail	• Accommodation		Gas Station
Other Trail	▼ Restaurant/Bar	≈ Waterfall	Glacier
Ferry	■ Other Location	⚑ Park	Mangrove
Pedestrian Walkway	▲ Campground	❶ Trailhead	Reef
Stairs		Skiing Area	Swamp

CONVERSION TABLES

°C = (°F - 32) / 1.8
°F = (°C x 1.8) + 32
1 inch = 2.54 centimeters (cm)
1 foot = 0.304 meters (m)
1 yard = 0.914 meters
1 mile = 1.6093 kilometers (km)
1 km = 0.6214 miles
1 fathom = 1.8288 m
1 chain - 20.1168 m
1 furlong = 201.168 m
1 acre = 0.4047 hectares
1 sq km = 100 hectares
1 sq mile = 2.59 square km
1 ounce = 28.35 grams
1 pound = 0.4536 kilograms
1 short ton = 0.90718 metric ton
1 short ton = 2,000 pounds
1 long ton = 1.016 metric tons
1 long ton = 2,240 pounds
1 metric ton = 1,000 kilograms
1 quart = 0.94635 liters
1 US gallon = 3.7854 liters
1 Imperial gallon = 4.5459 liters
1 nautical mile = 1.852 km

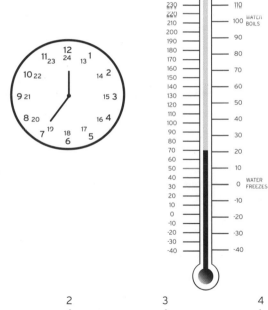

MOON GALÁPAGOS ISLANDS

Avalon Travel
Hachette Book Group
1700 Fourth Street
Berkeley, CA 94710, USA
www.moon.com

Editor: Kimberly Ehart
Series Manager: Kathryn Ettinger
Copy Editor: Linda Cabasin
Graphics and Production Coordinator: Krista Anderson
Cover Design: Faceout Studios, Charles Brock
Interior Design: Domini Dragoone
Moon Logo: Tim McGrath
Map Editor: Albert Angulo
Cartographers: Brian Shotwell, Karin Dahl, Albert Angulo
Proofreader: Kelly Lydick
Indexer: Greg Jewett

ISBN-13: 978-1-64049-288-2

Printing History
1st Edition — 2012
3rd Edition — November 2018
5 4 3 2 1

Front cover photo: Galápagos Land Iguana © David Santiago Garcia/ Aurora Photos

Printed in China by RR Donnelley

Avalon Travel is a division of Hachette Book Group, Inc. Moon and the Moon logo are trademarks of Hachette Book Group, Inc. All other marks and logos depicted are the property of the original owners.